The Boys of 1812

"The Cutlass Breaks at the Hilt".

The Boys of 1812
The Early Exploits of the United States Navy 1775-1846

James Russell Soley

LEONAUR

The Boys of 1812
The Early Exploits of the United States Navy 1775-1846
by James Russell Soley

First published under the title
The Boys of 1812 and Other Naval Heroes

Leonaur is an imprint of Oakpast Ltd

Copyright in this form © 2013 Oakpast Ltd

ISBN: 978-1-78282-086-4 (hardcover)
ISBN: 978-1-78282-087-1 (softcover)

http://www.leonaur.com

Publisher's Notes

Contents

The Beginnings of the Navy 7

Biddle and the "Randolph" 19

War on the Enemy's Coast 25

Paul Jones's Cruises 31

Barry and Barney 43

Hostilities with France 59

Tripoli 74

Impressment 105

The War of 1812.—The "Constitution" and the "Guerrière" 110

The First Sloop Action 124

Decatur and Bainbridge 128

Captain James Lawrence 136

The Cruise of the "Essex" 146

Perry and Lake Erie 171

The Sloop Actions 183

Macdonough and Lake Champlain 194

Stewart and "Old Ironsides" 202

The War With Algiers 212

The War With Mexico 219

BRIG, HEAD ON

CHAPTER 1

The Beginnings of the Navy

Simply to defend themselves against the tyrannical encroachments of the mother country was all that the thirteen colonies had in view when, in 1775, they took up arms against Great Britain. At this time the people hoped, and many of them expected, that by making a determined resistance they would induce the king and Parliament to treat them with fairness, and to give them their rights as English citizens. It was only gradually, during the summer and autumn of the first year,—after the battle had been fought at Bunker Hill, and after Washington had been for some time in command of the army which was laying siege to Boston, that they began to feel that they could make a new nation by themselves, and that independence was a thing that was worth fighting for, even though it cost a long and bloody struggle, in which all of them would pass through bitter suffering and many would give up their very lives.

As we look back upon it now, it is wonderful to think what a daring thing it was for this small and scattered people, living in their little towns along the seacoast from Maine to Georgia, or on farms and plantations in the country, without an army or navy, without generals, and above all without money,—for money is needed to carry on war more than almost anything else,—to have thus made up their minds to stand up bravely and manfully against such a power as Great Britain (one of the greatest in the world), with all her troops and ships and immense revenues.

That we should have come out successfully from a contest so unequal seems little short of marvellous; and we cannot but think that it was the hand of an overruling Destiny that enabled us to succeed, by giving us a general as skilful and prudent as Washington, statesmen as wise as Franklin and Jefferson and Adams, an enemy as indolent as Sir

William Howe, and allies as powerful as our good friends the French.

Still, even from the beginning the colonists had some reason to hope for success, at least in the war on land. They had no standing army, it is true, but they were not without experience in the business of fighting. In the Seven Years' War, which had come to an end only twelve years before, they had furnished the soldiers who filled the ranks of the English armies on American soil. These were the men who had fought the bloody battles at Ticonderoga and Crown Point, and whom the gallant Wolfe had led on the Plains of Abraham. The veterans of the old war were as ready to shoulder their muskets to protect themselves against the tyranny of the king as against the incursions of their Canadian and Indian neighbours. They knew something, too, of the soldiers who would be sent to subdue them, and what they had seen did not give them much reason to be afraid.

They knew how hard it was for an invading army, thousands of miles away from home, marching through a thinly-settled country that was filled with enemies, to protect itself from those incessant and harassing attacks that wear out its strength and destroy little by little all its confidence and pluck. They knew that these gayly-dressed redcoats, who made war according to rule, would find a new kind of work before them among the wooded hills and valleys of America, where every patriot was fighting for his own homestead, where every farmer was a woodsman, and where every woodsman was a crack shot. When that quiet but observant young Virginian, Major Washington, went out with Braddock on his expedition against Fort Duquesne, and saw how the gallant Colonel of the Guards insisted blindly upon following in the backwoods his Old World tactics, and how easily his regulars were defeated in consequence, he learned something that he never afterward forgot; for neither Howe nor Clinton nor Earl Cornwallis himself was the man to teach him a new lesson.

But all this was fighting on land. At sea, the colonists had had no such training. The mother country, with her great fleets, had needed no help from them in her sea-fights, and indeed was rather jealous of any attempts that they might make toward a colonial navy. The colonists in the old wars had fitted out a few privateers that harried the enemy's commerce, but real naval warfare was wholly unknown to them. They had had no ships-of-war of their own to serve in, and such of them as had been admitted into the Royal Navy under the king's commission remained in it almost to a man.

On the ocean, therefore, the colonists were badly off, for Great

Britain was here the worst enemy they could have. Her wooden walls had always been her chief reliance, and from the days when Drake and Howard and Raleigh defeated the Great Armada of Spain, they had asserted and maintained British supremacy at sea. During this long period of two hundred years the names of England's great naval captains had been a terror to all her enemies. There was Robert Blake, who beat off the Dutch, when Tromp sailed across the channel with a broom at his masthead as a sign that he would sweep the English from the seas. There were Sir Cloudesley Shovel and Sir George Rooke, who worsted the French in the great battle of Cape La Hogue; there was the doughty old Benbow, who, deserted by his captains, with his single ship kept at bay the squadron of M. Ducasse in the West Indies; there was Boscawen, who captured the fortress at Louisburg; Hawke and Anson, and finally Rodney and Howe, already famous, and destined to become yet more so in the war that was just begun.

The fleets that these famous admirals led into action were composed of line-of-battle ships,—immense structures, with two, three, or even four gun-decks, some of them carrying as many as one hundred guns, and the smallest of them rated at sixty-four. After these came the frigates, which had only one gun-deck, but which carried a battery on the spar-deck also. These were not thought of sufficient strength to be really counted as a part of the fighting force, although the largest size, the 50-gun frigates, were sometimes taken into the line of battle. But generally they served as scouts or outposts for the great fleets, or they cruised by twos and threes in light squadrons, or even singly, to attack privateers or unarmed merchantmen, or to make a raid on unprotected coasts and seaports, or to carry orders to the different stations. For all these uses they were of great service, being generally faster than the line-of-battle ships, and yet carrying guns enough to make them formidable to all the lesser craft.

After the frigates came the sloops-of-war, ship-sloops, and brig-sloops, as the English called them; not the little boats with one mast that we are accustomed to call sloops, but square-rigged vessels with three or two masts, as the case might be, and carrying twenty guns or so. With all these three classes of vessels the British were well supplied, and the larger ships carried what at that day were heavy guns, 18-pounders and 24-pounders. In 1775, when the war broke out, the Royal Navy numbered one hundred line-of-battle ships, one hundred and fifty frigates, and three hundred of the smaller vessels, and before the war ended it had two hundred and fifty thousand seamen in its service.

The colonies, on the other hand, began the struggle without a single armed vessel afloat. They had merchantmen which they could fit out as privateers to cruise against the British merchantmen, but they had nothing that could stand up against a ship-of-war. Even in guns they were sadly deficient; for though there were scattered here and there in the colonies a few 12-pounders and 9-pounders, they had to depend largely upon sixes and fours, which were not much better than popguns;while of eighteens and twenty-fours they had scarcely any for naval use. Sailors they had, to be sure, all along the coast from New England down; and especially in the northern part there were numbers of bold and hardy men who had followed the sea since they were boys, some in fishing-smacks that made long voyages to the Banks, some in coasters, and some in the large merchant-ships that traded at ports beyond the sea. But of what use are sailors without ships or guns? Besides, as the Continental Navy was slow in forming, many of the best men went into the army, which promised an easier life, or into the privateer service, which held out greater prospects of reward; and when the navy finally got to work, it was very hard to man the vessels.

In spite of all these discouragements, the leaders in the country boldly resolved that they would face Great Britain on the sea as well as on the land. They bought or built their little ships, fitted them out with guns and stores that were partly captured from the British, manned them with crews from the sturdy mariners along the coast, and sent them forth to war upon the enemy as best they might,—by capturing his transports and storeships, by fighting his smaller cruisers when they could be found alone, and sometimes even by daring raids upon his very coasts. Their officers were volunteers from the merchant service; and though hardly any had ever served in ships-of-war, there were some among them whose name and fame have lived to our own day, and will live forever,—Biddle and Manley, Paul Jones and Conyngham, Barry and Barney, and Wickes and Dale,—the first men to show that American naval officers can hold their own against any others in the world.

★★★★★★

The beginnings of the Continental Navy were made by Washington. When on July 3, 1775, he took command of the army under the old elm-tree at Cambridge in Massachusetts, he had a discouraging task before him. Not only was it necessary for him to organize the troops and train them in the art of war, but they had to be supplied

"BOLD AND HARDY MEN WHO HAD FOLLOWED THE SEA
SINCE THEY WERE BOYS."

with arms and ammunition and all kinds of equipments. Not only was there a scarcity of money to buy these things, but the things themselves were hardly to be got in the colonies either for love or money. At the battle of Bunker Hill the patriots had retired, not because they were beaten, but because their ammunition was exhausted. During the whole summer Washington was writing to the governors of the neighbouring colonies, entreating them to send him a little powder and lead. "No quantity," he said, "however small, is beneath notice."

All this time the British, securely established in Boston, were receiving supplies of all kinds from England. Though they were three thousand miles away from home, they could get what they needed with more certainty than the colonists, who were fighting in their own country: of such importance is it in war to have the control of the sea. Washington himself saw this, and he determined to dispute the control with the enemy by sending out little vessels, just strong enough to attack the transports and storeships coming to Boston. So he despatched to the north shore, as it is called, to Beverly and Salem and Marblehead, two of his trusted officers, Colonel John Glover of Marblehead, and Stephen Moylan, the Muster-master-general of the army, to procure and fit out the vessels.

Late in October the first two schooners got to sea, the *Lynch* and *Franklin*, under Captain Broughton, who sailed for the Gulf of St. Lawrence to intercept ships bound for Quebec. Ten days later Moylan and Glover, by dint of hard work, got off two more of these diminutive cruisers,—the *Lee*, under Captain John Manley, and the *Warren*, under Captain Adams of the New Hampshire troops. These were also schooners, and carried each four 4-pounders and ten swivels,—little guns throwing a half-pound bullet mounted on pivots on the gunwales, just as gatlings are mounted today. Each had fifty men, most of whom were drafted from the army; but there was hardly any ammunition to spare for them, and it went against the grain to give them twenty rounds for each gun, which was all they carried.

At Plymouth, also, Washington had his small navy-yard, but it gave him more trouble than it was worth. The schooner *Harrison*, under Captain Coit of Connecticut, was here, though she was old and weak; and a larger ship, the *Washington*. The *Washington* was a fine brigantine, and she mounted ten carriage guns which had been brought by boats and wagons from Bristol. But her captain, Martindale, was too ambitious, and wished his ship to have all the equipments of a real man-of-war. The general and his *aides*, Reed and Moylan, who had

12

the work in charge, were sorely tried by all this useless preparation, which delayed the vessel during the precious weeks of autumn, when she should have been at sea. "Shall we ever hear," wrote Moylan in the middle of November, "of Captain Martindale's departure?" For he knew that the captain's business was to seize the English stores, and to let ships-of-war alone.

Coit's schooner, also, the *Harrison*, was delayed in port, and the sailors were troublesome. "They are soured by the severity of the season," wrote the agent, "and are longing for the leeks and onions of Connecticut." By the third week in November the two ships got out; but the brigantine was presently captured by an enemy's frigate, which showed that the general's apprehensions had been right from the beginning. So the navy, especially the Plymouth fleet, was a source of much anxiety and discouragement to him during the month of November.

But suddenly the tide turned, for on the 29th of that month the news came from Cape Ann that the *Lee* was in, and that Manley had captured the brigantine Nancy, loaded with all kinds of military stores. We can fancy how the general must have felt as he read the invoice of her stores: two thousand muskets and bayonets, thirty-one tons of musket-shot, three thousand round shot for 12-pounders, eight thousand fuses, one hundred and fifty carcasses,—great frames for combustibles to set buildings on fire,—a 13-inch mortar, two 6-pounders, and several barrels of powder, besides great quantities of other valuable stores. No wonder he sent Colonel Glover and Mr. Palfrey in hot haste to the Cape to raise the minute-men from all the neighbouring towns and land the stores, and bring them under escort to headquarters! And the same day he wrote to the President of Congress to tell him of Manley's fine capture, and said: "I sincerely congratulate you, sir, on this great acquisition; it more than repays all that has been spent in fitting out the squadron."

Manley was off to sea again in a day or two, and a week later he captured three more vessels, the cargoes of which were sold, some of them bringing a high price. For these services Manley was placed by Congress on the list of Continental captains, and put in command of a frigate. His schooner, the *Lee*, was given to Captain Waters, who cruised in her for several months, capturing a number of transports with troops on board.

The other vessels also took their share of prizes, even the leaky old *Harrison* bringing in a sloop and a schooner. Broughton's ships, the *Lynch* and the *Franklin*, seized several vessels that were supposed to belong to Tories, but most of these were released. After their return the *Franklin* was given to James Mugford, a daring Marblehead captain. This was in the spring after the British had evacuated Boston, but ships laden with supplies were still coming to America. One of these, the *Hope*, of six guns, fell in with Mugford near Boston, and he determined to attack her, though an English squadron was in sight not many miles away. He had just boarded her, when the English captain ordered his men to cut the topsail-halliards, so that the ship would be delayed until the squadron could come up.

But Mugford roared out that any man who carried out the order would suffer instant death, and no one dared to move. The prize had fifteen hundred barrels of powder in her hold, and it was almost hopeless to try to get her into the harbour by the usual channel in the face of the enemy's fleet. But just then the *Lee* came up, and Captain Waters, who knew every shoal and winding passage in Boston harbour, told Mugford he would carry her in through Shirley Gut, a narrow channel where none of the English ships would dare to follow her. He made good his promise; for though the *Hope* did run ashore on Handkerchief Shoal, he got her off, and brought her with her precious cargo safely into Boston.

Poor Mugford did not long survive his exploit; for, leaving port a few days later by this same Shirley Gut, he too grounded, and while he was lying hard and fast, the boats from the enemy's fleet put off to capture him. There were three times as many men as Mugford had on board the *Franklin*; but he gave them a warm reception with his muskets and such guns as he could bring to bear. They came alongside and prepared to board; but as soon as any of them put their hands upon the rail, the crew hacked them off with cutlasses. Mugford himself was in the hottest of it, and as he leaned over the gunwale a bullet struck him in the breast. He called his first lieutenant and said to him, "I am a dead man: do not give up the vessel; you will be able to beat them off." And so he died; but the enemy were driven back, with two of their boats lost, and the ship was saved.

While General Washington was making his beginning of a Continental navy about Boston, aided by the Massachusetts people, the other colonies were working by themselves in the same direction. In Long Island Sound, on the Hudson River, in the Delaware and Chesapeake bays, and along the inlets of the southern coast, flotillas were fitted out to protect the towns and to prey upon the enemy's

"He Sent Colonel Glover and Mr. Palfrey in Hot
Haste to Raise the Minute-Men."

commerce. In October, 1775, the Continental Congress, which was then in session at Philadelphia, following the example of Washington, decided to have a navy for the general service of the colonies. With this early movement Stephen Hopkins, a delegate from Rhode Island, had much to do; for Narragansett Bay with its thriving farms and plantations offered a tempting prize to the British raiders, whom the little colony would find it hard to keep off.

There were others, too, who took a deep interest in the project,— above all John Adams, and Silas Deane of Connecticut, and Robert Morris of Pennsylvania. Through their efforts a beginning was made by purchasing two brigs, the *Lexington* and *Providence*. These were followed by two larger vessels, the *Alfred* and *Columbus*, carrying each about twenty 9-pounders. Then two more brigs were bought, the "*Andrew Doria*" and the "*Cabot*," which like Washington's schooners carried only 4-pounders, though they had more of them. The *Lexington* went to sea alone, but the others were assembled at Philadelphia in December, ready to start out as the first Continental squadron.

It was not an easy thing to select a commander for the new squadron, for there was hardly a man in the colonies who had seen any naval service. Young Nicholas Biddle, of Philadelphia, had been a midshipman in the Royal Navy, and had resigned his post to fight for his country; but he was thought to be too young, though he had seen more real service than his fellow officers. Finally, Hopkins's brother, Esek Hopkins, an old Rhode Island sea-captain who had been made a brigadier-general, was chosen to command the force. His son John was made captain of one of the ships, and his cousin Abraham Whipple of another, while Hazard, who was also a Rhode Islander, was assigned to the *Providence*. Biddle, who, as it turned out, was the best of them all, was given the little brig *Doria*.

From an obscure place in Virginia, far away in the country, came a letter from a young Scotchman named Paul Jones, who had followed the sea from his boyhood but had finally settled in America, asking them that he might have a commission. Although no one knew much of him, he was offered one of the smaller brigs; but he preferred to go at first as a lieutenant, and he was placed on board the *Alfred*, the commodore's flagship.

The squadron was fitted out to cruise upon the southern coast; but it was frozen up for six weeks in Delaware Bay, and when it sailed in February, 1776, it made first for the Bahama Islands. It came to anchor off Abaco, the northernmost of the islands. Here the commodore learned that there was a fort, with many guns and a great quantity of powder, but defended only by a feeble garrison, at New Providence, on the Island of Nassau, the same place which afterward gained such fame during the Rebellion as the refuge of the blockade-runners. Commodore Hopkins resolved to attempt its capture, but advancing incautiously with his whole fleet, gave a timely warning to the inhabitants; and the governor, who till that moment had not dreamed of the near approach of an enemy, succeeded in getting his powder to a place of safety. The marines were landed and marched to the fort, which they captured with little difficulty. The guns were taken, as well as all the stores except the powder, and the governor was carried off a prisoner.

The squadron had now accomplished such results that Hopkins thought it best to defer his operations on the southern coast, and made sail for home. He arrived safely in New London, meeting only one of the enemy's ships on the way, with which he had a battle; but neither side could claim the victory. The captured guns were sent off to the points where they were needed most, and Commodore Hopkins went to Philadelphia. But Congress was not very well satisfied with him, especially the Southern delegates, who had been promised protection for their shores. The old commodore, too, was fussy and impatient, and as he stayed on in Philadelphia, everybody began to grow tired of him; and finally Congress passed a resolution in which they announced to him, rather harshly perhaps, that they had no further use for his services. No doubt he had meant well; but he was too old to be the leader of the new Continental Navy, and this is the last we shall hear of him.

Before the squadron started on its cruise Congress had undertaken more ambitious measures. Thirteen frigates were ordered to be built, and different places were selected where the work should be done, so that whatever part of the country the British might overrun, some of the new ships might be finished and sent out. Thus the *Raleigh* was built at Portsmouth, the *Hancock* and *Boston* in Massachusetts, the *Warren* and *Providence* in Rhode Island, the *Trumbull* in Connecticut, and the *Virginia* at Baltimore. Of the other six, two were begun at Poughkeepsie, on the Hudson, and four at Philadelphia; but the only one of the six that got to sea was the *Randolph*, of Philadelphia, the others being destroyed at one time or another to prevent their falling into the hands of the enemy.

More vessels were built later, and a few were bought in Europe; but among them all there were no line-of-battle ships, and even for frigates they were not very large or strong. But they were the best that the colonies could get; there was not money enough to build great fleets, and there were not guns enough to arm them. Few and small as they were, they performed their part, and no small part it was, in showing the king and the Parliament that the colonies were thoroughly in earnest in the struggle upon which they had entered, and that they would spare no labour, and would encounter any danger, in order to secure their independence.

Chapter 2

Biddle and the "Randolph"

There were two men in Hopkins's squadron who far excelled all the others in those qualities of energy, courage, and intelligence that are most required in a naval officer. These were Biddle, the captain of the *Andrew Doria*, and Paul Jones, the lieutenant of the *Alfred*. Jones was at this time twenty-eight years old; the son of a Scotch gardener, he was born and brought up on the shores of the Solway Frith. Across the Frith lay the prosperous seaport of Whitehaven; and the boy when twelve years old was apprenticed to a merchant of the place, who traded with America, and his first voyage had been to Virginia. At a later time he had served in a slaver; but leaving this distasteful occupation, he became the master of a ship in the West India trade, and finally had drifted to Virginia, where he had made his home two years before the outbreak of the war.

After the squadron returned to New London, Jones was given command of the brig *Providence*, and in August he set off on a cruise to the eastward. His ship was small, but she was smart and handy, and Jones was the man to make her do her best. Presently he fell in with two frigates of the enemy; but he got away from them after an exciting chase. A few days afterward, while his ship was hove to, and his crew were fishing, another English frigate came up,—the *Milford*. Hastily calling his men to their stations, he started off to try his speed with the new-comer, for she was far too strong for him to attack or even to resist. He soon found that he could outsail her, which was just as good; and shortening sail, he allowed the *Milford* to come up a little.

Then he started ahead again, and so continued backing and filling, just to tease her, as it were. The frigate turned and gave him a broadside which fell short, and which he answered in derision by ordering a marine to fire a musket. Finally he left the *Milford* and went on his way to the fishing settlements in the eastern provinces, capturing the enemy's merchantmen right and left, wherever he could find them. He raided the harbour of Canso, to the great alarm of the inhabitants, and broke up the fishery. Then he crossed over to Île Madame, where he destroyed the shipping. By this time his ship was so loaded down with prisoners that he was obliged to put about for home, where he arrived safely in October, having been out six weeks and taken sixteen prizes.

After a month in port Jones started on a second cruise. This time he took with him the *Providence* and also the *Alfred*,—the ship of which he had been first lieutenant on the expedition to Nassau. Another raid was made on Canso, and another batch of prizes was captured. One of these, the *Mellish*, had a cargo of clothing which was intended for the enemy's troops, but which was needed even more by our own army, at this time just beginning its winter campaign. When he came home from this second cruise, Jones thought he had shown by what he had done that he deserved a better ship, and Congress thought so too; and after some little delay he was appointed to the new sloop-of-war *Ranger*, which was building at Portsmouth, and in which during the following year he entered upon a new and larger field of operations.

About the time that Jones took command of the *Providence*, his companion in the squadron, Nicholas Biddle, was sent out in the brig *Doria* on a cruise to the Banks. Biddle was at this time twenty-five years old. He was born in Philadelphia, and had begun life as a sailor before the mast at the age of fourteen. On his second voyage he was wrecked in the West Indies, and narrowly escaped with his life. Afterward he went to London, and in 1770, when a war was threatened between Great Britain and Spain, he obtained an appointment as midshipman in the Royal Navy under Captain Stirling. War did not break out, however, and young Biddle joined the exploring expedition under Commodore Phipps, which sought to reach the North Pole by the way of Spitzbergen.

On the same expedition was another youngster, by name Horatio Nelson, who was destined afterward to lead the English fleet to victory at the battles of the Nile and Trafalgar. After the return of Phipps's ships, Biddle left the navy and came home to take his part in the war that was now beginning. His first commission, from the Committee of Safety in Philadelphia, was signed by its president, Benjamin Franklin, and appointed him "Captain of the Provincial Armed Boat called the *Franklin*, fitted out for the protection of the Province of Pennsylvania,

NICHOLAS BIDDLE.

and the Commerce of the River Delaware against all hostile enterprises, and for the defence of American Liberty." But when Congress formed its first squadron, under Commodore Hopkins, he was transferred to the Continental Navy. The *Doria*, which Biddle commanded on the expedition to Nassau, and which he was now to take on her first independent cruise, carried an armament of fourteen 4-pounders, which, as I have said, were little better than popguns, and of course unfit for fighting with a ship-of-war. Her crew numbered one hundred men.

On her way out, the *Doria*" made three prizes. Off Newfoundland she captured two transports, with four hundred troops on board. Any ordinary man would have found it a difficult task to dispose of so many prizes and prisoners; but Biddle had served in the navy, and he knew what discipline meant. Manning the captured ships from his crew, he filled their places on board the *Doria* with prisoners, and started to return home. On the way back, six more vessels were taken. These were manned in the same way, by stripping the brig of her sailors and taking the best of the prisoners to do their work. Finally the *Doria* arrived at Philadelphia, with all her prisoners and with only five men left of her original crew. It would have been hard to find another man in the service, even if it were Paul Jones himself, who could have kept in check such a ship's company as that. One of the prizes was wrecked, and another recaptured, but the rest got safely into port.

Congress now began to realize that this young fellow of five-and-twenty was one of the very best officers in its employ; and indeed if he had been made at the start the commander-in-chief of our forces afloat, instead of an old weather-beaten merchant captain like Hopkins, his experience and skill and impetuous bravery would beyond a doubt have raised the navy to the highest point of excellence of which its scanty resources were capable. He was appointed to command the *Randolph*, which had lately been launched at Philadelphia. She was one of the best of the new ships, but she had been hurriedly built,—too hurriedly, as was shown on her first cruise; for no sooner had Biddle got out of sight of land than a gale sprang up, and all her masts went by the board.

To add to his difficulties, he discovered a mutinous spirit in his crew, several of whom were prisoners who had volunteered for the cruise. This was promptly checked, for the captain, as we have seen, was not a man to allow insubordination; and after rigging jury-masts he carried the ship safely into Charleston. Here she was refitted, and from here she again started on a cruise. She had been out only a few days when she captured the *True Briton*, a ship of twenty guns, and three West Indiamen that formed her convoy. The captain of the *True Briton* had been looking for the *Randolph*,—at least so he said,—and as the latter approached him, he received her with a warm fire; but the *Randolph* only waited till she got within pistol-shot, when she fired a single gun, and the English captain incontinently struck his colours.

Returning once more to Charleston with her prizes, the *Randolph* remained there for some time blockaded by the enemy's squadron. At last the State of South Carolina fitted out a force of vessels to raise the blockade and cruise with the *Randolph* under Biddle's command. Contrary winds and the want of a high tide detained them for some time in Rebellion Roads, and when they got over the bar the enemy had disappeared; so they set out in quest of adventures.

The squadron had cruised for more than a month in the Atlantic with no incident worthy of note, when on the 7th of March, 1778, being then to the eastward of Barbadoes, at one o' clock in the afternoon a large ship was seen in the distance, gradually approaching. By three o'clock she had come near enough for Biddle to make out that she was a ship-of-the-line. Knowing that the stranger must be an Englishman,—she proved to be the *Yarmouth*, of sixty-four guns,— and knowing too that the *Randolph*, even with the support of the smaller ships, was no match for her powerful battery, he signalled to the fleet to make sail. All the ships obeyed except the *General Moultrie*, which obstinately refused to leave her place, and remained hove to, giving no sign of moving.

This blundering conduct of the *Moultrie's* captain left Biddle no choice but to abandon his consort or to remain and fight what seemed to be a hopeless battle. He boldly chose the latter course; and as the *Yarmouth* ranged up on his weather quarter, he hoisted the American flag and opened on her with a succession of furious broadsides, giving four to the enemy's one, and inflicting dangerous wounds upon her sails and rigging. A few minutes after the action began, Biddle received a shot in the thigh. As his people, alarmed, gathered around him, he raised himself up, telling them it was only a slight touch, and calling for a chair seated himself on the quarter-deck, where the surgeon came to dress his wound. Here he was vigorously directing the course of the battle, and in spite of the disparity between the two ships he was gradually getting the advantage, when suddenly, without a moment's warning, the magazine of the *Randolph* blew up, scattering spars, hull, guns, officers, and men in a mass of fragments over the waters.

None ever knew how the accident happened. The other ships, seeing the disaster, made off as fast as they could; but the *Yarmouth* was too much disabled to follow them, and they made good their escape. Five days after the action the English ship, still cruising about the spot, came upon a floating piece of the *Randolph's* wreck, to which four of her crew were still clinging. They had been drifting in this way for four days with no sustenance except the rain-water which they had managed to collect. These were all the survivors of that fatal battle,—a battle which lost us not only a fine frigate, but, what was far worse, one of our best and most gallant officers.

Chapter 3

War on the Enemy's Coast

We have seen how the beginning of naval enterprise made by Washington in the summer of 1775 was taken up and borne along by the Continental Congress at Philadelphia, until little by little it had obtained a force at sea that was able to inflict serious loss upon the enemy. But a field for operations was now to be found in a new quarter; and happily for America, their direction was in the hands of its wisest and most far-sighted statesman. On the 7th of December, 1776, the United States brig-of-war *Reprisal* arrived at Nantes with Benjamin Franklin on board as a passenger, who had come over with a letter from Congress, naming him a commissioner to treat with France. The *Reprisal* was commanded by Capt. Lambert Wickes, a gallant naval officer who had been cruising during the summer before in the West Indies, where he had shown himself worthy of the people's trust. And indeed it was a heavy responsibility that rested with him on this voyage across the Atlantic; for had his ship with its passenger been captured, it is hard to say what troubles would have come upon the country, or how the Revolution would have held its own during the next five years.

But Franklin was carried safely to his destination; and not only that, but two English brigs laden with cargoes of wine were captured by the *Reprisal* on the voyage and came with her into port. It was in this way that Franklin's mind was turned to the benefits which his country might reap from ocean warfare,—above all, in the seas which English commerce most frequented,—and after he arrived in Paris he lost no time in putting in practice what he had learned.

At this early period, although the King of France was indifferent, if not hostile, to the American cause, the ministers and people warmly favoured it. The friendly feeling was strengthened by Franklin's coming, and his winning manners, simple and frank, but full of dignity, made him a favourite with all, both high and low. Persuaded thus by their own desires, and by Franklin's strong but gentle influence, they went just as far in their efforts to aid the Americans as they possibly could without declaring open war against England. Large sums of money were given; the departure of ships laden with arms and munitions of war was winked at; and when Lord Stormont, the English ambassador, complained of the admission of the *Reprisal* and her prizes into French ports, the Frenchmen gave evasive answers, and the vessels under one pretext or another were allowed to stay. Wickes even made a little roving cruise in the Bay of Biscay, from which he brought in as trophies three more prizes. To satisfy the English protests, he was forbidden to sell his prizes in the ports; but he took them just outside the harbour, where he held mock sales, and thus disposed of all of them. These little subterfuges were continued until the conclusion of the treaty, which came about in the following year.

In the spring after Wickes arrived, the brig *Lexington* came out, under Captain Johnston. She was the first vessel that had been purchased by the Continental Congress, and she had already done good service on the American coast. Johnston had with him as lieutenant one of the best and bravest of the Revolutionary officers, Richard Dale. Dale was at this time twenty years of age. Eight years before he had first gone to sea from his home in Virginia, and already since the beginning of the war he had been twice a prisoner; but the strangest part of his career was yet to come.

Franklin now thought it would be wise to join together the *Reprisal* and the *Lexington* and the little 10-gun cutter *Dolphin* in a squadron under the command of Wickes, who was to make a dash around the coast of Ireland and capture or destroy whatever he might find. The ships sailed from Nantes in June, and in August they came back successful from their perilous enterprise. They had captured fourteen prizes. Approaching the French coast on their return, they were discovered and chased by an English line-of-battle ship of seventy-four guns; but by separating they succeeded in making good their escape, though the *Reprisal* barely managed to get into port in time.

This expedition made so great a commotion that the French Government found itself obliged to notice it, and ordered the ships to leave the territory. Accordingly they set sail on the voyage home; but unhappily the *Reprisal*, upon reaching the Banks of Newfoundland, foundered in a gale, and only one of the crew was saved. The *Lexing-*

ton, soon after starting, fell in with the English cutter *Alert* in the Bay of Biscay. Both ships fought gallantly for two hours; but at length the *Lexington*, which was short of ammunition, had used up nearly all her powder and shot and made sail to get away from the enemy. The *Alert* had been badly cut up aloft in the fight; but she speedily bent new sails and in a short time overtook her antagonist. Captain Johnston held out as long as there was any hope, firing now and then a gun, and using every scrap of iron he could lay his hands on for a missile; but after he had fired his last charge of powder, and several of his officers had been killed, to prevent the useless slaughter he surrendered.

The prisoners were carried off to Plymouth, where they were confined in the Mill Prison. Here the harsh treatment and sufferings they underwent soon prompted them to devise a means of escape. A hole was dug under the wall, the officers and men working upon it with their fingers whenever an opportunity offered, but making slow progress, as they could only hide the dirt from the excavation by carrying it in their pockets when they went out for exercise, and scattering it when the sentry's back was turned. Finally one night, when all was ready, they passed out through the opening and escaped into the country.

But their troubles had only just begun. The hue and cry was raised, and parties were sent in pursuit of the fugitives. Separating into twos and threes, they were barely able to elude pursuit. One night Dale was concealed under the hay in a barn, when the officers entered it in search of him. At last he reached London and took passage in a vessel bound to Dunkirk; but before she had left the Thames she was visited by a press-gang, and poor Dale was seized, and when they found out who he was, sent back to prison. The captain, though, got safely off.

This was now the fourth time that Dale had been a prisoner. To punish him for trying to escape, he was thrown into the black hole—a dungeon that was only used for the worst offenders—and treated with the utmost rigor. After a time he was put on his old footing as a prisoner of war; but he was a reckless youth, and having roused the wrath of the jailers by singing what they called "rebellious songs," he served another term in the black hole. At length by some means, which to his dying day he never would disclose, he obtained the uniform of a British officer, and in this disguise he walked through the gates in plain sight of the sentinel. Rendered more cautious by what had befallen him after his first escape, he laid his plans with care, and at last succeeded in reaching France, after a year and a half of captivity. He came in good time; for it was just as he arrived that Paul Jones was setting out on his great cruise in the *Bon Homme Richard*, and Dale was made his first lieutenant. Here we shall leave him for the present.

About the time that the *Lexington* had come out from America, in the spring of 1777, the commissioners at Paris, finding that they could not get more ships in France, because the English made so great an outcry, bethought themselves that they would send a trusty agent across the channel to Dover, to see what he could get there. In this way they purchased secretly a swift English cutter, the *Surprise*, and they appointed to command her Gustavus Conyngham, a bold and adventurous officer. He started on a cruise in May from Dunkirk, and in a few days returned with two of the enemy's brigs,—one of them a mail-packet which he had captured off the coast of Holland. The English ambassador again protested, and the French Government told Franklin that, though much against its will, it would be compelled to restore the prizes. It even went so far as to imprison Conyngham and his crew; but this was only a make-believe, for they were shortly afterward released.

Unmoved by this event, Franklin immediately procured another cutter, the *Revenge*, and giving Conyngham a new commission, he sent him off from Dunkirk in charge of her. The second cruise was even more successful than the first. Conyngham roved about with his little ship as he pleased, keeping carefully away from the enemy's cruisers, which vainly sought to catch him, and capturing prizes on all sides. These he destroyed, or sometimes when he saw his chance sent into seaports on the Continent. Once during his cruise, being hard pushed for supplies, he touched at a small town in Ireland and bought them. At another time when off the English coast, finding his vessel unseaworthy and needing some repair, he took her into one of the smaller ports and refitted there, with the help of the inhabitants, without being discovered. Finally, when so many ships were sent out in pursuit of him that his cruising-ground became too hot, he made for Ferrol, in Spain, and after staying there awhile carried his ship safely to America.

The cruises of Wickes and of Conyngham, with their tiny craft, were the beginning of the great work that was to be taken up on a larger scale in the next two years by Paul Jones. The enterprise and hardihood of these bold captains, who carried the war, as it were, to the very threshold of the enemy's country, were not without results both in England and on the Continent. They showed foreign nations

He Touched at a Small Town in Ireland for Supplies.

that the rebels in America were making war in truest earnest, and that they would leave no honourable means unused to help them in asserting independence. In England they spread alarm among the merchants, and the insurers of English ships demanded double rates; while London traders, rather than run the risk of losing their goods by shipping them in their own vessels, were induced to employ their foreign rivals to carry cargoes for them,—a thing which before this time had been almost unheard of.

CHAPTER 4

Paul Jones's Cruises

Sometime in the summer of 1777 Paul Jones was ordered to command the sloop-of-war *Ranger*, at that time nearly completed at Portsmouth. The officers were detailed for their ships by resolution of Congress; and the same resolution that gave Jones his command, on the 14th day of June, is memorable as the first adoption of the flag of thirteen stars and stripes which was carried by Jones's ship, and which ever since has been the national emblem. The young captain had hard work before him to get his ship ready for sea; but at last everything was in order, and on the 1st of November he set sail for France. He had laid down for himself a clear plan of action. He knew that England's navy was too powerful to be met on the sea, but that all along the English coast were unprotected seaports where the people were not looking for attack, and where a sharp and sudden blow would take them off their guard.

He had hopes, too, that the commissioners in Paris would give him a larger ship,—perhaps two or three of them,—and he carried with him a letter from the President of Congress asking them to aid his enterprise. But in this he was disappointed. When he arrived at Nantes he found that the *Indien*, a fine frigate that Franklin was having built at Amsterdam, was to be presented to the King of France, whose friendship the commissioners were anxious to obtain, that by this means they might bring about an alliance against Great Britain. So after waiting awhile he thought it well to lose no more time, and on the 10th of April he started with the *Ranger* for a cruise in the Irish Sea.

The undertaking was full of danger. There was no knowing how large a force of ships the enemy might have stationed to guard the coast, for the cruises of Wickes and Conyngham had given the alarm, and the British might have known that their own waters were no longer safe. Besides, Paul Jones was a Scotchman who had lived only two years in America, though he had given himself heart and soul to his new country's cause, and if captured, especially near Kirkcudbright or Whitehaven, where many people knew him well, he ran a good chance of being hanged as a pirate and a traitor. But Jones was a man who cared nothing about danger, and a great deal about success and the rewards which it brings. He was never deterred for a moment by the risk he was running, and if he thought about it at all, he decided that the obstinate belief of the British in their own invincibility would lead them to neglect preparations; and for the rest he only asked to be allowed to take his chances. In this he proved to be right; for although the *Ranger* had been lying for months at a French port, preparing for her expedition, the narrow seas had been left with no protection except the *Drake*,—a sloop of the *Ranger's* size,—which lay snugly at anchor in the harbour of Carrickfergus.

On the fourth day out from Brest, in St. George's Channel, the *Ranger* made her first capture of a brigantine, which was burned on the spot. Three days afterward, as Jones was nearing Dublin, he took a London ship bound for that port, which he manned and sent in to Brest. Next day he moved over toward Whitehaven, whose port, crowded with shipping, he had known so well as a boy, and attempted to approach the harbour, so that his boats might go in and destroy the vessels. The enemy had burned and destroyed property wherever they could on the American coast, and it seemed to Jones that the best way to stop them was to do the like on theirs. But the wind began to blow fiercely toward the land, and the "Ranger" turned her head seaward again, to avoid the dangers of a lee shore. In the next two days she captured a schooner and a sloop, which were sunk one after the other.

This was small game for Jones; and learning from a fishing-boat just where the *Drake* was moored at Carrickfergus, he determined to run in and surprise her in the night. All was made ready. The decks were cleared for action, the lights were put out, the guns concealed, the grapnels at hand to hook on to the enemy's ship, and the boarders standing by with pikes and cutlasses to dash over the side. The *Drake* was lying with her head pointing seaward, and Jones's plan was to place himself athwart her cable and bring up on her bow. The *Ranger* came in silently but swiftly, with a captured fisherman to pilot her, and so approached the enemy. The order was given to "let go the anchor;" but either it was not quickly obeyed or the anchor hung from the jamming of the hawser, and the *Ranger* shot by in the darkness. It was of no use to try again, for a second attempt to get alongside would arouse suspicion; so Jones cut his cable and ran out, leaving his anchor in the bay behind him.

On the next night he made another trial at Whitehaven, but this too was a failure. The wind was so light that the ship could not come close in until much of the night had worn away, and the boats, with Jones and thirty of his men, only reached the outer pier at daybreak. One party, under Lieutenant Wallingford, was sent to the north basin, and another to the south, to burn the ships there; while Jones, with a handful of men, made his way into the fort, surprised the sentries, captured the little garrisons and spiked the guns, so that his retreat might be secure. When he returned to where the ships were lying, expecting to see them in a blaze, he was distressed to find that his men had let their candles burn away, and there was nothing left to kindle the fire.

At last one of the men brought a light from a house nearby; but by this time the people of the town had roused themselves, and began to move about the streets and to gather near the wharves. A fire started in one ship was helped on by a tar-barrel; and while his men were fanning it into a blaze, Jones stood before them on the wharf and kept the enemy away. But angry crowds were now collecting, and it was time to be off; so the captain manned his boats in haste, and embarking, pulled away to his ship, leaving the frightened inhabitants to wonder what this strange attack at their very doors could mean.

The *Ranger* now ran over to the Scotch coast, and was next seen off St. Mary's Isle, the country-seat of the Earl of Selkirk. Jones knew the spot, and he had formed the plan of landing with a boat's crew and carrying off the earl, whom he meant to keep as a hostage in order that the prisoners taken by the English might have better treatment. But the earl was not at home, and the men grumbled at having only their trouble for their pains. To quiet them, Jones told the party that they could go back and demand the silver plate that was in the house.

The Lady Selkirk, who, looking from the window of her house, had seen the men as they came on shore, had felt no alarm, thinking that they were revenue officers, or perhaps a press-gang; but she was undeceived when they came back to the house, and she hurriedly gave them the silver tea-service, just as it was, on the breakfast-table. So they carried it away. It was a shameful thing to do, only worthy of a tramp or a marauder, and Jones was heartily sorry for it afterward; so much so, that at the sale of the prizes he bought in all the earl's plate with his own prize-money, and sent it safely back to Lady Selkirk.

The last two exploits of the *Ranger* had alarmed the whole country-side; and as she came once more in sight of the coast of the three kingdoms, beacon-fires could be seen burning on every headland. The *Drake*, too, had caught the alarm, and came out from Carrickfergus to capture the bold American. She was looking for an encounter, and Jones had no wish to disappoint her. As the enemy came out, the *Ranger* was kept stern on, which caused her to be mistaken for a merchantman, and a boat put off from the *Drake* to gain some information. The boat's crew gained more than they bargained for, for they were no sooner alongside than the *Ranger* took them on board. Then, after drawing away for a while from the land, she waited for her adversary to come up. There was no doubt now about her character, and the two ships fired their broadsides as soon as they had come within range. It was a running fight, broadside to broadside, and the two enemies were fairly matched.

But the *Ranger's* men were better at the guns, and their steady fire soon began to tell, as the people who lined the shores could see to their dismay. The shots rained thick and fast upon the *Drake*, sweeping her decks, wounding her sides, and cutting up her rigging. Her ties were shot away and the fore and main top-sail yards fell upon the caps. The jib hung in the water ahead and the ensign drooped astern. Presently the captain received a shot in the head, and soon afterward the first lieutenant fell, mortally wounded; finally, after an hour of hot fighting, the *Drake* surrendered. On board the *Ranger* poor Wallingford was killed, but Jones had not been touched. Securing his prisoners and his prize, on board of which he found the anchor which had been left in Carrickfergus harbour, and which the *Drake* had fished up for herself, he made sail with the two ships around the north of Ireland. There was little time to be lost, for the enemy would soon have a squadron in pursuit of him. Off he went, and made his passage safely around the Irish coast, and on the 8th of May the *Ranger* and the *Drake* arrived at Brest, just four weeks after Jones had started.

With the great name that Jones had gained from his successful cruise, he now thought, and with reason, that his friends in France would bestir themselves to find for him a suitable command. He went to Paris, and received such fair promises from those in power, that he decided to send home the *Ranger* and wait abroad for the fine new ship which he expected to command. As the French had now openly concluded an alliance, they were ready to take part in any enterprise

The "Drake" Surrenders to the "Ranger."

against the common enemy but they wanted to use their ships for their own officers, and the commissioners had no money to build ships on their own account. Jones went back to Brest, determined to bide his time, and meanwhile to leave no stone unturned in his efforts to secure a vessel. From Brest he wrote most pressing and incessant letters to ever one in Paris who was likely to advance his scheme,—to Franklin, to M. de Sartine, the Minister of Marine, to the Prince of Nassau, and to Chaumont, a French official who had devoted much of his time and money to helping the American cause.

About this time Lafayette came over to France in a splendid new frigate, the finest ship in the American Navy, which had been named the *Alliance*, to show how much the Americans valued their French friends. For the same reason the command of the *Alliance* had been given to Pierre Landais, a French merchant-captain. This was a serious mistake, as it was no great compliment to France, and Landais was as poor an officer as could have been selected. It was now proposed that a descent should be made on the English coast, with Lafayette in command of the land forces and Jones as the leader of the fleet, which was to include the *Alliance* and several other vessels. But this plan also fell through.

Jones was not in despair, for he never was that, although he had good reason to be so now; but he was beginning to be very angry. He had been told to look about in the seaports and select a vessel, and he had selected several; but his letters all seemed to be pigeon-holed when they got to Paris. One day he chanced to take up an old number of the *Poor Richard's Almanac*, which Franklin had written years before, and read in it these words:

If you want a thing done, go and do it; if not, send!

Acting upon this advice he went to Paris, and in a few days after his arrival he was gratified by the announcement that one of the ships he had seen was to be fitted out for him.

The ship was the *Duc de Duras*, an old Indiaman; and Jones was so grateful for the advice which had prompted him to go to Paris, that he had her rechristened the *Poor Richard*, or *Bon Homme Richard*, as they called it in French. She was not a first-rate ship, but she would answer the purpose, and Jones knew that beggars should not be choosers. The larger frigates of that day carried 18-pounders, but the *Richard*, as we shall call her, had only 12-pounders. Jones managed, however, to get six 18's, which he mounted in the gun-room, cutting ports for them in the side. Besides his own ship he was to have four others,—the *Alliance*, under Landais, and three smaller vessels, the *Pallas*, *Cerf*, and *Vengeance*, commanded by French officers, and with crews of Frenchmen.

The crew of the *Bon Homme Richard* was made up partly of Americans, many of whom were exchanged prisoners, and she carried a considerable body of French marines. The rest of her people were taken from the foreign sailors of all nations and classes that are to be found in every seaport. Her officers were Americans. Of these the best was the first lieutenant, Richard Dale, one of the most gallant young officers that was ever borne upon the rolls of the American Navy, of whose career you have already heard something in the last chapter, and who, as I told you then, had made his final escape from prison just in time to set out in the *Richard*. The commodore, as Jones was now called, would have been badly off if it had not been for Dale; for through accidents he became short of officers on the cruise, and in the great battle that ended it, Dale was almost the only one of rank upon whom he could rely.

The squadron sailed from Lorient on the 14th of August, 1779. The plan was to sail to the northward along the Irish and Scotch coasts, thence to the east, and back by way of the North Sea, keeping near the shore, and so circling around the United Kingdom. When a few days out, at dusk one evening, off the Irish coast, the crew of the *Richard's* barge, which was towing at the time, cut the tow-line and pulled off. The master, Lunt, was sent in another boat in chase, but a thick fog coming up, he was unable to rejoin the ship. Next day the *Cerf* went in toward the coast to find him, the others remaining meanwhile outside in the track of vessels. Lunt saw the *Cerf* approaching him, but as she was flying English colours, he mistook her for an enemy, and made off to the shore, where he and his boat's crew were taken prisoners. The *Cerf* seized the opportunity to leave her duty and go back to France.

After this incident the squadron, now composed of the *Bon Homme Richard*, the *Alliance*, the *Pallas*, and the *Vengeance*, pursued its way, taking prizes and destroying them or sending them in. All the French captains were insubordinate, but Landais was the worst. Sometimes he flatly refused to obey the commodore's orders, and at all times he opposed and thwarted him as far as he dared. Still, the cruise was successful, the squadron doubled Cape Wrath, and about the 15th of September arrived off the Frith of Forth.

Jones was now eager to accomplish some great achievement, for so far he had done nothing that was more noteworthy than his cruise in the *Ranger*. As he came up the Frith, he decided to stand in toward Leith, the seaport of Edinburgh, and anchoring before the unprotected town, to demand a ransom of £200,000 as the price of sparing it. His plan was laid with care, and he had only to wait till night, when the *Pallas* and the *Vengeance*, which were a little behind, should join him. The *Alliance* at this time was away at sea, having been separated from the squadron. When the other ships came up, their captains demurred at Jones's plan, and the whole night was lost in tedious debate and argument. Finally the Frenchmen were won over to consent; but now that morning had come, the wind was contrary, and for two days all the ships were working up the Frith. At last they had nearly reached the anchorage, when a furious gale came on and drove them all out to the North Sea, running ashore one of the prizes they had taken. The commodore at first was for making a second trial; but when he found that the alarm had been given in the town, and that batteries had been thrown up along the shore, and arms had been served out to the trade-guilds so that they might be ready to receive him, he reluctantly gave up the attempt.

It was a few days after this, on the afternoon of the 23rd of September, as the four ships were working their way gradually to the southward along the English coast, that Jones's opportunity at length arrived. He had just passed Flamborough Head, a long promontory jutting out in the North Sea, when he descried a sail coming out beyond the point to the northward, then another, and another, then more, by twos and threes, until at last there were fifty of them. Fifty of the enemy's merchant-vessels in plain sight! It seemed almost too good to be true, for this was the great fleet of Baltic trading-ships, which it was the dearest wish of Jones's heart to meet. In an instant he had hoisted the signal to attack them; but presently the headmost merchant-ships, seeing the advancing enemy, put about and made off under the land, followed by the others like a flock of frightened geese.

Two of the vessels alone kept on their course, and it was presently discovered that these were ships of war convoying the fleet,—the fine 18-pounder frigate *Serapis*, just from the dock-yard, under Captain Pearson, and a smaller vessel, the *Countess of Scarborough*. These two vessels stood gallantly out to sea to get between the convoy and Jones's squadron. Jones held on his course to meet them; but Landais, either from cowardice or treachery, disobeyed the commodore's signals, and sailing off, left him in the lurch. The *Vengeance* being too small to be of any service, and the *Pallas* engaging the *Countess of Scarborough*, the *Bon Homme Richard* was left to fight the *Serapis* alone.

It was seven o'clock in the evening when the first shots were exchanged between the two frigates, and for three hours, under the bright moonlight of a clear September night, the battle raged between them with unremitting fury. At first Jones tried to get into a good position across the enemy's bow; but the *Serapis* was a much faster vessel than the *Richard*, and easily evaded her. After manoeuvring for a time the two vessels got foul, and Jones with his own hands made fast the jib-stay of the *Serapis* to his mizzen-mast. At the same time the English vessel's anchor hooked in his quarter, and the *Serapis* having let go her other anchor, the two ships, firmly lashed together, swung side by side to the single cable.

This position was much the best that Jones could have taken; for the *Serapis* outsailed him, and if the ships had remained apart, she would soon have knocked him to pieces with her heavy battery. As it was, her 18-pounders cleared the *Richard's* lower deck, knocking all her ports into one, and blowing out the two sides of the ship. At the beginning of the battle, two of the old 18-pounders which Jones had taken care to mount in his gun-room burst, and the crew refused to have anything more to do with them. Lieutenant Dale, who commanded the lower battery, fired his little 12-pounders as long as the men could stand to their guns, though in order to load them the rammers had to be run in through the enemy's ports, so close were the two ships. Presently word was brought to Dale that the ship was sinking, and he sent some men to man the pumps.

Then the master-at-arms, overcome by panic, set loose all the prisoners,—there were more than a hundred of them,—and the men stationed in the magazine, seeing them crowding up, were afraid to send up any more powder. But Dale was below again in a twinkling, and overawing the prisoners, he set them to work in gangs at the pumps. When he returned to the gun-deck he found it almost deserted, for the sides were nearly all open, and the cannon-balls were passing through and falling into the water beyond. Then indeed it seemed as if all hope was lost and the *Bon Homme Richard* was a beaten ship, and it would be folly to hold out longer.

But all this time another fight had been going forward on the deck above, where Jones himself was in command. Pearson, seeing the havoc that had been made on the gun-deck of the *Richard*, hailed the commodore to know if he surrendered; but Jones, though his ship was sinking, his gun-deck riddled, his prisoners loose, and, worst of all, a fire had broken out near the magazine, sang out in answer that he "had not yet begun to fight." And he was as good as his word. Though the purser, who had charge of the battery on the quarter-deck, had been shot in the head, and some of the guns had been disabled, Jones had others moved across the deck, and pointing them himself, poured round after round of grape-shot upon the enemy. The French marines, too, with their muskets, were stationed in the tops, and taking steady and deliberate aim killed man after man on the spar-deck of the *Serapis*, until Pearson was left there almost alone. Other marines and sailors lying out on the yard-arms of the "Richard," which overhung the enemy's deck, flung hand-grenades through the open hatchways. Finally one of these struck the piles of cartridges that were lying on the lower deck of the *Serapis*, and caused a series of deafening explosions, by which twenty men were killed and many more were wounded.

This last mischance was too much for Captain Pearson, and left alone and unsupported as he was on the quarter-deck, he surrendered, hauling down his flag with his own hands. Instantly Dale, who had been with Jones during the last part of the battle, caught a pendant that was hanging from the main-yard, and swung himself over to the enemy's deck. He was quickly followed by Midshipman Mayrant and a party of men who scrambled over the rail; but so little did those below know of what had happened, that a man ran Mayrant through the leg with a pike, and the English first lieutenant, rushing up on deck, asked Dale if the Americans had surrendered.

"No," said Dale, calmly; "it is you who have surrendered, and you are my prisoner."

The crew were then secured, the ships were disentangled, and the victory was won.

While the great fight was going on between the large vessels, the *Countess of Scarborough* had fallen an easy prey to the *Pallas*, which was a heavier ship. The *Alliance*, if Landais had done his duty, might have destroyed the enemy single-handed; but she took no part in the fight except to fire a few broadsides at the two ships as they lay together, which did more harm to the *Richard* than to her foe. Landais was led to this most treacherous conduct by his jealousy of Jones; but so far from injuring the commodore, it only benefited him, for it left to him alone all the glory of the victory.

The *Richard* was kept afloat with difficulty that night; but next day a gale sprang up, and seeing that it was impossible to save her, Jones took off all his people and their prisoners to the captured ship. Then the *Bon Homme Rich*ard, whose career had been so short and glorious, slowly settled, until at last the waves closed over her. The other ships made sail and put into the Dutch port of the Texel, where Jones took command of the *Alliance*, and soon after, carrying her through the midst of the Channel fleet, arrived safely at Brest. The miserable Landais was tried by a court-martial, and dismissed from the service in disgrace,—a punishment which he richly deserved.

In the whole war of the Revolution there was no event, excepting the battles of Saratoga and Yorktown, where Burgoyne and Cornwallis laid down their arms, that so encouraged our friends and wrought confusion to our enemies, as the victory of the *Bon Homme Richard*. The battle had been fought on the English coast, and in the sight of a thousand Englishmen. The *Serapis* was a noble ship, well armed, commanded by a gallant officer, while her victorious enemy was old and rotten, an India trading-vessel never meant for war, with guns of no great service. No wonder that when Paul Jones went to Paris after the battle the people of all degrees vied with one another in doing honour to the victorious commodore. He went to court, where he was graciously received, and the king presented him with a golden sword, and made him a *chevalier* of his Order of Merit,—an honour which it was said had only been conferred before that time upon those who had borne arms under the commission of France. The Continental Congress, too, was mindful of his great service, and caused a medal to be struck in commemoration of the victory.

It was Paul Jones's last exploit in the navy of his country. When the *America*, the first ship-of-the-line that was built by the United States, was nearly finished, Congress passed a resolution, without one dissenting voice, giving the command to Jones. But in 1782, when the ship was ready, the war was almost over, and it was then thought best to give her to the French, to take the place of the ship *Magnifique*, which had been lost in Boston Harbor. So there was nothing left for Jones to do; but if in his whole life he had accomplished nothing else but the conquest of the *Serapis*, that single act would have been enough to make his country hold him forever in grateful remembrance.

Some years after the end of the Revolution the Russian Empress Catherine, who was then fighting against the Turks, sent for Paul Jones to lead her fleet against the enemy. Thus it came about that he became a Russian Admiral, and commanded the squadron in the Black Sea, where he increased his fame by winning victories over the Turkish vessels. After this service he came back to Paris, where he died in 1792, in the midst of the French Revolution.

CHAPTER 5

Barry and Barney

During the time that Wickes and Conyngham and Paul Jones were carrying on the war with such success in the enemy's waters under the guidance of Franklin, the Continental Navy was cruising on the American coast as actively as was possible, in the neighbourhood of the great English fleets. But it was a work of the utmost danger and difficulty. Several of the ports at one time or another were in the enemy's hands, and in all of them the Tories, or Loyalists, as they called themselves, were ready to give information whenever a vessel was fitted out for sea. Outside the ports, and up and down the coast, from Halifax to Florida, were innumerable cruisers of the enemy, sailing alone or in light squadrons, ever on the watch, and ready to capture the insurgent ships, which almost always were of lesser force.

Of the thirteen frigates that were built by Congress in 1775, five never got to sea at all, and several of the others, like Biddle's ship, the *Randolph*, were captured or destroyed before they had had time to do much service. The first one taken was the *Hancock*, under Captain Manley, the same who, by his capture of the brig *Nancy*, had so rejoiced the army before Boston. He was cruising toward the Banks, and had made one good prize, the armed ship *Fox*, when, rashly looking into Halifax, he was chased out and captured by Sir George Collier in the *Rainbow* frigate. This was in 1777. The next year was full of disasters. First came the blowing up of the *Randolph* in March, the story of which has been already told. In April, the *Virginia*, which had been built at Baltimore, was taken while aground on her first passage down the Chesapeake.

In August, too, the *Raleigh* had to yield, but only after a hard-fought battle, of which we shall hear more presently. In the next year the *Warren*, under Commodore Saltonstall, sailing on an expedition against the British post on the Penobscot, fell in with a large squadron of the enemy and was burned to prevent capture. The *Providence* and *Boston* were taken a year later, at the surrender of Charleston; but, like the *Warren*, they had done good service and taken many prizes before they fell into the hands of the enemy. The last of all the thirteen frigates was the *Trumbull*, and she held on till 1781, when she was overpowered by a squadron and struck after a desperate resistance.

One of the Philadelphia frigates which never got to sea was the *Effingham*. Near the latter part of 1776 she was assigned to the command of John Barry, a Philadelphia sea-captain of Irish birth, who was much trusted and respected by the great merchants of his adopted city, and who had entered the navy at the beginning of the war. Under such difficulties did the Colonies labour in the preparation of their ships-of-war, that the *Effingham* was at this time far from being in a condition to proceed to sea, and while waiting for her during the winter, Barry saw some service with the army as a volunteer. The spring and summer passed away, and still his ship was not ready.

At last, in September, Sir William Howe suddenly appeared in the Chesapeake, and after landing and fighting the battle of the Brandywine, he marched across the country to the Delaware, and took possession of Philadelphia. The *Effingham* and the other ships which had been lying there were hurried away to places of safety either up or down the river. The British threw up works to command the river, and the frigate *Delaware*, attacking them, ran aground and was lost. The Continental troops in the river forts—Fort Mercer and Fort Mifflin—were vigorously assailed by the British and the Hessians; and though the invaders were repulsed with heavy loss, the forts were finally evacuated. The ships below the town—among them Biddle's famous little brig the *Andrew Doria*—were then destroyed, and the passage was opened to the enemy from Philadelphia to the sea.

The *Effingham* and *Washington*—the two unfinished frigates—had been carried up the stream, where they remained, as it would seem, secure from all attack. Barry grew impatient in his enforced idleness, and conceived a plan to use the frigates' boats for a cutting-out expedition down the river, where the enemy's freight-ships and transports, loaded with supplies and stores, were constantly passing and repassing on their way to and from the sea. Selecting thirty men on whom he could rely, he rowed down the stream, and evading all the lookouts, made his way successfully past the town.

Pausing now cautiously to reconnoitre, he presently discovered four store-ships which had anchored in the river before discharging their cargo. Stealthily he crept up to the nearest of them, boarded her with his men, overcame the watch, and in a few seconds had taken possession of her. The same course was pursued with the other three. Barry was strongly tempted to try to carry off his prizes; but by this time the alarm had been given and signals were displayed, and before long the enemy's patrol boats would approach. There was nothing left but to destroy the vessels; and Barry, taking only time enough to see that the work had been well done, made for the opposite shore, and after landing his men safely, returned without loss to the frigate.

The boldness with which Barry had performed this dashing exploit won for him a reputation with both friends and foes. The story goes that Howe, struck by the captain's daring, made overtures to him to join the British service, and even went so far as to promise him a reward of £15,000 if he would betray his trust. "Not the value or command of the whole British Navy," was Barry's prompt answer, "would seduce me from the cause of my country!"

The French alliance, and the change it wrought upon the face of the war, led the British to determine upon the evacuation of Philadelphia, which came about accordingly in the following summer. But before going away they struck one blow from which the Continental Navy could not easily recover. Major Maitland, with a force of gunboats and barges, accompanied by a detachment of infantry and artillery, made a raid up the river and sought out all the vessels which had been lying snugly concealed there during the winter. They had no batteries, and were in no way capable of offering resistance; and all, including the *Effingham* and *Washington*, were burned. A month later the British abandoned Philadelphia.

Barry was now appointed to the *Raleigh*, one of the best of the thirteen frigates, which had already been at sea under another captain. At this time she was lying at Boston, and on the 25th of September, 1778, Barry weighed anchor and sailed down the harbour, bound on a cruise to the eastward. She had been only six hours out of port, when two large ships were seen approaching her from a distance. These proved to be a British frigate, the *Experiment*, of fifty guns, and the sloop *Unicorn*. The *Experiment* alone was nearly double the *Raleigh's* size, and Barry used his best endeavours to escape from them. But they had seen him, and crowded sail in chase. Night fell, and concealed both pursuers and pursued. The next day was hazy; but at noon the fog lifted and showed the enemy still far away, but doing all he could to lessen the distance.

So the chase continued for the rest of the day and the whole of the night, and the next day too, the enemy occasionally lost to view, and so raising the hopes of Barry and his crew, but each time reappearing, and still in hot pursuit. On the morning of the third day the wind freshened, and the *Raleigh*, which now was off the coast of Maine, gradually increased her speed and seemed about to cast off her pursuers; but in the afternoon the breeze again fell light, giving them once more the advantage, until at five o'clock the larger ship, the *Experiment*, had barely managed to come up, and opened fire.

The chances of escape now seemed slight indeed; but Barry was not a man to let himself be taken without a struggle, even by an enemy that was twice his size, and boldly joining battle, he began a contest which was to last for seven long hours, and in which the steadfast courage and unyielding purpose of the commander would have done credit to Paul Jones himself. At the second fire of the enemy the *Raleigh's* fore-topmast toppled over and fell. Nevertheless, she kept up a furious cannonade at close quarters, pouring in broadside after broadside at her big antagonist. The latter now found herself badly injured, and moved to a point some distance off, keeping up her fire at long range. Never allowing himself to be discouraged for a moment, although he had little reason to hope, Barry took advantage of this breathing-space to repair his damages. Then he followed the enemy and attempted to close with her and carry her by boarding.

It was a desperate measure, but it seemed to be the only chance; for the *Unicorn* had now come up, and Barry found himself between two fires. The *Experiment*, however, discovered his purpose and avoided him successfully. It had now grown very dark, and as a last resort Barry sought to get away and elude his opponents among the islands which at this point are thickly dotted along the shores of Maine; but they hung to him closely, and as a crowning misfortune his vessel ran aground. The struggle was now hopeless, and it would have been madness to hold out any longer. Abandoning his ship, Barry made for the land. This, with great difficulty, he at length reached, and so succeeded in escaping with some part of his crew; but the frigate which he had so gallantly defended fell into the hands of the enemy.

Thus ended the cruise of the *Raleigh*,—a cruise which had lasted only three days, but of which every moment had been filled with intense excitement, alternating between faint hope and blank despair, ending in failure, but which gave to her captain a name and fame that lasted long after the close of the Revolution. No man of his day in the navy was more honoured by his equals and more beloved and reverenced by those below him in rank. His sailors adored him; there was nothing they were not ready to do for him. He was always frank and generous to his friends and humane to his enemies. On board his ship he exacted full obedience, and he got it, both from officers and men, but always by gentle means. With a fine and noble presence, and a face that bespoke a true heart and ready hand guided by a strong purpose and a lofty courage, there was none in all the navy more regarded and esteemed than John Barry.

After the cruise of the *Raleigh*, Barry served for a time in privateers. Like Paul Jones, he should have had a good ship, but there was none to give him. Finally in 1780, after Landais came back disgraced from Europe, Barry was ordered to take command of the *Alliance*, and in the following winter he sailed for France, taking with him as a passenger Henry Laurens, who went out as the new Minister to France. In May, 1781, he left Lorient on his return; and on the 28th, being then near the Banks of Newfoundland, in the evening he discovered in his neighbourhood two sail of the enemy,—the ship *Atalanta*, of twenty guns, and the brig *Trepassey*, of fourteen.

Barry waited for daylight to attack them; but the next morning the wind fell, and not a ripple broke the shining surface of the water; while the *Alliance*, with her tall and graceful spars, and her sails hanging loose in the dead calm, slowly rose and fell with the broad swell of the Atlantic. There she lay like a huge log, unable to move a yard this way or that. Her very size was a misfortune now, for her two antagonists, smaller and more handy, could manoeuvre as they pleased, with their long sweeps; and moving up they took positions on her quarter, and opened on her with their guns. The *Alliance* could not reply with a single cannon, her heavy battery was useless, and the *Atalanta* and her consort kept up a steady fire for the whole morning and well into the afternoon. It was a galling thing for Barry to be placed thus at the mercy of a lesser force, to see his men shot down around him, and to be powerless himself to fire a shot in their defence.

At two o'clock Barry, who had all this time been waiting with impatience on the quarter-deck for the unwilling breeze, received a wound in the shoulder from a grape-shot. Stung as he was by the sharp pain, he refused to leave the deck; but at length, fainting from loss of blood, he was carried below to the cockpit, where the surgeon set about dressing his wound. Presently the first lieutenant came down to report the condition of the ship, upon whose deck many of the crew were lying killed or wounded, and ending his report, asked if he should strike the flag. Barry indignantly refused. "If the ship," said he, "cannot be fought without me, they shall carry me again on deck."

This answer revived the drooping spirits of the crew and gave fresh vigour to their efforts. Soon after this a little wind sprang up. It barely gave the frigate way to bring her guns to bear upon the enemy; but it was enough, and only a few broadsides from her 18-pounders were needed to settle the result. The captain of the *Trepassey* fell, and his ship immediately surrendered. His comrade Edwards, who commanded the *Atalanta*, refused at first to yield, but a few more broadsides cut his vessel well-nigh to pieces, and at three o'clock his flag too was hauled down. As the brave Edwards came on board the *Alliance* to give up his sword, Barry, forgetting his wound and the anxious hours that his opponent had made him pass, generously gave it back to him, saying as he did so, "Keep it, my friend. You richly deserve it; and your king ought to give you a better ship."

The *Alliance* during the next year was still cruising under Barry's command. But the war, though in name it still continued, was almost at an end. It was now certain that the king would do the thing he most abhorred, which was to recognize the independence of America,— and hostilities on land had really ceased. The seas still swarmed with British cruisers, but none of them were able to capture the *Alliance*, and she was brought safely home. After the treaty was concluded, the government, no longer needing her, sold her to Philadelphia merchants, and she became a peaceful trading-vessel.

★★★★★★

There was one officer among the younger men of the navy who resembled Barry no less in bravery and seamanlike skill than in the winning frankness and generosity of his nature. This was Joshua Barney. Three years before the war broke out he had gone to sea on his first voyage, and had risen in two years to be the second mate of his vessel. Early in 1775, not dreaming of the hostilities that were shortly to occur; he had set out from Baltimore on a voyage to the Mediterranean. The captain died at sea, the chief mate had been left behind, and Barney found himself, when only sixteen years of age, in the command of a leaky ship, with a long voyage before him, and all the responsibility resting on his shoulders. It was a hard trial for him; but he had gained the good-will of his crew, and to a man they obeyed and supported him.

Just before sighting the coast of Spain he fell in with a gale of wind; and he only managed to get into Gibraltar as his ship was on the point of going down. Here he obtained assistance and repairs by giving bonds,—for he had no money,—and he was thus enabled to deliver his cargo at Nice, which was the port of destination. The firm to which the cargo was consigned refused to pay the bonds, although there could be no doubt that it was their duty. "Well, then," said Barney, "you shall not have your cargo."

The merchants were astounded at the attempt of this boy of sixteen to make resistance, and upon their presenting a complaint to the governor, the latter threw Barney into prison. Making his escape by a stratagem, young Barney went at once to Milan and laid his case before the British minister, with such effect that in three days he had returned to Nice, the governor had apologized, his bond had been paid, and his ship discharged.

After a short stay Barney set out on his voyage home. As he was coming up the Chesapeake, he learned for the first time, from an English sloop-of-war that boarded him, of the stirring events that had occurred,—that battles had been fought at Lexington and Bunker Hill, and that Washington was besieging Boston, and the war for independence was begun. As soon as he landed, he made the offer of his services to the government.

At first Barney served as a volunteer in small vessels; but he soon became a lieutenant, and he was ordered late in the summer of 1776 to the *Andrew Doria*, now under the command of Captain Robinson. In this ship he made a cruise to the West Indies. While here, the *Doria* put in at the Dutch island of St. Eustatius to get some ammunition that was stored there for the Continental Congress, and upon arrival she fired a salute to the governor's flag. The governor, without much thought perhaps, returned the salute. This was the first time that the flag of the new American State had been recognized by any foreign power, and the Americans were much rejoiced that it should come about. But the British, who still felt that the Colonies were a part of Britain, and who knew that Holland was bound so to regard them, were incensed at the governor's act, and demanded his recall. The Dutchmen, who did not dare refuse, ordered him home; and the poor governor lost his post in consequence of his unthinking courtesy.

Soon after this the *Doria*, now on her way home, met an enemy's sloop-of-war, the *Racehorse*, which had been sent by Admiral Parker to lie in wait for her off Porto Rico. But the admiral did not count upon the bravery of the Americans, or he would have sent a larger ship; for the *Racehorse*, after a hot engagement for two hours, was herself forced to surrender.

A few days later the *Doria* captured an English snow,—an armed merchant-vessel of peculiar rig,—and Barney was detached to take her home. As had happened before with the *Doria's* prizes when Biddle was in command, the brig's crew was too small to man them, and Barney made up the needed number from the prisoners. On the way north he had heavy weather, for it was now December,—a month in which no seaman likes to pass Cape Hatteras,—and day after day the vessel encountered a succession of furious gales and heavy seas. Keeping well out to the eastward until he had fetched a point from which he could reach the Chesapeake, Barney now headed for the land, and at last found himself, on Christmas night, in a driving easterly storm, close on the breakers of the Jersey coast. To keep his vessel away from the lee shore and its certain perils, the young prize-master, as his only course, resolved to ride out the gale and let go his only anchor.

So the night fell upon him and his men,—a fearful night, what with the roaring tempest, and the sea rolling mountains high, while every wave broke over the bows of the ship. It seemed each instant, from the violence of the sea, that the small cable must part, and with it she would lose her only hope. The men, yielding themselves to blank despair, were sinking into lethargy. It was then that Barney, though he had little cause to hope himself, talked to them with cheering words, trying to rouse them from their stupor. He called to mind the battles they had fought, and how they had been ready to stand up bravely before the enemy and face death in another form.

"I am not much of a chaplain, my good lads," he said, "but this I know, that the same Power that protected you then can protect you now; and if we are all to go to Davy Jones's locker, we might as well go with a bold face as a sheepish one."

Barney's good example shamed the men to greater courage; but the night wore on and the day broke, and still the fury of the storm kept up. The crew were in the tops, and Barney with them. Soon a cry was heard of "Sail ho!" and every eye was turned toward a small sloop, which appeared in sight driven before the gale, yet trying to make an offing. Anxiously the men watched the frail boat, one moment rising on the wave till they could see her keel, and the next plunging down till she was lost to view. Each time it seemed as if she could not rise again; but each time she shot up on the foaming crest, seemingly steadying herself an instant before the next downward plunge. Suddenly there was heard a long, shrill shriek of terror piercing through the din and crash of breakers, and the sloop was swallowed up in the seething waters.

After this sight no words of Barney's could rouse his men from their terrors. But fortunately toward the middle of the afternoon the wind abated and the sea gradually went down. Barney lost no time in getting his crew down from aloft as soon as it was safe, and they were only too glad to come.

"Up with the anchor! Man the capstan! Cheerily, my lads!" rang out from Barney; and the men went to their duties with a will, and getting underway, headed for the harbour of Chincoteague, nearby, where they found a temporary shelter.

After resting here for a few days Barney started for the Chesapeake. On the second day out he was discovered by the *Perseus*, one of the enemy's blockading vessels, which immediately started in pursuit. Barney would have got off, as he had the faster ship; but the prisoners in his crew, who had been planning mutiny, and were only waiting till they sighted an English ship-of-war, refused to go to their stations. Barney singled out the ringleader and ordered him to his duty, and as the man did not stir he shot him then and there, though without giving him a mortal wound. This put an end to the mutiny; but through the delay the *Perseus* had been enabled to overtake the prize-vessel, and so she was recaptured. The wounded mutineer told his story to Captain Elphinstone, the commander of the *Perseus*, thinking that he would at once have Barney put in irons; but the captain set his complaint at nought, and said that if he had been in Barney's place he would have done the same.

Barney remained a month on board the *Perseus*. Her captain, Elphinstone, who afterward became the famous Admiral Lord Keith, was a generous enemy, and treated his prisoners as became an honourable and gallant officer. Upon one occasion the purser, a hot-tempered Scotchman, struck Barney in the face, on the quarter-deck, whereupon the young lieutenant knocked him down. The captain, when he heard of it, sent word to them both to come to his cabin, and without asking any questions he commanded the purser to make apology on his knees to the unarmed prisoner whom he had affronted. So Barney fared well in the *Perseus*; but he was not sorry, soon afterward, at Charleston, to leave her on parole and go to Philadelphia, to which place his old ship the *Andrew Doria* had meanwhile come without mishap.

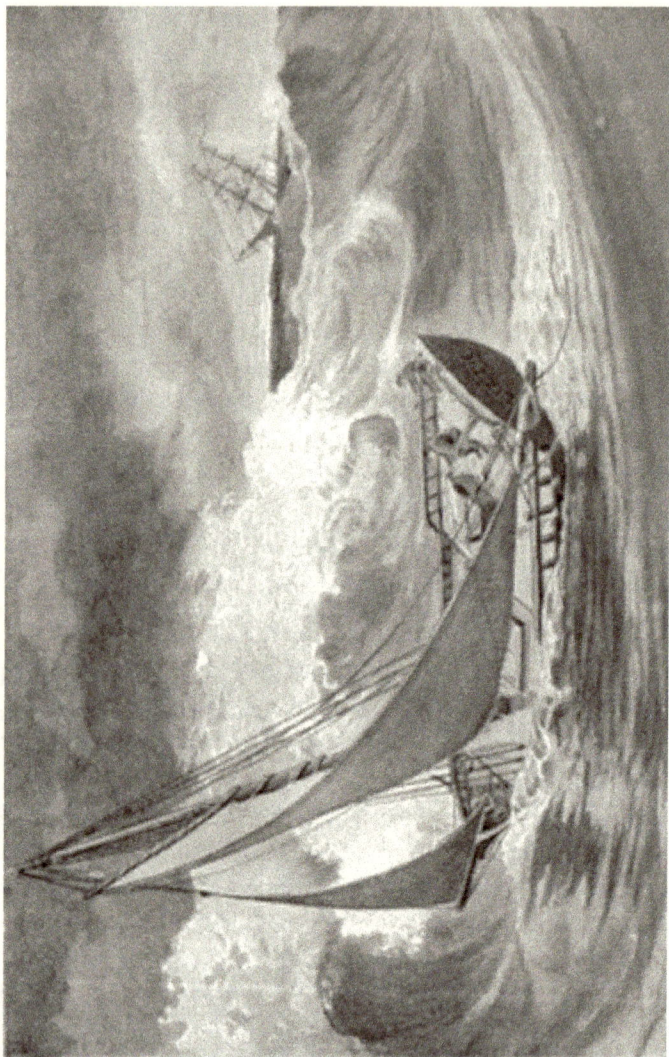

"The Sloop was Swallowed up in the Seething Waters."

For some months Barney could not join his ship, being bound by his parole, but at last an accident relieved him of it. It happened that Lieutenant Moriarty, of the English frigate *Solebay*, with a boat's-crew, had incautiously gone ashore for water somewhere in the Chesapeake, and had been seized and taken prisoner by a party of Virginians. Captain Elphinstone now made an agreement with Gov. Patrick Henry, of Virginia, to exchange the two lieutenants; and so Barney was released from his parole in time to bear his part in the actions in the Delaware River during the weeks that followed Sir William Howe's occupation of the city. How the *Doria* and the other vessels were destroyed after the surrender of the forts has been already told; and Barney, being now without a ship, was ordered to march with a detachment of his men to Baltimore, and there to join the new frigate *Virginia*.

It was just at New Year's, in 1778, that Barney arrived in Baltimore; and as the frigate of which he was to be the first lieutenant was not yet ready for sea, he took command of a pilot-boat to cruise about the bay and watch the movements of the enemy, who had then several ships in the Chesapeake. One night, as he was returning from a reconnoissance, he found a merchant-sloop from Baltimore on her way down the bay, and hailed her, telling her what dangers she would meet below. To his no small surprise he was answered by a volley of musketry. He tacked in order that he might the better return this unlooked-for fire, and presently discovered on the off side of the sloop a ship's barge lashed alongside.

It was now clear why his seeming friend had fired on him. The enemy had cut out the sloop, and they were using her as a decoy to capture Barney. But he served them the same turn that he had served the *Racehorse*; for after a short and sharp struggle he captured them and took them to the city. The barge belonged to His Majesty's ship *Otter*, and Barney, mindful of the treatment he had received on board the *Perseus*, took the best of care of his prisoners,—above all of Gray, the officer in charge, who had been wounded, and sent a flag-of-truce boat to the Otter, to bring them what they needed.

On the last day of March the *Virginia* left Baltimore, and attempted under cover of the night to pass the British lookouts in the bay, and so get out to sea. No doubt she would have done it safely had not the pilot, losing his way, run her ashore on the Middle Ground, a large shoal in the lower Chesapeake. The morning broke, and found her hard and fast aground, with three of the enemy's frigates close at hand. Nicholson, the captain of the *Virginia*, now called away his barge and left the ship, making his escape to land. It is a story that one must grieve to tell of an American officer; but it can only be supposed that, having but just entered the navy, he did not know what honour and duty meant. There was nothing left now but surrender, for the rest could not escape.

Barney was now a prisoner on board the *Emerald* frigate. It is clear that even in a bitter war not only one good turn deserves another, but secures another; for the kind treatment which Barney had received from Captain Elphinstone resulted in his kindness to the *Otter's* men, and this again, which was well known throughout the British squadron, gained for him equal favours in his new captivity. But this did not last long; for after a little while he was sent to New York, where for the first time he came to know the horrors of a prison-ship.

Late in August Barney was exchanged, and found himself again in Baltimore; but there was little now for him to do. After all the disasters of this disastrous year of 1778, only four frigates were left on the American coast, and the smaller vessels had mostly been destroyed or captured. While he was in this plight a merchant offered him the command of a privateer schooner, carrying two guns and a crew of eight men; and Barney, being so reduced for want of naval occupation, consented to take her to St. Eustatius with a cargo of tobacco. He must have been truly at his wit's end to have undertaken such a voyage in such a craft; for even if he could have carried out the undertaking, he would have gained neither glory nor profit from it. But he was not destined to carry it out; for even before he reached the capes he met a larger privateer, carrying four guns and sixty men, which speedily disposed of him after a running fight of a few minutes. The enemy, not caring to be troubled with prisoners, put him and his little crew ashore; and his voyage being thus curtailed, he found himself a few days later again in Baltimore. Here he remained for several weeks.

Strange as it must seem, Barney was now only nineteen years old, yet there had been crowded into his short boy-life more adventures and perilous enterprises than most men of three times his years have gone through. Since the war began, he had been thrice made a prisoner, but each time he had been fortunate in having humane captors. But the worst was yet in store for him. After a successful privateering voyage to Bordeaux, he sailed in 1780 in the *Saratoga*, under Captain Young. Early in October she captured four prizes, one of which was given to Barney to command. He left the *Saratoga*, and it was fortunate he did, for she was never seen or heard of afterward; but the prize which he commanded was herself captured only one day later by a British squadron. Barney was taken to New York, and soon after sent to England in the *Yarmouth*. On board this ship the prisoners were confined in the hold, in a space three feet high, and without light or air; and the horrors of the voyage, which lasted seven weeks, remind one of the fearful stories of the Middle Passage in the old slave-trading days. It was by comparison a happiness to be transferred even to the Mill Prison, after those wretched hours on board the *Yarmouth*; and the prisoners when they came ashore, weak from suffering and disease and want of food, were a most piteous spectacle.

How Barney, after three month's confinement, made his escape from prison; how he lived six weeks unrecognized in London, though all the time a price was set upon his head; how he sailed for Ostend in a mail-packet, and after various wanderings upon the Continent at last returned to America,—we have not time to tell. The spring of 1782 found him once more in Philadelphia, still ready for any service for which his country might call.

Although the war on land had at this time pretty nearly come to an end, the Delaware River and the bay below were still infested by Tory privateers and stray cruisers from the British fleets on the lookout for prizes. To clear its waters of these marauders, the State of Pennsylvania bought a merchant-vessel named the *Hyder Ali*, which had already started on her voyage with a cargo. She was brought back, her merchandise removed, a battery of sixteen guns was mounted, and she was fitted for a cruise under the command of Barney.

On the 8th of April she left Philadelphia with a large merchant fleet in company, which had been waiting patiently until the new cruiser should be ready to convoy them past the capes of the Delaware. All went smoothly on the way down the bay; but at Cape May, as the wind was southerly, the fleet anchored, waiting for a favourable breeze. They were in this position when suddenly a force of the enemy, composed of a frigate and a sloop-of-war, was seen rounding the cape on its way to attack them. Barney ordered the convoy to retire up the bay out of harm's reach, and the vessels tripped their anchors and made sail before the southerly wind, the *Hyder Ali* staying behind to cover their retreat.

Now it happened that there was—and still is, for that matter—in the lower part of the bay, a widely-spreading shoal called the Overfalls, which divided the water into two channels. The convoy on its way up took the eastern channel, and thither it was followed by the *Hyder*

Ali. The frigate went up on the western side, hoping by this means to overtake and cut off some of the merchantmen without hindrance at the upper end of the shoal. But the sloop, her captain being more ambitious or more reckless, followed in the wake of the convoy; and thus it came to pass that in a short time she had caught up with the *Hyder Ali*, which, seeing that the enemy's force was divided, was taking no great pains to get away from her. The sloop was the *General Monk*, which under the name of the *Washington* had once been an American privateer, but had been captured by the enemy.

Although the *Monk* alone was considerably heavier in force, as she carried twenty 9-pounders to his sixteen 6's, Barney waited for her to join battle. His object was to get her so to place herself that he would be able to rake her; that is, by lying across her bow or stern, to make his broadside sweep her decks from one end to the other. This he accomplished by a stratagem. As the *Monk* approached his quarter, he sang out to his helmsman to "port the helm," so loud, that the enemy could hear him. If the quartermaster had obeyed his order, it would have given the *Monk* an advantage by enabling her to rake his stern; but Barney had arranged beforehand that the helmsman should do just the opposite of what he said. The result was that the *Hyder Ali* was thrown squarely across the bow of the sloop, so that a moment later her jib-boom was entangled in the American's rigging, where she was held fast, and Barney had her at his mercy. He poured his broadside the whole length of her decks, and she could barely answer now and then with a single gun. After half an hour's contest she surrendered.

Meantime the frigate, seeing what was going on, endeavoured to help her consort; but the shoal lay between, and it took her a long time to round its lower end. Barney, knowing that he could not sustain a fight with her, decided to make off, and did not stand upon the order of his going. Hastily throwing a prize crew on board the *Monk*, he held his course up the river; while the frigate, which had turned back, was seen in the distance doubling the southern end of the shoal. But she was too late, and the *Hyder Ali* arrived with her convoy at Philadelphia, bringing with her as a trophy the sloop which had been captured with so much skill and gallantry.

The engagement between the *Hyder Ali* and the *General Monk* was the last of any importance during the war. Indeed, since the beginning of the French alliance in 1778, hostilities on the American coast had been chiefly carried on by the great English and French fleets of line-of-battle ships, which cast into the shade the small operations of the

HEAVING THE LEAD ON BOARD THE FRIGATE.

Continental Navy. In this very month Sir George Rodney won his great victory over the Count de Grasse in the West Indies,—a battle between two opposing fleets larger than had ever before been brought into action. Early in the next year the Treaty of Paris was concluded, which recognized the independence of the United States; and the navy and the army were disbanded, the ships that remained were sold, and the officers and men returned again to private life.

CHAPTER 6

Hostilities with France

Just at the close of the Revolution the country found itself independent, but labouring under a heavy burden of debt, and with a government that had hardly enough authority to be called a government at all. In fact, at this period the nation was little more than a collection of separate States, with a kind of league or confederation to hold them together. Each of these States had its own government, which paid little attention to the wants of the others. After a few years, however, it became clear that the jealousies and rivalries of the States would break up the league unless they were held together by some stronger bond; and as they could attain strength and greatness only by union, they wisely laid aside all their little differences, and acting through their delegates at Philadelphia, formed that wonderful plan of a united nation called the Constitution, which went into force in 1789, and under which we still live; for so skilfully was it framed, that it has stood every shock and trial, and the time will soon arrive to celebrate the hundredth anniversary of its adoption.

It is clear that a country under such conditions could not possibly keep up a navy; and so it was that after the Revolutionary War the whole establishment gradually passed out of existence. Even when the Constitution was adopted, and Washington became the first President of the United States, there were other matters that required attention first, and the new government rightly gave its thoughts to these. Besides, it was so short a time since the people of the Colonies had suffered from the oppressions of the Royal Army and Navy, that they had a dread and almost a hatred of any kind of standing military force. Therefore, though one of the officers of the new government was a secretary of war, he had not much of an army to look after, and no navy at all. But soon the government found it necessary to make a

59

change in its naval policy, and the change came about in a very unexpected way.

There were at this time four small States on the southern shores of the Mediterranean Sea called the Barbary Powers, which had for many years derived much profit from the detestable practice of sending out piratical ships to plunder the merchant-vessels of all nations. The European States from time to time made an attempt to put the pirates down, and sometimes a great nation had even paid them money on condition that they should not molest its commerce. There is some ground for thinking that England, of whom the Barbary Powers were most afraid, rather encouraged their depredations than sought to check them, because it was for her advantage, as a trading State, that foreign merchant-fleets should suffer, in order that the field might be left clear to her. However this may be, the English had never put forth their naval strength against the corsairs; yet English merchantmen were mostly spared by them. Before the Revolution the vessels of the Colonies, bearing as they did the English flag, had all the privileges of other English ships; but when the war was over, and the merchantmen of the young American State began to reappear in the Mediterranean with a new and hitherto unknown American flag, the Barbary cruisers pounced upon them as their lawful prey.

The first piratical capture was made in 1785, and was a Boston ship, the schooner *Maria*. Soon afterward the *Dolphin*, of Philadelphia, was seized. These were carried into Algiers, where the ships and their cargoes were confiscated by the *Dey*, and the crews were held in slavery. It seems strange that there should not have been enough of public spirit in the country to fit out ships at once and send them over to set free the Americans who were enslaved by these Turkish outlaws, or at least to protect from their barbarities other Americans navigating the seas. But no such measures were taken, and the prisoners were left to languish in captivity until their buccaneering captors received a heavy ransom. Agents were indeed sent out, who did much chaffering with the Algerines, mostly through foreign officials; but for a long time this brought about no result, and several of the captives meanwhile died.

During the next few years the Portuguese were at war with Algiers, and her ships were in consequence unable to venture far from port; but in 1793 a peace was concluded, and thereupon an Algerine squadron, suddenly appearing outside the Strait of Gibraltar, fell upon and captured ten unsuspecting American merchantmen. This was too much for any State to bear, however long-suffering or impoverished it might be; and Congress resolved at once to begin the building of a new fleet. Accordingly plans were made for the construction of six frigates of a much larger size than any which the navy had possessed during the Revolution. In fact, some of them were of about the largest size that were then afloat, and led our enemies in later wars to declare that we had misled them by building ships-of-the-line under the name of frigates; which, even if it had been true, would not have been a reproach to us, as it was their business to find out what our ships were like. It was a most wise measure to build these large frigates, as the country afterward realized; and great credit is due to Joshua Humphreys, a Pennsylvania ship-builder, upon whose suggestion the plan was adopted.

Even this small provision was made only after much debate and opposition, because there were many men who thought that a navy would make the central government too powerful, and would be used to destroy the liberties of the people: and although the building of the ships was begun, negotiations with Algiers were continued, and large sums of money were expended in presents,—or, to speak plain English, in bribes,—to influence the *Dey* to make a treaty. These were so far successful that in the next year the treaty was concluded, and all the prisoners were ransomed. Such violent objections were now made to keeping up the naval force, that it was decided to finish only two out of the six frigates, and the work on the others was stopped.

One member of Congress even went so far as to say that he hoped "the ships would rot upon the stocks as an instructive monument of national folly."Yet it was certainly much greater folly to spend a million dollars—which was what the treaty cost—in presents and bribes to Turkish officers, and in the ransom of American citizens, rather than in building ships and fitting out a navy to punish the marauders, and to deter them from a repetition of their outrages. For, as we shall hereafter see, the money that was paid was not enough to satisfy the Barbary Powers, who, however much they got, were always wanting more; while the navy, so far from overturning liberty, has ever since been one of its greatest bulwarks, by the glory and honour which, through all its history, it has brought upon the Republic.

★★★★★★

In 1793, some time before the Algerine trouble was settled, a war had broken out between France and Great Britain. It was only ten years after the close of the Revolution, in which the French had been our trusted friends and the British our bitter enemies; and the French, like ourselves, and partly influenced by our example, had cast off their monarchy and had established a republic. There seemed at first sight to be every reason why we should side with them against the old enemy, and in the beginning most of our people were ready to give them the warmest sympathy and support. But the French Revolution, with its Reign of Terror, soon took such a turn that men shrank with horror from its bloodstained course; and meantime France, presuming too far upon the services which she had rendered in our own struggle for independence, demanded of us favours in return which we could not give without going again to war with Britain.

It was Washington's desire then, and it has been our wise policy ever since, that we should avoid entangling ourselves in European broils, so that we found it necessary to give France a refusal, though it was very hard to do it. Thereupon the French, knowing our weakness, especially at sea, took advantage of it to inflict upon us every kind of injury and insult. They used our ports to fit out privateers, and captured vessels of the enemy in our own waters, which, as we were neutral in the war, they ought to have held sacred; they seized our merchantmen upon frivolous pretexts, to the great damage of our commerce; and when we made respectful protests and complaints about it, our ministers were treated with such indignity as the world has rarely seen in the dealings of Christian States.

The British too were guilty of aggressions on their side, but not at this time to the same extent. So the people of America were divided,— some siding with the French, partly for old friendship's sake, and some with the British, because from them had come the lesser evil. Between these two factions party spirit raged with bitterness and rancour; so that it sometimes almost seemed as if men thought themselves the citizens of one or the other of the opposing States, and forgot that they were all Americans. Finally, matters came to such a pass that something must be done to protect our commerce, and as a war with both States at once seemed to be too great an undertaking, and France was at this time the worse offender, the new President, John Adams, whose party leanings were all upon that side, urged that a navy should be fitted out to make reprisals upon the French cruisers and privateers.

In this way the summer of 1798 came to be a time of preparation for war. The larger frigates were completed, and several small ones were begun. The merchants in the different cities raised large sums of money to build ships by subscription, to be repaid later by the government, and everywhere the ship-yards were busy getting ready the

"Everywhere the Ship-Yards were Busy."

new fleet. Congress declared that the treaties with France were at an end, and authorized the President to instruct our ships-of-war to seize all French armed vessels that might be found at sea. Officers were selected, crews were recruited, and the Marine Corps, which has always since that day done most efficient service, was first created. A new department of the navy was established as one of the great divisions of the government; which showed that all this preparation was not the mere whim and fancy of the moment, but that the country was at last resolved to have a naval force which should continue for all time.

The new Secretary of the Navy, Benjamin Stoddert, proposed that a small force should remain to defend the coast, and that all the other ships should go to the West Indies, which swarmed with French cruisers and privateers, and attack the enemy on his own cruising-ground. Thither they all went in the summer or fall of the year, until we had assembled there what was for us a powerful force, composed of four squadrons, and numbering all together more than twenty vessels. The largest of the squadrons, with the new frigate *United States*, of forty-four guns, as flagship, was placed under the command of John Barry, the story of whose Revolutionary fights was told in the last chapter, and who had been chosen by Washington to be the first captain of the new navy to hold the President's commission. Besides some smaller vessels, Barry had with him another frigate, the *Constitution*, a forty-four like the *United States*, which was destined to become our most famous ship, by winning in the War of 1812 a succession of splendid victories.

The second squadron, with the 38-gun frigate *Constellation* as flagship, was given to Captain Truxtun, who had also seen much service in the Revolution while in command of privateers. The third and fourth were lighter squadrons. By means of these four detached groups of vessels the ports and harbours of the West India Islands were closely watched, every nook and corner was visited, and in the passages between the larger islands, which form the great highways of commerce, our merchant-ships had convoy and protection. It was a different kind of service from that of the earlier war; for our ships now were equal to any frigates in the world, and the enemy's great fleets of line-of-battle ships were fully occupied by the war in Europe; while our older officers were veterans who had passed with credit through their first trial, and the younger could have no better masters from whom to learn their early lessons.

The first prize of the war was the French privateer *Croyable*. The sloop-of-war *Delaware*, under Capt. Stephen Decatur,—not the one who afterward became so famous, who was then only a midshipman in Barry's flagship, but his father,—went to sea in June, 1798, and had been out but a few days when she captured the *Croyable*, which had been seizing several of our vessels on our own coast. She was taken into the navy and named the *Retaliation*, and the command of her was given to Lieut. William Bainbridge. Bainbridge was a young man who had only been a merchant captain, but he was a daring fellow,—almost too daring for prudence, as the result showed; for soon after he had reached the West Indies with his new command he one day unguardedly approached two French frigates, the *Insurgente* and the *Volontier*, supposing for no good reason that they were English, and his little ship was quickly captured.

The *Insurgente* was the smartest ship on the West Indian station, and indeed one of the finest and fastest frigates in the French navy, and the government expected great things of Captain Barreault, who was in command of her. But the captain was destined to disappoint them. Early in February of the next year, as the *Constellation* was cruising to the eastward of the island of Nevis, she discovered a large ship to the southward, and immediately bore down for her. In the old war, when our officers sighted a large ship, the best thing they could do was to take to their heels, for the enemy was sure to overmatch them. But the *Constellation* was a frigate of a different sort from those which we had sent to sea in the Revolution; and Truxtun, though he believed the stranger was an enemy, boldly advanced to meet her. She proved to be the "*Insurgente*," and soon she hoisted the French flag and fired a challenge gun to windward.

Though the *Insurgente* hailed him several times, Truxtun made no reply, but continued to bear down upon her until he was sure that every shot would tell; then he delivered his whole broadside, and the *Insurgente* answered him. The fight continued for an hour, the *Constellation* always gaining the advantage; for Truxtun was a better seaman than Barreault, and again and again he placed himself where he could rake the enemy, while she could not reply, her broadside being turned away. The Americans, too, were better gunners, for they killed and wounded the *Insurgente's* men, while the Frenchmen, pointing their guns too high, only damaged the *Constellation's* spars and rigging. At last, after seventy of the *Insurgente's* crew had fallen, and Truxtun had taken a position squarely athwart her stern, so that the next broadside would sweep her decks, she struck her flag and so surrendered.

DAVID PORTER.

The *Constellation* had only two men killed in the battle, and one of these was shot by his own lieutenant, Sterrett, because he saw him flinching at his gun. One of the midshipmen, a gallant fellow named David Porter, of whom we shall hear again later, at this time only eighteen years of age, was stationed in the *Constellation's* fore-top during the engagement. A cannon-ball struck the topmast above him, and it was in danger of falling under the weight of yards and sails. The midshipman hailed the deck, and reported to the officers what had happened; but they were too busy to send men up to repair the damage. So Porter, without waiting longer, climbed the mast himself amid a shower of bullets, and cut away the stoppers, which let the yard go down, and by this means the mast was saved.

After the battle the first lieutenant of the *Constellation*, John Rodgers, was sent on board the prize, with Porter and eleven men, to see to the removal of the prisoners. A fresh breeze blowing at the time delayed the work, and soon the night closed in, the wind increased to a gale, and the ships were separated. There were still one hundred and seventy of the Frenchmen on board the *Insurgente*, with no one but Lieutenant Rodgers and his handful of men to guard them. Rodgers was a young man of muscular frame, which is a good thing at such times as these; and both he and Porter were cool and determined, which is a better thing. But they had no easy task. The gratings covering the hatchways had been thrown overboard. There were no means of securing the prisoners. The spars and rigging and sails of the prize had been cut and torn, and her decks and sides still bore the marks of battle: and here was Rodgers separated from the *Constellation*, in a gale of wind, with only his faithful midshipman and eleven seamen, and with nearly two hundred prisoners who knew the weakness of their guards, and who were ready for any effort that would help them to retake the ship.

Difficult as his position was, Rodgers proved himself equal to it. He stationed a sentry at each hatchway with musket and pistols, ordering them to shoot the first man that attempted to come on deck, and with the other men he took care of the ship. For three sleepless days and nights—for neither he nor Porter could snatch a moment's rest—he sailed this way and that, almost at the mercy of the storm, and finally brought the vessel into St. Kitt's, whither the *Constellation* had gone before him.

During the next six months the war—for such we may call it, though in truth it was only a series of reprisals for injuries received—

continued with unabated vigour. Nothing could show more clearly the importance of a navy than these same reprisals of 1798 and 1799. During the twelve months ending in July of the latter year many privateers of greater or less force had been taken, and France was now more ready to treat on equal terms. The frigate *United States*, still under Barry, was selected to take out the new envoys sent by our government to Paris, and her place on the windward station was taken by the *Constellation*, Commodore Talbot in the *Constitution* relieving Truxtun at St. Domingo. New ships were sent out to both squadrons, which were instructed to go on with their captures in order that the French might see that we were in earnest and would put up with no more trifling.

Our merchant-ships still needed protection, for the privateers continued their aggressions, and besides the privateers there were in the West Indies many small armed vessels belonging to no State in particular, whose business was to seize and plunder anything they could. These last were little better than pirates, who made this or that island or bay a place of refuge for the moment, and were ready to change their character according to the ships that they fell in with. To serve against these *picaroons*, as they were called, two small but swift schooners were built,—the *Enterprise* and the *Experiment*. They carried twelve guns each, and were exactly what was needed for the purpose. The *Enterprise* alone during her short cruise captured nine vessels carrying all together more than seventy guns and five hundred men; and besides this she recaptured eleven American merchantmen, and beat off a Spanish brig which sought to attack her. This was more than any of the frigates had accomplished.

The severest action of the war was yet to come, and this fell also to the lot of the *Constellation*. In February, 1800, just a year after his fight with the *Insurgente*, Commodore Truxtun was cruising to the west of Guadeloupe, when he came in sight of the *Vengeance*, a heavy French frigate of the largest size, carrying fifty guns. Although she was much more than a match for Truxtun, she avoided an engagement and made sail to leave him. Truxtun without hesitation followed in pursuit; but the chase lasting several hours, it was twilight before he came up with her. Then he hoisted his ensign, lighted his battle lanterns, and gave his orders not to throw away a single charge of powder, but to take good aim, firing directly into the enemy's hull, loading with two round shot, and now and then a round shot and a stand of grape; and he told his officers "to encourage the men at their quarters, and to cause or suffer no noise or confusion, but to load and fire as fast as possible, when it could be done with certain effect."

As the commodore approached, his guns loaded and his gunners ready and waiting, he stood in the lee gangway to speak the *Vengeance*, and demand her surrender to the United States of America. But at that instant she opened a fire from her stern and quarter guns directed at his spars and rigging. Truxtun gained a position on her weather quarter, and returned the enemy's salute; and now for five long hours of the tropical night the battle raged, a running fight, the two vessels keeping side by side within pistol-shot. The *Constellation's* gunners, bearing in mind their orders, planted one hundred and eighty shot in the enemy's hull; but their guns were light, and they could not inflict a fatal wound upon the great frigate's heavy side. But the slaughter on the Frenchman's decks was fearful, for fully one third of his crew lay killed or wounded. Three times his flag was struck during the battle, but in the darkness of the night it was not seen, and there was no cessation of the combat.

At last, about an hour after midnight, the enemy was silenced, and no answer came from his fifty guns. Both ships were still under way, the *Vengeance* sheering off; and Truxtun, knowing that the fight was over, was about to follow her as well as his torn and ragged sails would enable him, when he learned that all the rigging of the mainmast had been shot away, and that the mast was tottering. The men were called to repair the rigging and secure the mast; but it was too late, they could not save it. The officer of the maintop was James Jarvis, the youngest midshipman on board the ship. With him was an old bluejacket, who told him of the danger they were in because the mast must surely go. But little Jarvis had been stationed by his captain in the top, and he only answered: "I cannot leave my station; if the mast goes, we must go with it."

So the mast fell: and Jarvis, the midshipman who would not leave his post, fell with it and was killed,—the only officer who perished in the action.

The *Constellation's* loss, all told, was forty killed and wounded. The *Vengeance*, which she had so nearly captured, arrived a few days later at Curaçao in great distress, and almost a wreck.

In memory of this great battle, one of the most obstinate that our navy ever fought, Congress passed a resolution which should be read by all who care that gallant deeds should be remembered. This was the resolution:—

"It was Twilight Before He Came up With Her."

Resolved, by the Senate and House of Representatives of the United States of America in Congress assembled, That the President of the United States be requested to present to Captain Thomas Truxtun a golden medal, emblematical of the late action between the United States frigate *Constellation*, of thirty-eight guns, and the French ship-of-war *La Vengeance*, of fifty-four, in testimony of the high sense entertained by Congress of his gallantry and good conduct in the above engagement, wherein an example was exhibited by the captain, officers, sailors, and marines, honourable to the American name, and instructive to its rising navy.

And it is further Resolved, That the conduct of James Jarvis, a midshipman in said frigate, who gloriously preferred certain death to an abandonment of his post, is deserving of the highest praise, and that the loss of so promising an officer is a subject of national regret.

The active occupations of the navy in the West Indies continued for the next eight months, its last important capture being the fine corvette *Berceau*, which yielded after a two hours' fight to Captain Little, in the *Boston*. Already, a month before, the treaty with France had been concluded, and after it was ratified, a vessel was sent to the station with orders of recall for the whole squadron. During its service there it had taken or destroyed over ninety French vessels, mounting in all more than seven hundred guns, and had recaptured numbers of Americans. Among its trophies there were the frigate *Insurgente* and the corvette *Berceau*, and not the least splendid chapter in its record was the long battle between the *Constellation* and the *Vengeance*; while in the two years but one ship had been lost,—the little schooner *Retaliation*, and that was only a recapture.

It was this work of the navy which gained us the respect of France, from which State we had hitherto received only threats and insolence: and it teaches us the lesson that it is to our navy that we must always look in times like these to secure for us a proper treatment and consideration from domineering foreign powers. It would be well for us Americans, especially those who are ready to cry down the navy, to take to heart these words of the President, which he said in November, 1800, but which are just as true today, and which will be true to the end of time:—

Seasonable and systematic arrangements, so far as our resources

THOMAS TRUXTUN,—FROM MEDAL VOTED
BY CONGRESS.

will justify, for a navy adapted to defensive war, which may, in case of necessity, be *quickly brought into use*, seem to be as much recommended by a wise and true economy as by a just regard for our future tranquillity, for the safety of our shores, and for the protection of our property committed to the ocean.

CHAPTER 7

Tripoli

The truth of President Adams's words was shown the very next year after they were uttered, when new difficulties arose with the Barbary Powers. We have seen how the old difficulties with Algiers had been settled, at least for a time, by a treaty which cost the government a million. Under this treaty we agreed to send every year to the Dey of Algiers a present of naval stores of the value of twelve thousand sequins, or about twenty thousand dollars. In the autumn of 1800 this present—or tribute, as it was well called, for it was little else than a tribute—was carried to Algiers by the ship *George Washington*, commanded by Captain Bainbridge. While his ship was lying in the port, the Dey commanded Bainbridge to go to Constantinople with an Algerine ambassador and presents for the Sultan of Turkey; for Algiers was then a vassal of the Ottoman Porte, although the Porte allowed the *Dey* to do much as he pleased in most things.

It was a grievous outrage that a ship of the United States should be compelled to do such a service for a barbarian prince; but there is no doubt that Bainbridge chose the better part in complying with the demand. Though sometimes rash in war, he was wise and prudent in diplomacy; and as our government, by yielding to the clamour of the Algerines for tribute, instead of chastising them for their outrageous conduct, had pointed out the line of action that it meant to follow, Bainbridge was right in conforming to the same rule. If he refused, unnumbered evils might happen: our unprotected commerce would be swept away; more of our countrymen would be captured and enslaved, or kept for years confined in dungeons; and fresh payments must be made for ransom. So he went to Constantinople.

It was then the rule—and it still is, for that matter—that foreign ships-of-war wishing to enter the Turkish straits of the Dardanelles and Bosphorus must first ask and receive permission from the *sultan*. Bainbridge, who felt that he had had enough humiliation on the voyage, did not stop for this, but passing by the forts at night, anchored unannounced in the harbour of Constantinople; and here he lay, flying a strange flag which no one in the place had ever seen borne by a ship of war.

A Turkish officer was sent off to find out to whom this new craft belonged, and Bainbridge in reply told him, "the United States." When this was translated by the interpreter, and reported to the Turkish officials on shore, they shook their heads,—thinking the national appellation somewhat vague, as perhaps it is,—and sent a second time to gain more definite information. Bainbridge now answered that he came from "the New World." This statement seemed greatly to impress the Turks, and the ship was piloted into the inner port, and Captain Bainbridge and his officers were treated thereafter with deep respect, as was becoming toward anyone who came from so remarkable a region.

When the *George Washington* had fulfilled her mission and had returned to Algiers, the captain found that the *Dey* had suddenly declared war against France, and had ordered all the French in his dominions to be put in prison. The foreign consuls, seconded by Bainbridge, implored the *Dey* to revoke his cruel order; and they were so far successful that he consented to put off its execution for forty-eight hours. But the *Dey* swore by his beard that if every soul—man, woman, and child—that belonged to France had not departed by that time from his territories, he would put in irons those that remained. The *George Washington* was at the moment the only ship in the harbour, and she was shifting ballast in the mole. But Bainbridge would not leave the Frenchmen to their fate; and by working night and day with all his officers and men he got the ship ready, took the fugitives on board, and sailed away, glad to get out of the clutches of this Oriental despot. He had no time to spare; for in less than an hour after his departure the limit had expired. Sixty Frenchmen were thus rescued by the captain's efforts, and after a short passage they were safely landed at Alicant, and the *George Washington* returned home.

About this time a new and very serious trouble began with another of the Barbary powers. This was Tripoli. When the *Pasha* of Tripoli had made his treaty with the United States some years before, he had received a large amount of money, but no agreement had been made for tribute. As soon, however, as the *pasha* found that the Americans were sending every year a shipload of presents to Algiers, of whose power he was always jealous, he became enraged beyond all bounds; and he wrote to the President insolent letters demanding money and arms and naval stores. In one of these he said:—

> We could wish that these your expressions were followed by deeds, and not by empty words. You will therefore endeavour to satisfy us by a good manner of proceeding. We on our part will correspond with you with equal friendship, as well in words as deeds. But if only flattering words are meant, without perform-ance, everyone will act as he finds convenient.

As no attention was paid to these demands, the *pasha* announced to the American consul that he would declare war; "For paid I will be," he said, "in one way or another." The consul tried to smooth over the difficulty, but without success; and on the 14th of May, 1801, just a week after Bainbridge had landed the French refugees at Alicant, the *pasha* cut down the flagstaff of the American consulate at Tripoli, by which act he declared war against the United States.

It had been known at home for some time that trouble was brew-ing at Tripoli, and as the French war was now entirely over, a squadron was at this very time fitting out to go to the Mediterranean. It was commanded by Com. Richard Dale, that gallant veteran of the Revo-lution who had been the first lieutenant of the *Bon Homme Richard* in her fight with the *Serapis*. But in this cruise Commodore Dale, though he had a good squadron, was not allowed to show what he could ac-complish; because, although Tripoli had declared war, Congress had not yet recognized the fact, and the President was of the opinion that until Congress had passed an act making a declaration, the navy could not carry on war against a foreign State. The commodore was there-fore prevented by his orders from capturing any prizes or prisoners; and from this singular arrangement it resulted, as might be expected, that nothing of any great importance was accomplished.

One event, however, took place in August of this year which at least showed the Tripolitans that war with the Americans was no child's play. That fine little schooner the *Enterprise*, which had done such good service in the West Indies, was one of the ships of Com-modore Dale's squadron, under the command of Lieutenant Sterrett. While cruising about in the Mediterranean, on the lookout for pirates, she chanced upon a Tripolitan *polacca* called the *Tripoli*, of about the same force and size. The *rais* or captain who commanded the *polacca*,

Mahomet Sous, thought he would try the mettle of the American schooner, and made a furious attack upon her. The Tripolitans fight desperately; for they are little better than cut-throats, and, as their *pasha* says, war is their trade. But they have not the skill of the Americans. Sterrett placed his schooner where he pleased. When the battle had fairly begun, he took the offensive himself; he attacked the enemy on her quarter, on her bow; he raked her fore and aft.

After a bloody fight the *Tripoli* had received several shot in her side, and was badly cut up in her rigging. Then she hauled down her flag. The crew of the *Enterprise* left their guns, and gave three cheers, thinking that the victory was won. But the Tripolitans, though brave, were treacherous villains, and no sooner was their enemy off his guard than they hoisted their flag again and opened fire on the *Enterprise*. So the battle began anew. This time the Turks attempted to board, crowding on the rail with their scimitars. But they were driven back, and again they made a pretence of surrendering, only to renew the fight at the first favourable moment.

The American blue-jackets were now in no humour for trifling. Their blood was up, for they were indignant at such unheard-of treachery, and it looked as if there would be no question to settle about prisoners, for the reason that none of the Tripolitans would be left alive. But the *polacca* was by this time in a sinking condition, her mizzen-mast was shot away, her deck was slippery with blood, and the dead and wounded were lying about in heaps; and the *rais*, Mahomet, himself wounded and disheartened, convinced that the time had come when neither ferocity nor fraud could help him, threw his flag into the sea and prostrated himself upon the rail, begging for quarter. Then Lieutenant Sterrett, who was as generous as he was gallant, ordered the firing to cease and took possession of the enemy.

As the *polacca* could not be made a prize, the Americans cut away her masts, threw overboard her guns, and left her with the surviving fragment of her crew to make the best of her way back to Tripoli. Upon her arrival, the *pasha* was so incensed at the news of her defeat that he had the *rais*, wounded as he was, mounted on a jackass and paraded up and down the streets of the city, after which he was given five hundred blows of the *bastinado*. Such was the result of the first fight between the Americans and their piratical enemy, and it was a long time before the latter forgot the lesson.

By the autumn of 1801 the terms of enlistment of Dale's crews having nearly expired, his ships were ordered home, and in the next

"Crowding on the Rail with Their Scimitars."

spring a new squadron was sent out under Commodore Richard Morris, Congress having meantime passed an act that was to all intents a declaration of war. But the new commodore was not an energetic man, nor did he seem to concern himself much about what was to be done; and a whole year was passed by the squadron in fruitless cruises among the Mediterranean ports, sometimes convoying merchantmen, sometimes merely lying in harbour, but doing little or nothing against the enemy. At the end of this time the President found it necessary to replace Commodore Morris by a more active man; and in the summer of 1803 he was ordered home, and upon his arrival was dismissed the service.

Already the government had determined to fit out a new squadron, and to take more vigorous measures against Tripoli; for the people were rightly impatient at the dallying which had prolonged through two years this war with a little barbarian State, and it was against the navy that this impatience was mainly directed. Strange as it may seem, party feeling had run so high that the gallant exploits of the French war were thought by many Americans to be the bad results of a mistaken policy, rather than a source of pride and satisfaction to the country; and the officers and seamen of the navy, who were then and who have always been the single-minded and devoted servants of the people, were looked upon simply as the instruments of an odious party that meanly cringed to England and sought to embroil us in a war with France. In the last general election this party had been defeated and broken up, and the navy came in for a large share of the popular condemnation; which, as we at this day can clearly see, was exceedingly unjust to the brave men who composed the service.

Whatever men may have thought and said about the navy, it was evident that nothing but a naval war would bring Tripoli to terms, and the government set about the work in earnest. Four new ships were built, which, though they were small, were well suited to their purpose,—the brigs *Argus* and *Siren*, and the schooners *Nautilus* and *Vixen*. Two of the larger frigates were sent out,—the *Constitution* forty-four, and the *Philadelphia* thirty-eight, the latter commanded by Captain Bainbridge; and last, but not least, one vessel of the old squadron remained, the schooner *Enterprise*, which had already made herself famous under Sterrett, but which was to acquire still greater fame under Lieut. Stephen Decatur, who now commanded her.

The new squadron was strong in its ships, but its efficiency was mainly due to the officer who was ordered to take the chief command, Com. Edward Preble. Although not an old man, he was one of the few veterans of the Revolution that were still in the service; and though he had been a mere lad when he first sailed as a midshipman in the Revolutionary cruisers of Massachusetts, he had served throughout the war, and had learned well the lessons of naval discipline. What Paul Jones was in that war, and what Truxtun was in the West Indies, Preble became in the campaign against Tripoli,—the central figure of the war. He had around him the best and bravest of the young officers of the new navy,—as good as any navy the world has ever seen, but up to this time untried and unknown,—and it was Preble who in great measure made them what they afterward became.

Among the first of the new vessels to come out was the *Philadelphia*. She had no sooner arrived in the Mediterranean than she made a most unexpected discovery. She had left Gibraltar to search for some Tripolitans that were reported to be cruising somewhere off the coast of Spain. One evening after dark, off Cape de Gatt, she fell in with two vessels,—a ship and a brig. Captain Bainbridge hailed the ship, which proved to be the *Mirboka*, a cruiser of Morocco; and allowing her to suppose that he was English, Bainbridge ordered her to send him her passports. The Moorish officer who came on board the *Philadelphia* fell into the snare, and told Bainbridge that the brig which he had with him was an American.

This was an extraordinary piece of news, for Morocco was then at peace with the United States; yet here was one of her ships-of-war preying on American commerce. The Moors must have thought that a State which could not protect its vessels from the attacks of Tripoli need not be much respected, and that the time was ripe for them to take a hand in the plundering which their neighbours were carrying on with such success and profit; so they had sent out their cruisers, and this was the first that had made a prize. The captured ship was the brig *Celia*, of Boston, whose crew and captain were at that moment confined in the *Mirboka's* hold, to be carried to Morocco and sold as slaves or held for ransom. Fortunately Captain Bainbridge had arrived just in time to rescue the prisoners; and seizing the *Mirboka*, he took her with him to Gibraltar.

This was the state of affairs when a few weeks later Commodore Preble, with the *Constitution*, came out to take command of the squadron. He saw the situation at a glance, and he was not a man to hesitate long about taking action. If the Moors, who had seaports on the Atlantic, were not put down and the strait opened, it would be of no

COMMODORE EDWARD PREBLE.

great use to clear the inland sea of pirates. The commodore immediately assembled all his ships, gave them orders to capture every Moorish vessel they could find, and himself proceeded in the *Constitution* directly to Tangier, in Morocco. The emperor was expected to arrive here shortly with his army. He sent to know whether Preble would fire a salute in his honour. The commodore sent back his answer by the consul.

"As you think," said he, "it will gratify His Imperial Majesty, I shall salute him and dress ship; and if he is not disposed to be pacific, I will salute him again!"

The resolute tone which Preble took in this and other communications had the desired effect. In three days after the emperor arrived he had consented to renew the treaty his father had made with the United States, and had ordered the release of all the Americans that had been seized, together with their property. At the same time the orders which had been given to capture American vessels were revoked; whereupon Preble restored the *Mirboka*, and withdrew his own order to seize the vessels of Morocco. This done, he sailed for Tripoli.

Already the *Philadelphia*, with the schooner *Vixen* in company, had taken her station before the enemy's port, and preparations were made to maintain a strict blockade. It needed two vessels at least for this service; for if any accident happened to one alone, she would certainly be lost, being so far from help and close to the watchful guards of the enemy's harbour. Nevertheless, immediately after his arrival Captain Bainbridge heard from a Neapolitan merchantman that one of the enemy's *corsairs* had sailed the day before, and he sent the *Vixen* off to find her.

Next day, it being the 31st of October, a Tripolitan vessel was descried to the eastward of the city, attempting to work into the harbour. Captain Bainbridge at once gave chase. The wily Tripolitan kept on his course, not far from the shore, where he knew the water was full of reefs and sunken rocks which he could easily avoid, but which he hoped might prove a trap for his unsuspecting enemy. And so it came about; for the captain, whose zeal, as we have already seen, was sometimes greater than his prudence, forgetting the dangers of the treacherous coast, followed the Tripolitan, with a fair breeze and a good eight-knot speed, until suddenly the water began to shoal. Then realizing for the first time his peril, he turned his vessel's head off shore. But it was now too late; and an instant later the *Philadelphia* had shot up on a sunken reef, where she hung hard and fast, her great stem

"He Cut Away the Anchors. . . . But Still the Ship Hung Fast."

and bowsprit pointing upward in the air.

Even now the captain did not lose his confidence, and setting all sail he tried to force the vessel over; but this only had the effect of thrusting her higher on the rocks, and making escape more hopeless than ever. It was clear that this plan would not work. The boats were then sent out with leadsmen, who found deep water astern of the ship, and the yards were braced aback, and every one watched anxiously to see if she would not back off; but she did not move an inch. Then Bainbridge tried to lighten her. He cut away the anchors and threw overboard the forward guns, but still the ship hung fast.

Meantime the enemy discovered that their stratagem had proved successful, and word having been sent to the city, the Tripolitan galleys could now be seen in motion, evidently preparing to make an attack upon the helpless frigate. Soon they came out in a long line, their white lateen sails glistening in the afternoon sunlight, and their decks crowded with men eager for the splendid prize that chance and craft, combined with their opponent's over-confidence, had thrown within their reach. But they were wary, and they remembered the lesson which Sterrett had given them, that the Americans were stubborn fighters, and this time they meant to run no risks. Taking up their positions on the stern and quarter of the *Philadelphia*, at a little distance, where no guns could be brought to bear on them, they opened fire with their heavy cannon; for each of these gunboats carried a long eighteen or twenty-four pounder in her bow, and the whole flotilla was a hostile force not to be despised even by a ship that could manoeuvre.

As it was, the *Philadelphia* had heeled over, and the few guns that remained on board were useless, even after great holes had been cut with axes in her side to enable the crews to point them. The enemy fired high and only cut the spars and rigging; but all the same their ultimate success was sure if the ship could not get off the reef. In spite of the shot that rained upon them, the officers did not relax their efforts. The tanks of water in the hold were pumped out, and finally the foremast was cut away, carrying with it the main top-gallant mast. But it was all of no use, for the ship obstinately refused to budge; and as the sun was sinking in the horizon, Captain Bainbridge, to prevent what seemed likely to be a useless sacrifice of men, hauled down his colours.

No sooner was the flag lowered than the Tripolitans, setting up a shout, rowed quickly to the frigate and swarmed on board, over the rail and through every port-hole. Then there was a scene which has never before or since been witnessed upon an American ship-of-war. The pirates, intent first of all on plunder, looted every chest and locker in the ship. Nor did they stop here. The officers were forced to give them all that they demanded, and like so many highway robbers they took watches, epaulets, money; and when all the valuables were given up, coats, waistcoats, and cravats, until all the prisoners were stripped to their shirts and trousers.

In this condition they were thrust into the boats and carried to the city. Here they were taken before the *pasha*, who was so much elated by his capture that he received them in high good-humour, and as he counted over the number,—three hundred and seven officers and men,—he stroked his beard, and his avaricious eyes glistened as he thought of the heavy ransom that the United States would have to pay him before it could get them back. So he ordered them to be well cared for, and sent the officers to be quartered in the building which before the war had been the American consulate, where they were to remain during many months of captivity.

It was bad enough that so many officers and men should have been taken; but the mischief did not end here. For the next two days the Tripolitans worked away at the grounded frigate with their gunboats and lighters, and anchors carried out with hawsers from the stern; and by these means, with the help of favouring wind and tide, they at last succeeded in getting the *Philadelphia* off into deep water. Bainbridge, before he abandoned her, had ordered the carpenters to bore holes in her bottom; and if this had been well done, she would never have got afloat again. But the carpenters in their excitement and flurry had only half performed their task, and the ship was now in the enemy's hands in as good condition, barring a little needed repair, as she was before the accident. Even the anchors and guns which had been thrown overboard were discovered lying on the reef, where the water was only twelve feet deep, and the Tripolitans got them up without much trouble.

******

Meantime Commodore Preble, having despatched his business at Morocco to the great satisfaction of his government, was now on his way to Tripoli in the *Constitution*. Falling in one day with the British frigate *Minerva*, he received the first news of the disaster; and going directly to Malta, he found there a letter from Captain Bainbridge confirming the report. It was a staggering blow to all his hopes at the very outset of his command. The Tripolitans, who had already become tired of the war and of the annoyances of the blockade, and whom he had hoped by resolute attacks speedily to overawe into submission, were encouraged by this their first great success to renewed efforts. Not only would they stand more firmly to their previous demands for tribute, but they would clamour for an enormous ransom for the three hundred prisoners; and unless they could be utterly crushed, they would get it, for they had the prisoners in their power, and in some way or other those three hundred Americans must be set free.

The squadron, none too powerful at the beginning, had now lost one of its two principal vessels, and the force of the enemy was correspondingly increased. No wonder that Commodore Preble, writing to the department of the loss of the frigate, should say in the bitterness of his heart, "It distresses me beyond description." But however great his distress, he never yielded to despondency, and the loss only urged him on to greater efforts to harass and reduce the enemy.

For the next two months the commodore and all the ships of his squadron were busy making preparations for the coming campaign. The first blow to be struck was against the captured frigate, and Preble resolved upon her destruction from the very moment when he heard of her loss. But he bided his time, patiently waiting until a good opportunity should arrive. Meanwhile a rendezvous for the squadron was established at Syracuse. The *Argus* was stationed at Gibraltar, to watch the Moors and guard the strait. The other ships were cruising about from point to point, giving protection and convoy to American vessels, and seizing any Tripolitan vessels they could find, though there were few of them that dared to venture out. About Christmas-time the *Enterprise* fell in with one of these craft, a ketch named the *Mastico*, which was on her way to Constantinople with slaves on board,—a present from the *pasha* to his master the *sultan*. The slaves were not a capture of much benefit to the commodore, but the *ketch* was; for she had once been a French gunboat, and he saw how she might be of service in carrying out his most cherished scheme. So he made a tender of her and called her the *Intrepid*.

All this time the prisoners at Tripoli were not forgotten. The Danish consul in the city, a kind-hearted and generous man, Nissen by name, was pleased to do all that he could to help the Americans. Through him Preble and Bainbridge were enabled to get letters to and from each other, and supplies were sent from Malta through an agency established there by the commodore. The secret parts of the letters were written in sympathetic ink, so that one only saw the writing when the letter was held before a fire. In this way the commander of the squadron was kept informed of all that went on in Tripoli, as far as Bainbridge knew it; and Bainbridge in his turn was much cheered by getting word from time to time that his friends outside had not forgotten him. He needed it badly, for what with the loss of his ship, and the gloomy prospect of a long captivity, he was at this time in great despondency; so that it did him good to hear from Preble the words the latter wrote in January from Malta: "Keep up your spirits, and despair not; recollect 'there's a sweet little cherub that sits up aloft'!"

When Preble returned to Syracuse after this visit to Malta, he had completed his plan for the destruction of the *Philadelphia*. Lieutenant Decatur, of the *Enterprise*, had volunteered to command the expedition; and although he was very young, and had been only five years at sea, no better man could have been chosen than this gallant and true-hearted officer. He was to take the *Intrepid*, whose Tripolitan rig would make a good disguise, and whose small size would enable her safely to navigate those dangerous waters, and with seventy-five officers and men to attack the frigate. The *Siren* was to go with him to support and cover his retreat.

It was a perilous enterprise; almost rash, one would think, for the *Philadelphia* was lying fully armed and manned in the inner harbour, under the guns of the *pasha's* castle and all the neighbouring forts, and around her lay the galleys of the enemy's flotilla. Decatur took three other lieutenants, Lawrence, Joseph Bainbridge, whose brother was in prison in Tripoli, and Thorn; and six midshipmen were told off to go with them. Among these last were Thomas McDonough, who afterward won the great battle of Lake Champlain in the war with Great Britain, and Charles Morris, who in the same war was first lieutenant of the *Constitution* in her fight with the *Guerrière*. Morris was at this time a boy of nineteen; and I shall tell the story of the attack as nearly as may be in his words.

A Maltese pilot, Catalano, who knew the harbour of Tripoli, and who could speak the language, had been engaged to go with the expedition. When the two vessels arrived off Tripoli, the wind was fresh and the sky lowering, and all seemed to threaten a storm. The *Siren* and *Intrepid* anchored under cover of the night, and Morris and the pilot were sent in with a boat to see if the passage to the harbour was safe, of which the pilot was doubtful. They found the surf breaking in a long line of foaming waves across the entrance, and Morris coming back reported that it would be dangerous to make the attempt. "It was a severe trial," said the poor boy, "to make such a report. I had heard many of the officers treat the doubts of the pilot as the offspring of apprehension, and the weather was not yet so decidedly boisterous as to render it certain that an attempt might not be made, notwithstanding our report; should such be the case, and should it succeed, the imputations upon the pilot might be repeated upon me, and, unknown as I was, might be the cause of my ruin in the estimation of my brother officers." Still, in spite of their murmurs of dissatisfaction, Morris, being a brave and independent lad, stood firm in his opinion, and the attempt was given up.

It was well that this was done; for before morning a furious gale had come up, and the ships, with difficulty getting away from the shore, were driven far to the eastward. For six days the storm continued, the officers and men being all this time cooped up in the little *ketch* with hardly room to breathe, and overrun with vermin which the slaves had left behind them. The midshipmen slept on the top of the water-casks on the lower deck, while the sailors were berthed in the same way in the hold.

At last the wind abated, and on the 16th of February the ships were once more in sight of Tripoli. The breeze was light and the sea smooth, and the *Intrepid* stood in slowly toward the town. The *Siren* stayed outside to lull suspicion; but in spite of all precautions she was seen and noticed from the harbour. The plan was for the *Siren's* boats to come in after dark and join in the attack. All through the afternoon the *Intrepid* kept on sailing slowly in, her drags in the water astern checking her headway so that she might not reach the town too early. Her crew remained below, that no suspicion might be roused by the unusual numbers, and only six or eight, dressed as Maltese, were allowed to come on deck. As the sun went down, the breeze grew fainter; and Decatur, fearing that if he delayed longer he might not be able with the light wind to reach the frigate, decided that he would not wait for the *Siren's* boats, saying to his officers, like Henry V. at Agincourt, "*The fewer the number, the greater will be the honour.*"

It was now dark, and the lights could be seen glittering in the houses of the town and on the boats in the harbour, throwing bright reflections over the water. The last preparations were made on board the *Intrepid*, and the officers, speaking in low tones, told each man once more his allotted duties, and cautioned all to steadiness and silence. The watchword for the night was *Philadelphia*, by which they were to recognize one another in the confusion of the attack. There was no need to enjoin silence, for each man was busy with his own thoughts. "My own," said Morris, "were now reverting to friends at home, now to the perils we were about to meet. Should I be able to justify the expectations of the former by meeting properly the dangers of the latter?" These thoughts, mixed with calculations to get a good place in boarding, were passing through the minds of all as they waited in breathless expectation.

Gradually the *Intrepid* was borne along by the gentle breeze toward the inner basin. Her boat was towed astern. The young moon gave light enough to show her movements, but nothing could be seen upon her deck except Decatur and the pilot standing at the wheel, and here and there a man whose Maltese cap and jersey gave no indication of his hostile character. From end to end of the little ship the rest of the crew, crouching under the shadow of the bulwarks, were lying concealed from view, each man with his eye fixed on Decatur, waiting for him to give the order. Before them could be seen the white walls of the city and the forts.

The first battery is now passed in silence, every man holding his breath. Right in the path of the *Intrepid* towers the *Philadelphia*, with her great black hull and lofty spars, and around her lies the circle of batteries. The little craft speeds on noiselessly, steering directly for the frigate. Suddenly the anxious silence is broken by a hail from the enemy demanding the name and purpose of the *ketch*, and ordering her to keep away. Among the officers and men stretched on the deck can be seen the eager movements of heads bending forward to hear the colloquy. The pilot, speaking the language of the country, answers for Decatur, who prompts him in low tones. He says that he has lost his anchors in the gale,—which, as it happened, was the truth,—and asks to be allowed to run a hawser to the frigate and to ride by her during the night. To this the captain of the *Philadelphia* consents, and the *ketch* is approaching, when suddenly the wind shifts, blowing lightly from the ship, and leaves the *Intrepid* at rest not twenty yards away, motionless under the enemy's guns.

It is a moment of terrible suspense. The least mistake, the least disturbance or excitement, must mean detection, and detection now will seal the fate of all. But Decatur has that perfect calmness and clearness of judgment which is the highest bravery. There is no flurry. In his low quiet voice he orders the boat manned. His calmness calms the men, and with an air of lazy indolence they get in and take the oars, car-

"THE LIGHTS COULD BE SEEN GLITTERING IN THE HOUSES."

rying a rope to another boat which meets them from the frigate. The work is done in silence; the ends are fastened, and the boat returns. The hawser is passed along the deck; the crew lying on it pull noiselessly, and the *ketch* slowly, slowly but surely, nears her place and lies fast alongside the enemy.

Suddenly a piercing cry breaks the stillness. "*Americanos!* The Americans are upon us!" The enemy has now discovered the disguise. But at the same moment Decatur's voice is heard ringing out, "Board!" and he and Morris, who has been watching him, leap to the enemy's deck. Springing to their feet as one man, the crew follow them, each with his cutlass and pistol. The Tripolitans are panic-struck; for a moment they huddle in a frightened crowd on the forecastle. One instant Decatur pauses to form his men, and then at their head he dashes at the enemy. The few who stay to offer resistance are cut down; one is made prisoner; the rest, driven to the bow, leap from the rail into the water.

The ship is now captured, and the victorious crew hurry to their appointed stations. Two parties are told off to the berth-deck, one to the forward store-rooms, and one under Morris to the cockpit. Each prepares its supply of combustibles, and when all is reported ready, the order is given to set fire. This done, each party leaves the ship, but Morris and his men barely escape through the smoke and flame with which the lower deck is already filled. Decatur, standing on the *Philadelphia's* rail, while the smoke rises around him and the flames are bursting from her ports, waits till the last man has returned, and as the *Intrepid's* head swings off, he leaps into her rigging.

By this time all the Tripolitans have caught the alarm, and from batteries and gunboats in quick succession, all around the wide sweep of the harbour, are seen the sudden jets of flame followed by clouds of smoke, and the shores resound with the roar of cannon. One hundred guns are firing upon the little *ketch*, whose white sails are lighted up by the flames of the burning frigate. The harbour is a circle of fire, and the gallant band seem doomed to pay the penalty of rashness. The frigate is herself a source of danger, for her magazine must soon explode. But the crew of the *Intrepid*, after giving three rousing cheers for their success, man the long sweeps and head their vessel seawards.

The *Philadelphia*, which reveals them to the enemy, lights them on their way. Her appearance is magnificent. The flames illuminate her ports, and mounting up the rigging and masts form columns of fire, which, meeting the tops, branch out in beautiful capitals. Behind her, thrown out into strong light by the burning ship, are the city walls

"The 'Philadelphia' Lights Them on Their Way."

and roofs, with dome and minaret rising above them,—bright points against the sky.

The guns of the *Philadelphia* commanding the harbour have been loaded and double-shotted. As the fire reaches them they are discharged, but their missiles do more injury among the Tripolitans than among their foes. The *Intrepid* seems to bear a charmed life under the converging fire of the enemy. The cannon-balls fall thickly in the water, ahead, astern, alongside, throwing up columns of spray; but only one shot touches her, and all the harm that does is to make a hole in her top-gallant-sail. A favouring breeze now springs up, and aided by the strong arms of the rowers at their sweeps, the *ketch* is carried out of range, and in a short time she has reached the open sea and joined her consort.

******

Meantime in the squadron lying at Syracuse the officers and men, and above all the commodore, had undergone profound anxiety. It had been thought that a week, or ten days at most, would be sufficient time for the two vessels to accomplish their work and return to the station. But as the time wore on and day after day passed by, the hopes of all began to turn to apprehension; for no one knew that for a week after they reached the enemy's coast the *Siren* and *Intrepid* had been driving about before the gale, their efforts for the moment directed only against the elements. Each day the horizon was scanned by the lookouts aloft, and as the second week came to an end with no sign of the expedition, the most hopeful shook their heads, and all were filled with a sense of dull foreboding. But on the morning of the fifteenth day the fleet was startled by the cry of "Sail ho!" from the mast-head, and every face peered anxiously toward the southern horizon. First one ship was seen, then two; and as they came nearer, and little by little their spars and rig could be distinguished, the hope that they might prove to be the missing vessels grew slowly into certainty.

Now a signal could be descried from the *Siren's* mast-head. What did it mean? Was it success, or failure? At length there was no doubt; and when from alternations of despair and hope the news was spread that Decatur had successfully achieved his purpose, and that the *Philadelphia* was indeed destroyed, the men's excitement knew no bounds, and cheer upon cheer of welcome and of exultation went up from all the vessels.

One thing is certain: that no exploit of our navy since that time has surpassed in bravery and finished excellence this of Decatur,—"the

STEPHEN DECATUR.

most bold and daring act of the age," as it was called by Nelson, then commanding the fleet off Toulon. The commodore wrote his despatch to the department, asking that Decatur might immediately be raised to the same grade as himself; and when the government heard the news, it lost no time in granting Preble's generous request. In this way it came about that young Decatur, though barely five-and-twenty, became a post-captain in the navy, which he had entered less than six years before; and among all the officers of Preble's squadron, who were in all things like a band of brothers, there was not one that grudged him his promotion.

******

After the destruction of the *Philadelphia* the commodore desisted for the time from further enterprises; for it was now midwinter, and at this stormy season the dangers of the rocky coast made it imprudent to attempt active operations against the enemy. But there was no slackening in preparations for the campaign of the next summer, and meantime the blockade was maintained with strictness. By this means was captured a brig of sixteen guns which belonged to the Tripolitan consul at Malta, and which was seeking to smuggle powder and other contraband into the enemy's port. The prize was re-named the *Scourge* and taken into the service, making a useful addition to the squadron.

All this time the commodore was on the alert,—at Syracuse, Messina, Malta, Naples, as occasion called him, but never long in one place. At one time he appeared off Tripoli and gave the *pasha* an opportunity to reduce his terms; but the *pasha*, sulking after the loss of the *Philadelphia*, would not yield one jot in his demands. The commodore next took three of his ships to Tunis, to quiet threatening demonstrations in that quarter, and to let the *Bey* know that the Americans, though occupied with Tripoli, still had time to keep an eye fixed upon him. Some of the vessels needed repairs, and these were in turn attended to. The weakness of the squadron in small gunboats, wherein lay so much of the enemy's strength, was a source of great concern; and Preble in his letters to the department entreated that permission might be given him to buy or build them in the Mediterranean ports.

But to this the government would not consent; and Preble, as a last resort, went to Naples and obtained from the King of the two Sicilies, who was an enemy of the Tripolitans, a loan of six gunboats and two bomb-vessels, or mortar-boats, as we should call them now. They were not very seaworthy or efficient, and "required careful nursing," as the commodore said. "However," he added in his report to the department, "as they were the best I could obtain, I have thought it for the good of our service to employ them, particularly as the weather in July and August is generally pleasant, and without them my force is too small to make any impression upon Tripoli."

★★★★★★

At last all the preparations were completed, and the commodore toward the end of July set out to begin operations against the city. His whole force consisted of one frigate, three brigs, three schooners, and the eight small gunboats and mortar-boats which he had borrowed at Naples. Taking these last, the *Constitution*, *Nautilus*, and *Enterprise* set out from Syracuse, and arriving before Tripoli were joined by the blockading squadron, composed of the *Argus*, the *Siren*, the *Vixen*, and the *Scourge*. The ships made a brave display as they all appeared before the enemy's city; but in reality they were an insufficient force to bring to the attack of such a place, with its hundred guns protected behind massive walls, its fleet of nineteen gunboats, and its army on shore of twenty-four thousand soldiers.

For they were desperate fighters, these Turkish bandits, when it came to a hand-to-hand conflict, as we have already seen from their fight with Sterrett; and in all the American fleet there were not above one thousand men. But the assailants were strong in one thing, and that was in their officers. Young as the officers were, they counted among their numbers the flower of the navy. There were Somers and the two Decaturs,—Stephen and James; Lawrence, the brave captain of the *Chesapeake* in the War of 1812; Hull, who captured the *Guer-rière*; Stewart, who took the *Cyane* and the *Levant*; Charles Morris, Macdonough, Warrington, Blakely, Spence, Henley,—all of them preparing now for the greater war that was to come, in which they were to win new renown for the navy and the country. They believed in their commander-in-chief, who they knew would lead them to victory if any man could. They believed too in each other, and they fought side by side like true and generous comrades.

For several days the wind blew violently on shore and prevented any active operations. The ships hastened to gain an offing; but the gale increased, and on the last day, when it was at its height, the gunboats pitching and tossing in the heavy sea seemed on the point of foundering. The foresail and main-topsail of the frigate, though close-reefed, were blown out into ribbons from the bolt-ropes. Fortunately before any worse accident happened the gale subsided, and the squadron was once more able to approach the town.

At last came the 3rd of August,—a day ever memorable in the annals of our naval history. There was a light breeze blowing from the southeast as the squadron stood in slowly for the town, whose white walls, surmounted by glistening mosques and minarets, and surrounded by gardens and groves of palms, seemed to the Americans like some fabled city of old myths, which they were always approaching and which never could be reached. There is no fable about it on this day, however. Within these walls are three hundred of their companions confined in prison by a barbarian despot who calls himself a *pasha*, but who is little better than the leader of a gang of pirates. His hundred cannon are frowning from the walls, his batteries are manned, and his fleet of galleys is drawn up in battle order outside the bristling line of rocks that covers the entrance of the harbour. They are there to have a fight, and the commodore is not a man to balk them in their purpose.

The fleet is now advancing, the bombs and gunboats still in tow. Presently the ships wear, with their heads off shore. The *pasha*, on the battlements of his castle, surrounded by his courtiers, is watching the movements of the Americans, and says to his officers, "They will mark their distance for tacking; they are a sort of Jews, who have no notion of fighting." But he is going to find out before night. The ships are now passing within hail of the commodore, and each captain is receiving his final orders for the attack. Officers and men are transferred from the larger vessels to the gunboats. The latter are arranged in two divisions,—the first under Somers, the second under Decatur. There are only six of them in all, and they are to attack nineteen of the enemy, while the mortar-boats shell the town, and the *Constitution* and her attendant brigs and schooners deliver their broadsides at the batteries.

At half-past one in the afternoon, the ships, wearing in succession, are headed for the batteries. As they approach silently and steadily, the bombs and gunboats are cast off. The batteries give no sign of life, there is no sound to break the stillness of the clear midsummer afternoon; and looking at the picture as the sun shines peacefully from the bright blue sky upon the white city walls, and the ships under their clouds of canvas, and the sparkling waters, one can hardly fancy that in a few moments it will be transformed into a scene of mortal combat.

At length the bombs have taken their position and come to anchor, and the signal for battle is displayed at the mast-head of the *Constitution*. Each of the mortars flings out a little curling puff of smoke.

97

An instant later, with a deafening din and uproar, all the guns in the squadron and in the batteries on shore, as if directed by one man, have opened fire with their heavy round shot. The gunboats, led by Decatur and Somers, dash out against the enemy, and soon they are lost to view beneath the smoke of battle.

The cannonade continues. Meantime Somers, though his boat is a dull sailer, by dint of hard work with the sweeps has reached the enemy's rear division, and single-handed as he is drives them in confusion behind the rocks. Decatur, followed by his brother James, by Trippe, and by the younger Bainbridge, attacks the van. The bowsprits have been unshipped so that there will be nothing to impede the boarders, for it is by boarding that Decatur means to gain his prizes. Bainbridge in his advance loses his lateen yard by a shot, and can only support the attacking column from a distance. Trippe dashes up alongside one of the enemy's boats crying out, "Board!" and leaps over the rail, followed by Henley, his midshipman, and nine of his crew. The others are about to jump, when the boats fall apart. It is hot work for the little handful of Americans. The enemy is more than three times their number. But there is no time for thought, and without a second's hesitation the boarders make a rush upon the crew of the galley with pike and cutlass.

For a few minutes the struggle is desperate. Trippe singles out the leader, a tall and well-built Turk, as his own antagonist. As he comes up, the Turk makes a swift cut at him with his scimitar; but Trippe parries the blow skilfully with his sword, receiving only a slight wound. Stroke after stroke descends, as the enemy, swinging his curved blade with the rapidity of lightning, cuts savagely at his opponent. But Trippe is a cool and expert fencer, and though he is gashed and cut again and again, he holds his ground until he has passed his weapon through the body of the Turk. His companions, in the fury of their attack, have killed thirteen of the enemy; and though there are still more than twenty left, the rest seeing their leader fall are panic-struck and fall on their faces begging for mercy. Trippe carries off with him eleven honourable scars, and three of his men are wounded; but none have fallen, and the Tripolitan gunboat is a prize.

Meanwhile the two Decaturs, in the other gunboats, are not idle. The elder, Stephen, runs on board the largest of the enemy's boats, taking with him his whole crew of Americans, twenty-three in number, and leaving the Neapolitan gunners to guard his boat. For ten minutes they are fighting pell-mell on the enemy's decks,—another bloody hand-to-hand encounter with the same result. Despite their numbers, the Turks cannot resist the impetuous charge of the Americans. Many of them are killed, some jump into the sea, a few rush in terror to the hold, the rest surrender. The flag is lowered, and Decatur takes his prize in tow, to draw her out of the battle.

At this moment Lieut. James Decatur's gunboat comes up under his stern and he learns that his brother, after receiving the surrender of one of the galleys, has been shot through the head by her commander. Decatur has left most of his crew on board the prize, but he does not stop to think of that; his brother has been murdered by a treacherous enemy, and he must meet the Turk and exact from him the penalty. The boat is pointed out; she has taken refuge within the enemy's line. But this is nought to Decatur. Plunging into their midst, he finds himself beside the object of his search, and in a moment he has leaped upon the galley's deck. He does not look to see whether he is followed; but young Macdonough has joined his leader with a handful of men, and at his side they charge the enemy.

As Decatur rushes upon the Turkish captain, the latter makes a thrust at him with a boarding pike. Decatur parries with his cutlass, but the blade breaks at the hilt. The Turk makes another lunge, and this time wounds Decatur in the breast. The American wrenches the weapon from his antagonist, and they grapple and fall to the deck, Decatur uppermost. At this moment another Tripolitan makes a cut with his scimitar at Decatur's head; but as the weapon is raised in the air a young blue-jacket, Reuben James, whose name will ever be remembered for this act of self-devotion, since he cannot stop the blow with his wounded arms, stoops down and intercepts it with his head.

The fight now goes on around the two prostrate captains. The active and sinewy Turk, making one last effort, turns and gets Decatur under him. Drawing a knife from its sheath, he is about to bury it in the captain's throat. But Decatur is as cool as he is valiant. Seizing the Turk's uplifted arm with a grip like iron, he feels with his right hand for the pistol in his pocket. Quickly it is cocked, and without drawing it, Decatur aims and fires. The dagger drops from the Turk's hand, and his body, limp and lifeless, rolls over on the deck. Another prize has been captured, and Decatur has avenged his brother's death.

While the gunboats are thus actively engaged, the ships keep up a steady cannonade. Twice the reserve division of the enemy, stationed behind the rocks, endeavours to come out, and by rallying and supporting the defeated rear, to renew the contest; but each time it is covered and checked by the guns of the *Constitution*, and after losing three more galleys which are sunk by the frigate's fire, it gives up the attempt.

Presently the wind comes out from the northward, freshening, and the gunboats are signalled to retire from action. The *Constitution*, now only two cables' length from the batteries, tacks, and firing two broadsides in stays, drives the Tripolitans from the castle and sends a minaret in the town crashing down about the people's heads. The gunboats, bringing with them their three prizes, rejoin the squadron. The commodore sends his barge to bring Lieut. James Decatur on board the flag-ship, and he is tenderly lifted in and rowed swiftly to the frigate. He lies in the stern-sheets, his head in Morris's lap, and with him is his brother. But his strength is going fast, and he dies before they reach the ship.

The squadron now takes the gunboats and bombs in tow, and all the ships stand out to sea. The last gun has been fired, the batteries are silent, and the first attack on Tripoli is ended.

★★★★★★

Soon after the battle of the 3rd of August Commodore Preble received a letter from the French consul intimating that the *pasha* would be ready to lower his terms and treat for peace. But the commodore refused to make the first advances, and on the 7th he was ready for another attack. The enemy's gunboats wisely kept their stations within the rocks, where it would have been folly to engage them, and the attack was directed only against the town and batteries.

The bombs were ordered to take their position in a bay to the westward and throw shells into the city, while the gunboats, now increased to nine by the addition of the three prizes, were to silence a heavy battery that commanded the entrance to the bay. At nine in the morning the *Constitution* lay at anchor six miles from the city. The smaller vessels lay three miles within her. It was nearly calm, but with a strong current setting in to the eastward. The gunboats and bombs advanced slowly to the attack with sails and oars. The *Constitution* had her top-sails set ready for the first breeze; and at half-past one, when a light wind sprang up from the northeast, she weighed and stood in. As the wind was on shore, it was imprudent for any of the larger vessels to join in the movement; for if a mast were shot away, it would be almost impossible to save the ship.

At half-past two, signal was made to begin the attack, and the bombs and gunboats opened a heavy fire upon the town, to which the batteries replied. In a short time the walls of the seven-gun battery were nearly demolished. The small vessels kept their stations steadily under an annoying fire. Suddenly on board one of the prize gunboats was seen a burst of flame followed by a terrific crash; a hot shot had passed through the magazine and exploded it. The young commander of the gunboat, Lieutenant Caldwell, and Dorsey, one of the midshipmen who stood with him on the quarter-deck, with all the seamen near them, were killed, and the stern of the boat was blown to atoms. In the bow was the gun's crew under Midshipman Robert Spence. The crew had just loaded the gun, and for a moment stood paralyzed, as the boat was sinking fast.

"All right, boys!" sung out Spence as he coolly pointed the gun. "We'll give them one more, anyway. Fire!"

Crack! went the gun.

"Now, then, three rousing cheers for the flag! Hip, hip, hurrah!" The gallant tars gave three cheers, and the boat sank from under them. Spence, who could not swim, seized an oar as he plunged into the water, and so kept himself up until help came to him from one of the boats nearby. In this way were rescued all whom the explosion had left alive.

The eight remaining gunboats, which though here and there cut up were not disabled, continued the action until late in the afternoon, when the freshening wind warned the squadron to retire. During the engagement a strange sail had been seen to the northward, and the *Argus* was sent in chase. It proved to be the frigate *John Adams*, Captain Chauncey,—the first ship of the new squadron that was coming out from the United States. Unfortunately she had left her gun-carriages to be brought out by the other ships, so that she could not be used for active operations. Still more unfortunately it turned out that the authorities at Washington, who were somewhat given to red-tape, had thought it necessary to send an officer in command of the squadron of reinforcement who was higher in rank than Preble, and who would therefore upon his arrival replace the latter in the command. It was a cruel blow to the commodore to be cast aside after having done so much where others had accomplished little; and in his private journal, written with his own hand in the solitude of his cabin, and meant only for his own eye, we find these words:—

How much my feelings are lacerated by this supersedure at the moment of victory cannot be described, and can be felt only by

101

an officer placed in my mortifying situation.

At first the commodore thought it only right that he should now wait for his successor to arrive. But in a day or two the *pasha* sent him a message through the French consul, offering to treat for peace if the United States would pay one hundred and fifty thousand dollars for the ransom of the captives. The last proposal before this had been for a ransom of half a million; all which showed that the two attacks had lowered the Tripolitan demands to less than one third of what they had been, and that in time they would come down still further.

Preble therefore renewed his operations, making the same zealous and eager efforts that he would have done had the department not superseded him. Decatur, whose new commission as captain had come out in the *John Adams*, and Chauncey rowed into the harbour one dark night in two small boats to find out how the enemy's flotilla was arranged at night. When this was ascertained, a night attack was planned, and the gunboats and bombs were sent into the harbour, where they bombarded the town from two o'clock till daylight. It was a beautiful sight to one who could watch it from a distance; but it filled the people of the city with terror, and if the *pasha* had had any concern for the feelings of his subjects, he would have made peace then on any terms. But as long as his castle stood, and taxes could be wrung from his people, and he had plenty of food and slaves, it mattered little to him that the town should suffer from the horrors of a night bombardment.

A few nights later the attack was repeated, and it was shortly followed by a warm engagement with the forts and gunboats in the harbour, in which the enemy was repulsed and great damage was done in the town. This last attack, the fifth which the squadron had made, exhausted nearly all its ammunition; and as the bad season was coming on, the commodore determined to use up what was left in carrying out a plan which he had some time before projected, and which was to inflict a final blow on the enemy. The plan was to load the *Intrepid* with gunpowder and shells, making a kind of infernal machine of her, and send her in to explode among the Tripolitan shipping. One hundred barrels of powder were stowed in her magazine, and one hundred and fifty fixed shells were placed in different parts of the vessel. The whole was to be fired by a fuse calculated to burn a quarter of an hour.

The direction of this hazardous undertaking was intrusted to Lieut.

Richard Somers, a gallant and devoted officer who had shared with Decatur the command of the gunboats in all the attacks upon Tripoli. Lieut. Henry Wadsworth went with him; and at the last moment young Israel, another of the "Constitution's" lieutenants, begged so hard to be allowed to go that the commodore consented. They took with them the two fastest boats in the squadron, one of them from the *Nautilus* with four men, the other from the *Constitution* with six men.

On the evening of the 4th of September everything was ready, and the *Intrepid* got under way and stood for the entrance of the harbour. The *Argus*, *Siren*, and *Nautilus* went with her as far as the rocks, and remained there to pick up the boats on their return. The night was thick, and there was a faint starlight, and the *Intrepid* was gradually lost to sight in the gathering gloom as she passed between the rocks at the entrance. But the Tripolitan sentries on the mole were on the watch, and presently the batteries opened fire upon her. Still she held silently on her course, steering straight for the mole, where the enemy's flotilla lay at anchor. Suddenly, before the allotted time had passed, the explosion came. There was a quick flash, a sheet of flame, a deafening report, then the sound of bursting shells and cries of alarm as for an instant the city walls, the harbour, and the vessels were lighted up by the blaze, and then—darkness and silence.

The three ships remained for hours off the entrance watching anxiously for some signs of the returning boats or men. Every ear was strained to catch the plash of the oar in the water or its dull rattle in the rowlock, and every eye strove to pierce the shroud of mist that hung over the waters; but in vain. None of that devoted band were destined ever to return. They had given up their lives as a sacrifice for their country; and whether their destruction was caused by one of the enemy's shot, or whether, finding himself attacked by boarders, Somers had lighted the fuse, as he had resolved to do in such an event, and had blown up himself and his assailants together, no man knows to this day. Thirteen bodies drifted ashore the next morning, and Captain Bainbridge was taken from his prison to see them; but they were scarred and burned beyond recognition.

With this melancholy tragedy Commodore Preble's operations before Tripoli came to a close. The bad season was upon him, when attacks were impossible, and the *pasha* on his stormy coast was secure behind his barriers of rocks and shoals. A week later the new squadron came out and the commodore gave up his command.

In the following spring, when the season again opened, Commodore Rodgers, who was now at the head of the squadron, appeared before Tripoli with an overwhelming force. There were six frigates, two brigs, three schooners, and twelve bombs and gunboats. At the same time an adventurous expedition had been led from Egypt by General Eaton, and had captured the city of Derne, an outlying dependency of Tripoli. Against such a force the *pasha*, after what he had been taught by Preble in the summer before, knew that he could not long hold out; and the negotiations for peace, which were conducted on board the flagship, lasted only a week. On the 3rd of June, 1805, the treaty was signed. Bainbridge and his companions were set at liberty, and the war with Tripoli was over.

Chapter 8

Impressment

Europe, at the period which we have now reached, was engaged in a general war. This had begun with the French Revolution, when France bade defiance to the rest of the world; and, kept alive by the aggressive policy and military ambition of Napoleon, it continued, with occasional interruptions, until the power of the French emperor was overthrown at Waterloo. During all this time England was the most persistent and successful enemy of the French,—fighting them sometimes alone, sometimes in coalition with the great States of the Continent, but always fighting. It was on the sea that the English were most successful. Here the French and the Spaniards, brave as they were, seemed to be no match for the islanders; and the splendid victories of Lord Howe off Ushant, of Sir John Jervis at Cape St. Vincent, and last and greatest of all, of Nelson at the Nile and at Trafalgar, won for the English Navy an imperishable renown, and destroyed the naval power of France and Spain.

The wonderful battles between the French and English navies were fought with great fleets, numbering sometimes thirty or forty ships-of-the-line, carrying each from sixty to one hundred and twenty guns, and the largest of them as many as one thousand men. To keep these fleets manned with sailors was no easy task. After all who would volunteer were gathered in, there still remained a great dearth of men; for it was a hard life that the sailors led on board the ships-of-war, especially if, as often happened, the captain, or the second in command, was a harsh and tyrannical officer. How bitterly the men hated the service was shown by the mutinies at Spithead and the Nore. So it became necessary to resort to compulsion to recruit the crews.

If the government had established a draft or conscription to obtain its seamen, enrolling all the population, or all the seafaring part of it, and drawing names by lot, as sometimes must be done even in free countries, things would not have been so bad. Instead of that it got them by a method which was called "impressment." A press-gang composed of a party of armed sailors under a lieutenant or a warrant officer was sent ashore to seize any stray men it could find, and run them in for His Majesty's service. In all the seaport towns were crimps and runners, rascally fellows who knew the town and the inhabitants, and who frequented all the sailors' lodging-houses; and these were employed to put the press-gangs on the track of likely men who could be forced into the service.

In such towns, after dark, when these prowlers scoured the streets, it was hardly safe for anyone to go out alone; for if he were caught and made remonstrance, a gag and a pair of handcuffs were ready to stay both voice and arm. Even when a sailor had shipped for his voyage in a merchantman and had got out to sea, he was not safe from capture. For the merchantman falling in with a ship-of-war was obliged to heave to, when a lieutenant came on board and took such men as suited his fancy.

But with all this the English fleet was still short of men. So the officers or the government, or both together, hit upon a new device. In time of war the naval ships of either party have the right to stop and search all merchant-vessels on the high seas, to see if they are enemies or neutrals, and whether they are pursuing any illegal trade; and the foreigners must submit, because if their own country were at war its naval ships would do the same. As England was all this time at war, it came about that any American merchantman falling in with English cruisers must undergo a search. If the merchant-ship had any natural-born Englishmen in her crew, although they might have emigrated long before, and have become citizens of the American Republic, the English Government held that they were still subjects, and that they might be taken out if they were needed for the service of the king.

This was an outrage, because no such right of taking persons out of neutral ships exists. But this was not the worst. As the two nations were of the same blood and spoke the same language, their sailors could not easily be told apart; and thus Americans were sometimes taken on the pretence that they had formerly been English. The cruiser's officer when he mustered the crew was never very particular about the selection if he wanted the men, as he was always sure to do. Often, indeed, he did not care much whether they were Americans or not, and having a force behind him, he could not be gainsaid or resisted.

The Government of the United States protested against this practice, but as it did not believe much in naval armaments, and never followed up its protests by making a show of force, little heed was paid to them; while England, being in such great necessity, and not over-scrupulous as to the means of relieving it, continued the practice. The American Government then granted to its sailor-citizens passports or certificates of nationality, which were called "protections," but which nevertheless did not always protect. At any rate a man who had not taken out the "protection"—and sailors, as everybody knows, are careless in such matters—was sure to be impressed, whatever evidence he might give of birth or nationality. So the men were seized, and where they could they made complaint, though it often happened that they did not have the chance; and when the complaints reached home, the State Department kept on filing them, and entering its futile protests and arguments and counter-arguments. But still, as might be expected from such a course, the practice of impressment never ceased, until finally there were several thousand native-born Americans serving under constraint in the Royal Navy.

On one or two occasions the English had even gone so far as to take seamen out of our ships-of-war, which is perhaps as gross an affront as one nation can offer to another. This was done by Commodore Loring, who commanded a powerful squadron off Havana in 1798, and who removed five men from the sloop-of-war *Baltimore*, of twenty guns. As the English force was composed of the *Queen*, of ninety-eight guns, and several frigates, they could have sunk the *Baltimore* with a single broadside. So the American ship made no resistance. Gross as it was, this injury did not bring on a war or even reprisals; although reprisals might have been used with good effect, as they were about the same time against France.

Again in 1807, when the *Chesapeake* was starting from Hampton Roads for a cruise in the Mediterranean, she was followed out to sea by the British frigate *Leopard*, which sent an officer on board to demand that some of the *Chesapeake's* men, who were supposed to be deserters from the English navy, should be given up; and when the demand was very properly refused, she attacked the *Chesapeake*, in sight of our own coast, and in time of peace,—discharging broadside after broadside at the vessel of a friendly State. The *Chesapeake*, which had gone to sea unprepared to fight, through hurry in preparation, and also it must be said through negligence on the part of certain of her officers, could not fire a shot in reply, the powder-horns and matches for priming and setting off the guns not being ready, and the men not having been called to quarters at the proper time. So she made a very poor showing, even allowing, as was the case, that her assailant was superior in force; only one gun being fired in reply, which was touched off by a live coal which Allen, one of the younger lieutenants, carried in his hand from the galley, to save the honour of the flag.

After the *Chesapeake* surrendered, four men were taken from her to the *Leopard* and she returned to port. This galling insult, which makes one blush to hear of even after so great a lapse of time, was only atoned for four years after it was given. And yet the country forbore to go to war, or even to make such preparations that if war came the navy might be ready for it.

One would think that the government must have grown very tired of making complaints, for during all these years its foreign correspondence was chiefly made up of protests and requests for redress. To all these evasive answers were given, or hopes held out which never were fulfilled. Besides the outrage of impressment, there were many grievous wrongs inflicted on American commerce through the Orders in Council which the British issued; and France, too, through Napoleon's Berlin and Milan decrees, did us serious injury. The French decrees were finally revoked, as were also at the last moment the Orders in Council; but England never would give up the right she claimed to take out of American vessels seamen that were supposed to be English.

At last matters reached such a point that the nation refused to submit longer to these repeated insults. The British frigate *Guerrière*, cruising off New York, had impressed a seaman from an American coaster almost in sight of Sandy Hook. Commodore Rodgers, in the frigate *President*, was now employed in patrolling the coast, and he was resolved, if he should meet the *Guerrière*, to demand the man's surrender. One evening he fell in with a British cruiser, the sloop-of-war *Little Belt*, which in the dark he mistook for a frigate. His ship was cleared for action, the crew were at their quarters, and the guns were loaded and double-shotted; for the *President* was not going to be caught unprepared, as the *Chesapeake* had been four years before. Ranging up to her, Rodgers hailed the *Little Belt*, but in reply his hail was only repeated; and as he hailed the second time, the sloop fired a shot at him. The *President* returned the fire before Rodgers could give an order, for the crew were only waiting for the chance; and no wonder, considering what American seamen had suffered from English ships-of-war. The firing continued on both sides, until at last the *Little Belt* was silenced. In the morning the commodore sent his boat to her with offers of assistance; but these were refused, and the *Little Belt* proceeded on her way to Halifax, where she arrived almost a wreck.

This incident, though not important in itself, added fresh fuel to the fire that was already kindled. There was now a strong party of younger men in Congress, who were resolved that the United States should no longer submit tamely to foreign aggression. These at last succeeded in making themselves heard, and they carried Congress with them. Unhappily but little had been done in all these years of encroachment to prepare the navy, the nation's principal arm of defence, to resist an enemy; and although the dominant party was now active and alert about rousing a war spirit, they seemed to be exceedingly dull of comprehension about the necessity of preparations for defence.

Therefore, except for the few noble frigates which Washington's foresight had provided, and the fine corps of naval officers whom Jefferson had selected and Preble had trained, we were as ill-prepared for war as it was possible to be. Nevertheless, the war party, rightly conceiving that the country could not endure forever the alternate bullying and subterfuge of foreign States, were determined to make an armed resistance; and on the 18th of June, 1812, war was declared against Great Britain.

CHAPTER 9

The War of 1812.—The "Constitution" and the "Guerrière"

Difficulties which finally led to the outbreak of war had been growing for several years; and the government, as I have said, had all this time done little or nothing in the way of preparation for defence either on land or at sea. The navy was opposed as bitterly as ever, and the money that was needed for its support was given grudgingly. After the war with Tripoli, in which gunboats had been found of so much use, the administration had begun to build great numbers of vessels of this class. This was a great mistake. Gunboats were useful and even necessary for operations in bays and rivers and shoal waters, but they could not take the place of frigates in making war. But it seemed to be a pet scheme with the President to transform the navy into an immense gunboat flotilla, and one hundred and seventy-six of these little craft were built, which turned out to be of no more service in war than so many mud-scows. The money which was wasted by this mistaken policy would have built eight frigates of the largest class, and would have added immeasurably to our power upon the sea.

When the war broke out, there were in the navy, besides the gunboats, only eighteen vessels, of which three—the *Chesapeake, Constellation*, and *Adams*—were repairing, and one was on Lake Ontario. Of the other fourteen there were those three fine frigates of forty-four guns,—the *Constitution*, the *United States*, and the *President*; and three smaller frigates,—the *Congress*, of thirty-eight guns, the *Essex*, of thirty-two, and the *John Adams*, of twenty-eight. The rest were sloops, brigs, and schooners carrying from ten to twenty guns apiece. To make war on this puny force, the British Navy possessed two hundred and thirty line-of-battle ships, of from sixty to one hundred and twenty guns each, and over six hundred frigates and smaller vessels.

What could the United States now do with its eighteen ships against nine hundred of the enemy? It seemed a hopeless situation,—so hopeless, that there were some statesmen in the country who thought it would be best to lay up and dismantle our little fleet as the only way to enable it to escape capture. It happened that when this plan was broached, Captain Bainbridge and Captain Stewart were in Washington, and hearing of it they went to the secretary and implored him not to do so suicidal a thing.

"What are our ships for," said they, "if not to fight and attack the enemy when their country goes to war? If when a war comes they are all to be laid up, it would be better to give up altogether this pretence of a navy, which seems to be only used in peace-time, when there is no real work for it to do. No doubt if one of our frigates falls in with the enemy's squadron it will be captured; but English frigates do not always sail in squadrons any more than our own; and if one of us meets one of them alone at sea, we shall be able to give a good account of ourselves. Let the frigates go to sea to show what they can do: at the worst, they can only be captured, and the country will be no worse off than if they were laid up to rot in idleness."

Persuaded by these arguments the government consented, though with many forebodings of disaster, to send the ships to sea; and fortunate it was that this wise decision was reached. For never in the history of the world was a naval war conducted with greater skill and gallantry, and success in proportion to its means, than this which the little navy of America waged in 1812 against Great Britain. Despite the comparative force of the two navies, it often happened, as Bainbridge and Stewart had predicted, that single ships met single ships in naval duels, as it were; and as through the wisdom of our first constructors our frigates and sloops were the best of their class afloat, they were often more than a match in strength of resistance and in power of attack for their antagonists.

Besides, under the thorough training of their captains, who had learned what naval warfare meant in the school of Preble at Tripoli, the crews were more careful and more skilful gunners than the enemy, and far exceeded them in their ability to make their firing tell. The English, on the other hand, whose conquests over the French and Spaniards had led them to belittle and despise the navies of other States, thought that they had an easy victory before them,—or, as we might say now, a "walk-over,"—and they ridiculed the American frigates, calling the *Constitution* a "bundle of pine boards under a bit of striped bunting," until they found out to their cost that they had in their enormous list of ships hardly a single frigate that compared with her in all those qualities which a frigate ought to have.

★★★★★★

On the 21st of June, 1812, three days after the declaration of war, a squadron sailed out of New York, under the command of Commodore Rodgers, composed of the *President*, as flagship; the *United States*, under Commodore Decatur; the *Congress*, Captain Smith; the *Hornet*, Capt. James Lawrence; and the *Argus*, Captain Sinclair. The object of the cruise was the capture of a fleet of one hundred merchantmen known to have sailed from Jamaica sometime before for England, under convoy of some ships-of-war. When two days out, the squadron fell in with and chased the British frigate *Belvidera*. When the chase began, the frigate was some six miles off; but in the course of the afternoon the *President*, which was the fastest ship of the squadron, gradually neared her, until she was within half a mile.

Then the *President* opened with her bow-guns; but, most unfortunately, one of these guns after being fired a few times exploded, killing and wounding several officers and men, the commodore himself being among the wounded. The *Belvidera* held on her course, returning the fire from four guns which she had shifted to her stern-ports. The *President*, delayed by her accident, lost ground; and though a running fight was kept up for several hours, the *Belvidera*, by cutting away her anchors and throwing overboard her boats, lightened herself so much that she soon left the squadron far behind. At midnight the pursuit was abandoned.

The squadron now resumed its course in chase of the Jamaica fleet, from which it had been turned aside in attempting to capture the *Belvidera*. But the delay proved fatal to its enterprise. Intelligence was gained off the Banks of Newfoundland that the Jamaica-men were ahead, and soon the ships knew from the quantities of orange-peel and cocoanut-shells floating in the water that they were on the enemy's track; but they never sighted him. At last, upon reaching the British Channel, the pursuit was given up, and Commodore Rodgers, after a ten-weeks' cruise, returned with six prizes to Boston.

The cruise of Commodore Rodgers had one good effect, in compelling the ships-of-war of the enemy then on our coast to keep together for their own safety. Among these was one sixty-four, the *Africa*, two large frigates, the *Shannon* and the *Guerrière*, and the small frigate

"Among These was One Sixty-Four, the 'Africa.'"

Æolus, all under the command of Com. Philip Broke, of the *Shannon*. These were presently joined by the *Belvidera*, and all were cruising together near New York, and off the Jersey coast. About the middle of July the little schooner *Nautilus*, of twelve guns, left New York on a cruise, and running into the midst of the squadron was made a prize after a six-hours' chase.

On the 12th of July, four days before the capture of the *Nautilus*, the *Constitution* had sailed from Chesapeake Bay, under Captain Hull, bound for New York. Late on the afternoon of the 16th, the day on which the *Nautilus* was taken, she too fell in with the British squadron. For three long and weary days and nights the enemy pursued her, and during all that time the zeal and courage of her officers never flagged, and no means were left untried that might assist in her escape. The untiring efforts of Captain Hull were seconded by his first lieutenant, Charles Morris, the same who had been with Decatur when he burned the *Philadelphia* in the harbour of Tripoli, and certainly one of the best officers that ever fought under the American flag. He shall tell in his own words the story of

THE CHASE OF THE *CONSTITUTION*.

We had proceeded beyond the Delaware, but out of sight of the land, when on the afternoon of the 16th we discovered four vessels at a great distance to the northwest and a single ship to the northeast, from which quarter a light wind was then blowing. The wind changed to the southward about sunset, which brought us to windward, and we stood for the ship, the wind being very light. The chase was evidently a frigate, and the first impression was that she might be a part of Commodore Rodgers's squadron. By eleven p.m. we were within signal distance, and it was soon apparent she was not an American vessel of war.

There being no apprehension that a British frigate would make any attempt to avoid an engagement, Captain Hull felt justified in delaying any nearer approach till daylight, when our newly-collected and imperfectly-disciplined men would be less likely to be thrown into confusion. The ship was accordingly brought to the wind with her head to the southward and westward under easy sail, with a light wind from the northwest. The other ship did the same at about two miles' distance. The watch not on duty were allowed to sleep at their quarters, and the officers slept in the same manner.

As the following morning opened upon us it disclosed our companion of the night to be a large frigate just without gunshot, on the lee quarter, and a ship-of-the-line and three other frigates, a brig, and a schooner, about two miles nearly astern, with all sails set standing for us, with English colours flying.

All our sails were soon set, and the nearest frigate, fortunately for us, but without any apparent reason, tacked and immediately wore round again in chase,—a manoeuvre that occupied some ten minutes, and allowed us to gain a distance, which though short, proved to be of the utmost importance to our safety. By sunrise our ship was entirely becalmed and unmanageable, while the ships astern retained a light breeze till it brought three of the frigates so near that their shot passed beyond us. The distance was, however, too great for accuracy, and their shot did not strike our ship.

Our boats were soon hoisted out, and the ship's head kept from the enemy, and exertions were made to increase our distance from them by towing. This and occasional cat's-paws, or slight puffs of wind, enabled us to gain nothing. A few guns were fired from our stern-ports; but so much rake had been given to the stern that the guns could not be used with safety, and their further use was relinquished. All means were adopted which seemed to promise any increase of speed. The hammocks were removed from the nettings, and the cloths rolled up to prevent their unfavourable action; several thousand gallons of water were started and pumped overboard, and all the sails kept thoroughly wet to close the texture of the canvas.

While making all these exertions, our chances for escape were considered hopeless. For many years the ship had proved a very dull sailer, especially during the late cruise, and it was supposed that the first steady breeze would bring up such a force as would render resistance of no avail; and our situation seemed hopeless.

At about eight a.m. one of the frigates called all the boats of the squadron to her, and having arranged them for towing, furled all sails. This brought her toward us steadily and seemed to decide our fate. Fortunately for us, a light breeze filled our sails and sent us forward a few hundred yards before her sails could be set to profit by it.

With our minds excited to the utmost to devise means of escape, I happened to recollect that when obliged by the timidity of my old commander, Cox, to warp the *President* in and out of harbours where others depended on sails, our practice had enabled us to give her a speed of nearly three miles an hour. We had been on soundings the day before, and on trying we now found twenty-six fathoms. This

115

depth was unfavourably great, but it gave me confidence to suggest to Captain Hull the expediency of attempting to warp the ship ahead. He acceded at once; and in a short time the launch and first cutter were sent ahead with a kedge, and with all the hawsers and rigging, from five inches and upward, that could be found, making nearly a mile of length.

When the kedge was thrown, the men hauled on the connecting hawser, slowly and carefully at first, till the ship was in motion, and gradually increasing until a sufficient velocity was given to continue until the anchor could be taken ahead, when the same process was repeated. In this way the ship was soon placed out of the range of our enemy's guns, and by continued exertions when the wind failed, and giving every possible advantage to the sails when we had air enough to fill them, we prevented them from again closing very near us. The ship which we had first chased gained a position abeam of us about nine *a.m.*, and fired several broadsides; but the shot fell just short of us and only served to enliven our men and excite their jocular comments.

The exertions of neither party were relaxed during this day or the following night. There was frequent alternation of calms and very light winds from the southeast, which we received with our heads to the southwestward. When the wind would give us more speed than with warping and towing, the boats were run up to their places or suspended to the spars in the chains by temporary tackles, with their crews in them, ready to act at a moment's notice.

At daylight of the second day, on the 18th, it was found that one frigate had gained a position on our lee bow, two nearly abeam, one on the lee quarter about two miles from us, and the ship-of-the-line, brig, and schooner, three miles from us in the same direction. The wind had now become tolerable steady, though still light. The frigate on the lee bow tacked about four a.m. and would evidently reach within gunshot if we continued our course. This we were anxious to avoid, as a single shot might cripple some spar and impede our progress. If we tacked, we might be exposed to the fire of the other frigate on the lee quarter; but as she was a smaller vessel, the risk appeared to be less, and we also tacked soon.

In passing the lee frigate at five, we expected a broadside or more, as we should evidently pass within gunshot; but from some unexplained cause Lord James Townshend, in the *Æolus*, of thirty-two guns, suffered us to pass quietly and tacked in our wake, while the others soon

"A Squall of Wind and Rain Passed Over Us."

took the same direction.

We had now all our pursuers astern and on the lee quarter; and as the wind was gradually increasing, our escape must depend on our superiority of sailing, which we had no reason to hope or expect. Exertions, however, were not relaxed. The launch and first cutter, which we dared not lose, were hoisted on board at six a.m. under the direction of Captain Hull, with so little loss of time or change of sails that our watching enemies could not conceive what disposition had been made of them. This we afterward learned from Lieutenant Crane, who was a prisoner in their squadron. The sails were kept saturated with water, a set of sky-sails was made and set, and all other sails set and trimmed to the greatest advantage, close by the wind. The ship directly astern gained slowly but gradually till noon; though, as the wind increased, our good ship was going at that time at the unexpected rate of ten knots an hour. At noon we had the wind abeam, and as it gradually freshened, we began to leave our fleet pursuer. Our ship had reached a speed of twelve and a half knots by two p.m. Our hopes began to overcome apprehension, and cheerfulness was more apparent among us.

Though encouraged we were by no means assured, as all the ships were still near and ready to avail themselves of any advantage that might offer. About six p.m. a squall of wind and rain passed over us, which induced us to take in our light sails before the rain covered us from the view of the enemy; but most of them were soon replaced, as the wind moderated. When the rain had passed, we had evidently gained a mile or more during its continuance. Still the pursuit was continued, and our own ship pressed forward to her utmost speed. The officers and men again passed the night at quarters. At daylight on the morning of the 19th our enemies had been left so far astern that danger from them was considered at an end, and at eight a.m. they at last relinquished the chase and hauled their wind. Our officers and crew could now indulge in some rest, of which the former had taken little for more than sixty hours. . . . The result may be remembered as an evidence of the advantages to be expected from perseverance under the most discouraging circumstances so long as *any* chance for success may remain.

After the prolonged labour and anxiety of the three days' chase, the people of the *Constitution* needed some relaxation of the strain, and Captain Hull put into Boston, where he remained a week. From there he sailed to the Gulf of St. Lawrence, where he took and burned some prizes; but hearing that the squadron from which he had just escaped was in the neighbourhood, he steered for the southward. All the time the sailors were kept exercised at the guns, under the careful oversight of the officers; for the captain knew that the result, in any battle he might be called upon to fight, depended mostly upon skill in firing, which practice alone could give.

On the 19th of August, at two o'clock in the afternoon, while cruising about in the ocean somewhere in the latitude of New York, the *Constitution* made a strange sail to the southward and eastward. Captain Hull had just before received information that an English frigate was cruising alone to the southward of him, and suspecting that this stranger was the object of his search, he bore down for her under all sail, she meanwhile making no attempt to get away. At three o'clock the ships were near enough to make each other out, and Hull's conjecture proved to be right. The stranger was the frigate *Guerrière*, under Captain Dacres, which had now left the squadron of Commodore Broke, and was on her way to Halifax.

By four o'clock the *Constitution* was gaining rapidly on her opponent, and three quarters of an hour later, being then about three miles off, the *Guerrière* backed her main-topsails and waited for the Americans to come up. Upon this the *Constitution* took in her topgallant sails, staysails, and flying jib, took a second reef in the topsails, hauled the courses up, sent down the royal yards, cleared ship for action, and beat to quarters. At the same time she bore up, and steered for the *Guerrière's* quarter.

At five o'clock the *Guerrière* hoisted her colours and opened fire, but her shot fell short. Then for nearly an hour the two ships manoeuvred, Hull doing his best to get into a good position to rake, and the English frigate each time deftly evading him by "wearing ship," as it is called,—that is, by turning quickly on her heel, with the wind astern. But all this drew the ships apart, when both really wished to close and fight; and presently by a common impulse Hull and Dacres concluded to give up manoeuvring, and both ran off to the eastward, with the wind free, the *Guerrière* a little ahead, but the *Constitution* quickly crawling up on her.

Now began the real battle, for before this it had been little more than the play of fencers, each feeling his way to discover his opponent's skill and strength. But the ships were now side by side, and the *Constitution's* practised gunners were firing terrible broadsides in quick succession, her guns double-shotted with round shot and grape. The

Captain Isaac Hull.

Guerrière answered, but her guns were not so heavy as the Americans, nor was her gunnery so skilful. In just ten minutes after the real fight began, her mizzen-mast toppled and fell over the side, the shrouds holding the wreck of mast and spars and sails, which dragged behind in the water.

The *Guerrière's* speed was now slackened, and Captain Hull ranged ahead; and putting his helm hard aport, he lay across her bows and raked her with his broadside twice from stem to stern. But as he swung round again, the *Guerrière's* jib-boom and bowsprit crossed his quarter-deck and got entangled in his rigging. It was a critical moment, for the bow-guns of the enemy were so close that their wads, entering the *Constitution's* cabin, set it on fire. By dint of great exertions the fire was put out, and Lieutenant Morris, standing on the taffrail, attempted to pass some turns of the main brace over the *Guerrière's* bowsprit, to keep her fast and give his men a chance to board. But Morris in his exposed position had not yet finished his task, when a marine on the *Guerrière*, taking deliberate aim, put a bullet through his body. The brave lieutenant fell, though happily not killed but only badly wounded, and the two ships were separated.

All thoughts of boarding were now given up, but there was no need of it. Hull kept up his heavy fire, and in ten minutes more the *Guerrière's* foremast and mainmast had also gone, and she lay a helpless wreck in the trough of the sea, rolling her main-deck guns under water. The *Constitution*, knowing that the enemy was at her mercy, now hauled off for half an hour to repair the slight injuries she had received; and after completing this task in a leisurely way, and making everything shipshape, she came back to receive the enemy's surrender. It was a bitter task for Captain Dacres to acknowledge himself beaten in the first frigate fight between the veteran navy of England and the derided vessels of the young Republic; but it was all that he could do, for he had fought his ship until she was little better than a dismantled hulk, and it was vain to think of trying to prolong resistance. So the captain came on board the *Constitution* and delivered up himself and all his men as prisoners; and the next day the *Guerrière*, being so shattered that it was of no use to take her into port, was burned where she lay, and left to sink in the ocean.

Great were the rejoicings when the *Constitution* arrived at Boston with her trophies and prisoners. Men, women, and children vied with each other in demonstrations of delight. We can hardly realise today what the people felt at the news of the destruction of a British frigate.

"She Lay a Helpless Wreck in the Trough of the Sea."

To understand the feeling, we must look back at the twenty years during which American ships and American seamen had suffered repeated outrage at the hands of British ships-of-war,—outrage which had been borne only because the young country felt too weak to cope with those forces which had conquered all the navies of the Continent. At the outset, war with such foes offered a dismal prospect. And to think that in the first real encounter on the seas, a veritable pitched battle, these redoubtable champions of the ocean had been so utterly crushed and annihilated that not one fragment remained of their good ship the *Guerrière*, which had harried with impunity our very coasters, was something more than men's minds could at once grasp.

For Hull and his companions no reward seemed too great. Feasted in Boston at a great civic banquet, received with an ovation at every town through which he passed, he was for the moment the country's hero. Congress struck a medal in his honour, and votes of thanks were passed by the legislatures of New York and Massachusetts, and by many municipal bodies. The Society of the Cincinnati elected him an honorary member. The citizens of Philadelphia presented to him a great silver vase, and a golden sword whose engraved hilt bore a picture of the battle; the vase and sword may be seen today, (as at time of first publication), in the hall of the State Department at Washington. Morris was promoted to the rank of captain; and finally Congress passed an act appropriating fifty thousand dollars as a bounty for the officers and seamen of the *Constitution*.

CHAPTER 10

The First Sloop Action

What American ships could do in battle, Captain Hull had now shown; and the hopes of the country were aroused, and it began with reason to look for fresh successes. Nor was it destined to be disappointed; for during that memorable autumn of 1812 and the early months of winter there came such a rapid and unbroken succession of naval victories as has fallen to the lot of hardly any nation before or since. And that these victories should have been won by a service that for fifteen years had been treated with derision and contempt even by those in the highest station in the country, who should have given it both honour and support, and that they were won too over the mistress of the seas, made them in people's eyes tenfold more marvellous. It mattered little that the force engaged was small, that in comparison with the great fleet actions of European navies these encounters seemed the battles of pygmies; for their significance as victories was not thereby diminished; whether the force engaged was one ship or fifty ships, the same qualities in officers and men were needed to achieve a victory. The English had been beaten,—beaten in part no doubt by the better quality of American ships, but beaten too by the superior skill and training of American seamen.

The second victory of the naval war[1] was won by the sloop-of-war *Wasp*, which left the Delaware on the 13th of October under the command of Capt. Jacob Jones. She had been out only five days, when one Sunday morning she fell in with the British brig *Frolic*, convoying a small fleet of merchantmen, somewhere to the eastward of Albemarle Sound. At the first sign of battle the convoy made off under a press of sail. It was blowing fresh at the time, with a heavy sea, so that

---

1. This was really the third victory, counting the unimportant action between the *Essex* and the *Alert* as the first.

the ships came into action under short canvas.

At eleven o'clock in the forenoon the *Frolic"* hoisted Spanish colours, but Captain Jones knew that this was a ruse; and as he came down to windward of her and hailed, she displayed the English flag and opened the battle. The ships were very close, so that in spite of their pitching and tossing the firing told severely on both sides; but the Americans, following the same wise rule of aiming low that Truxtun had put in practice in the *Constellation*, fired while the engaged side of their ship was going down with the swell, and the enemy fired while theirs was rising; so that the *Frolic's* wounds were on her decks or in her hull, and the *Wasp's* chiefly aloft. In a few minutes the American's main-topmast fell, followed by his gaff and mizzen-topgallant-mast. Nevertheless, Captain Jones succeeded in placing himself on the port bow of the *Frolic*, where he raked her with terrible effect, and man after man fell upon her decks, dead or dying, until her fire began to slacken. By this time the masts of the *Wasp* were almost unsupported, so much of the rigging had been cut away; and the captain, fearful lest the enemy should escape him, prepared to board notwithstanding the heavy sea.

Presently the ships fell foul, the *Frolic's* bowsprit running over the quarter-deck of the *Wasp*, which was just the position most favourable for accomplishing the captain's purpose. The men were eager to board, and could not wait for the order. Jack Lang, a brave American blue-jacket, who had sometime before been the victim of a British press-gang, and who thus had old scores to wipe out, leaped first upon the enemy's bowsprit. Next to him came Biddle, the first lieutenant of the *Wasp*, who climbed upon the bulwarks; but his foot caught in a rope and he lost his balance. Behind Biddle came a midshipman, who, by way of helping himself up, in his eagerness seized the lieutenant's coat and so dragged him back to the deck. Biddle was on his feet in a twinkling, and getting on board the enemy, he rushed with a handful of men along her deck. But there was no force to oppose him, only the quartermaster at the wheel and three officers who threw down their swords in token of surrender.

Biddle hauled down the British flag himself, and in a short time the shattered remnant of the crew on the gun-deck below were made prisoners. It had been a most heroic defence of the *Frolic*, one that has few parallels in the whole range of naval history, for more than three fourths of her people were strewn about the decks; but it only shows that heroism alone without care and skill cannot always win a battle,

"Jack Lang, a Brave American Blue-Jacket, Leaped First."

for the Americans, with better knowledge of their art, had gained the victory, and it had only cost a loss of five men killed and as many more wounded.

The *Wasp* was not to gather the fruits of victory, however. Soon after the battle an English line-of-battle ship, the *Poictiers*, came in sight, and her great battery of seventy-four guns, before which both the little sloops would have fled had they been able to make sail, found them an easy capture. But all the same the real battle had been fought and the real victory won; and the loss of the two disabled ships in the face of such an overwhelming force was as nothing in its real import to the added proof which Captain Jones had given that American ships could meet and conquer on the seas an equal foe.

CHAPTER 11

Decatur and Bainbridge

Just before the *Wasp* had set out on her short but eventful cruise, Commodore Rodgers had put to sea again with his squadron. Soon after leaving New York, the *United States*, still under Capt. Stephen Decatur, separated from the other ships, and steering to the southeast, proceeded alone across the Atlantic. The *United States* was now in the highest condition of efficiency: the captain had taken great pains to train the crew in all that was needed to make them good fighting men; and his efforts had been seconded most worthily by his first lieutenant, William Henry Allen, the same who had proved his gallantry in the affair of the Chesapeake.

About two weeks after leaving port, on the 25th of October, when in the neighbourhood of Madeira, the *United States* sighted a strange vessel to the southward, which turned out to be the British frigate *Macedonian*. She was considered at this time to be the finest frigate in His Majesty's Navy, and was, commanded by Capt. John Carden. It seems that when Decatur had been cruising off our coast in his frigate before the war, he had met the *Macedonian*, and he and Carden had become good friends,—at least as far as could be in those troublesome times,—and had often exchanged good offices and hospitality. Thus they had talked from time to time about the strength of the two frigates, and of the probable result in case they should one day meet in battle. In these friendly conversations Captain Carden would dwell upon the disadvantage, as he thought it, of the American batteries; seeing that they carried 24-pounders where the English carried eighteens, which last, so he thought, were handled more easily and quickly, and were as heavy as a frigate ought to carry.

"Besides, Decatur," he added, "though your ships may be good enough, and you are a clever set of fellows, what practice have you had in war? There is the rub. We now meet as friends, and God grant we may never meet as enemies; but we are subject to the orders of our governments, and must obey them. Should we meet as enemies, what do you suppose will be the result?"

"I heartily reciprocate your sentiment," replied Decatur,—"that you and I may never meet except as we now do; but if as enemies, and with equal forces, the conflict will undoubtedly be a severe one, for the flag of my country will never be struck while there is a hull for it to wave from."

These two good friends and gallant companions were now to meet in the trial of arms over whose issue they had talked and speculated. The *Macedonian* came on before the wind, with studding-sails set, rapidly approaching the American. The *United States* then wore, to delay the fight, and perhaps to complete her preparations; but having cleared ship for action, she wore again so that she might close with the enemy. At this point, had Captain Carden held on his course, having much the faster ship, he might have run across the bow of his antagonist and raked her. But he wished to keep the weather-gage, and so hauled by the wind; and at nine o'clock the two ships passed each other in opposite directions, and exchanged their first broadsides at long range.

On board the *United States*, everything was now ready for action, and the men were waiting eagerly until the real battle should begin, for they were confident of making a good fight. At this point a boy, Jack Creamer by name, who had been allowed to make the cruise in the ship, although too young to be regularly enrolled, came to Captain Decatur as he stood upon the quarter-deck watching the enemy, and touching his forelock, said,—

"Please, Commodore, will you have my name put on the muster-roll?"

"Why, my lad?" asked the captain, amused and interested at the boy's eagerness.

"Because, sir," answered Jack, "then I shall be able to draw my prize money."

So the order, was given, and Jack went back contented to his station.

The firing at long range was doing no good, and the ships having passed each other, the *Macedonian*, after going a little way, wore round, and followed the *United States*, overhauling her rapidly, as her superior speed enabled her to do with ease. But as she approached nearly bows on, Captain Decatur was able to oppose the guns on his quarter to those on the enemy's bow in a running fight, and every now and then, by shifting his helm a little, to bring his whole broadside to bear, raking her with his diagonal fire. In a short time her mizzen-topmast was seen to totter and fall, and as this made the sailing of the two ships equal, Decatur backed his maintopsail and allowed her to come up.

As soon as the two ships were abreast there began that tremendous disabling fire which was the secret of the Americans' success. The *United States* fired two broadsides to the enemy's one, and seemed to be in sheets of flame; so much so that the English thought her on fire and gave three cheers in their delight. But they were mistaken, and they soon found that the American fire was as accurate as it was rapid. It was now the turn of the Americans to cheer, as the *Macedonian's* mizzen-mast went by the board.

"Ay, ay, Jack," called out one of the gun-captains, "we have made a brig of her!"

"Take good aim at the mainmast, my lad," said the captain, overhearing him, "and she will soon be a sloop;" and in a little while, when her two remaining topmasts came down with a crash, he added: "Aim now at the yellow streak; her masts and rigging are going fast enough. She must have more hulling."

And indeed it was a hulling that the *Macedonian* got that day, for one hundred shot had entered her sides, her upper battery was disabled, and all her boats were cut to pieces. Her people still held on with stubborn courage, though one third of their number were by this time killed or wounded, and tried to board, but the ship would not answer the helm. At last, finding the contest hopeless, the gallant Carden struck his colours and surrendered.

His ship was like a slaughter-house. Out of his crew of three hundred men more than one hundred were killed or wounded. "Fragments of the dead," said the lieutenant whom Decatur sent on board, "were distributed in every direction, the decks covered with blood, one continued agonizing yell of the unhappy wounded; a scene so horrible, of my fellow-creatures, I assure you, deprived me very much of the pleasure of victory." On board the *United States* there were hardly to be seen the signs of battle. Some little damage had been done aloft, but nothing that was not easily repaired. Two or three round shot were in her hull; but her crew were almost unhurt, for out of four hundred and seventy-six men she had but seven killed and five wounded. The difference in force, both in guns and men, was greatly in her favour; but the difference in the injuries that she inflicted and received went far beyond it.

As Captain Carden came on board the *United States*, Decatur advanced to meet him, and the two friends recognized each other. The vanquished captain, filled with the bitterness and mortification of defeat, offered his sword in silence.

"Sir," said his young conqueror, with the gentle courtesy that so became him, "I cannot receive the sword of a man who has defended his ship so bravely."

So the sword was returned, and all that lay in Decatur's power was done to soothe the feelings of his enemy. The captured frigate was fitted out with jury-masts, and together the two ships made for the United States, where they arrived in safety early in December. The despatches containing a report of the victory were carried to Washington by Midshipman Hamilton, of the *United States*, the son of the Secretary of the Navy; and as he travelled post-haste from New London to New York, and on through Jersey and Pennsylvania and Maryland, everywhere the news of "another victory over the British frigates" was borne onward and spread from lip to lip and from house to house, until the whole country from New England to Georgia was filled with joyous and triumphant acclamations.

★★★★★★

On the very day of the battle between the *United States* and the *Macedonian*, the *Constitution*, now commanded by Captain Bainbridge, was making her final preparations at Boston to set sail on a cruise. On the next day, the 26th of October, all was ready; and the frigate, whose name was already endeared to Americans by the victory over the *Guerrière*, started forth to win for herself fresh renown. The sloop *Hornet*, under Capt. James Lawrence, sailed in company with the *Constitution*, and the two ships shaped their course for the coast of Brazil, where the *Essex*, under Captain Porter, was to meet them. From this point, if no mishap occurred, they were to sail as a flying squadron for a cruise in the Pacific. As it turned out, the junction was never made, and the proposed plan was not carried out; but perhaps it was just as well in the end, for even if they had been together it would have been hard for them to accomplish more than they did separately, as we shall see by following the adventures that befell them.

Soon after reaching their first cruising-ground the *Constitution* and *Hornet* put into San Salvador, where they found the sloop-of-war *Bonne Citoyenne* lying in the harbour. The English sloop could not be induced to come out and fight, although Bainbridge promised not to

"The Ships were Steering to the Eastward on Parallel Courses."

interfere; so leaving the *Hornet* to blockade her, the *Constitution* sailed away on a cruise. She had been out only three days, when, on the 29th of December, being then about ten leagues from the coast of Brazil, at nine in the morning she sighted two vessels to the northeast. These were the British 38-gun frigate *Java*, under Capt. Henry Lambert, and an American merchantman, a prize of the *Java*. The *Constitution* stood for the strangers; but at eleven she tacked to the southward and eastward to draw the "*Java*" away from the coast, and also to separate her from the prize, which in the distance Captain Bainbridge mistook for a ship-of-war. This course was kept up for some time, the *Java*, which had now hoisted English colours, gradually lessening her distance; when at about half-past one Captain Bainbridge hauled up his courses and took in his royals, tacked ship, and stood for the enemy. Half an hour later the battle began with a broadside from the *Constitution*.

The ships were now half a mile apart, steering to the eastward on parallel courses. The *Constitution* had the advantage in guns, and she carried fifty more men than the *Java*; but they were so nearly a match that the difference could not have affected the result, whichever way it turned out. The *Java* was a faster ship, and she had therefore greatly the advantage in manoeuvring. She was constantly trying to get in position to rake, and the *Constitution* was constantly on the watch to baffle her. The wheel of the American frigate was shot away early in the action; but this injury was quickly remedied, and never was a vessel handled with greater skill.

Soon after the attack began, Captain Bainbridge was wounded by a musket-ball in the hip, but he refused to leave his post. A few minutes later a piece of langrage entered his thigh, causing intense pain; but still he stayed on deck directing the movement of his ship as calmly as if his men were at drill instead of in battle. The firing had now lasted forty minutes, and no great damage had been done, owing to the distance between the ships; Bainbridge became impatient, and determined to close with the *Java* in spite of her raking. So he set his foresail and mainsail, and luffed up close to her, pouring in that furious fire for which the American frigates were to acquire their greatest fame.

In a few minutes the head of the *Java's* bowsprit was shot away. Bainbridge now wore ship, and the *Java*, as the quickest way to get about, tacked; but unfortunately for her, her headsails were gone, and after coming up in the wind she paid off slowly. The American captain, ever on the watch, saw his opportunity, and luffing up astern of her, as she was in the midst of her manoeuvre, raked her deck; then wearing again, he resumed his course and the *Java* was once more alongside. But she had better be anywhere else; for the American gunners, cool and steady, were now firing with fatal precision. She seemed to have become a mere target floating alongside.

Captain Lambert bore up toward the *Constitution*, trying to get on board; but at this instant his foremast fell and his design was frustrated. A few minutes more, and the *Java's* maintopmast tottered and came down; next the gaff and spanker boom were shattered; and finally down came the mizzen-mast, leaving her nothing but the ragged stump of the main-mast above the deck. On all sides the men were falling at the guns, under the withering fire of grape-shot from the *Constitution*. Captain Lambert was mortally wounded, and the command fell to Lieutenant Chads, the first lieutenant, who refused to believe himself beaten. But he could do nothing; his fire ceased, and as the clouds of smoke rolled away they disclosed on the one hand a dismasted wreck, and on the other a frigate sound and whole, except for some slight damage to her spars and rigging. So there was nothing left for him but surrender.

In this gallant action—gallant on the enemy's side as well as on our own—the *Constitution* had thirty-four killed and wounded, and the *Java* one hundred and fifty. Captain Lambert died soon after of his wounds. Among the prisoners was General Hislop, the Governor of Bombay, who was on his way to assume his post. The general and all the other prisoners, whom Captain Bainbridge treated with the utmost courtesy and kindness, were paroled, and landed at San Salvador. The ship could not be taken into port, and two days after the action, on New Year's eve, she was set on fire and blown up. The *Constitution* now gave up her cruise in the Pacific and returned to the United States.

With this battle ended the year 1812, the most memorable that ever occurred in the history of our navy. For though gallant things had been done before this time, during the Revolution and the war with Tripoli, and though in the later wars, as well as in the later years of this same war, the record of naval achievements showed no falling off in brilliancy, there was a splendour so full, so dazzling, and so unexpected about this uninterrupted succession of triumphs on the ocean, that it would be hard to describe in words the depths to which it stirred the nation. That despised and belittled navy,—despised alike at home and abroad,—which the government had proposed at the outbreak of war to lay up, that it might be kept out of harm's way as a plaything and an ornament fit only for peaceful use, had shown itself a most terrible engine of offensive war.

Those much-abused frigates, of which we had but half a dozen for the nation's defence, had met the frigates of Great Britain in battle, and had conquered,—conquered the victors of Camperdown and Cape St. Vincent, of Aboukir and Trafalgar; beaten them on their own ground in honest hard fighting, beaten them thrice over, and beaten them as they had never been beaten before. The bitter strife of political parties, the truckling to this or that foreign State, which had vexed the councils of the nation for twenty years, and lowered the self-respect of Americans, was cast aside in united rejoicings at the success with which Hull, Decatur, and Bainbridge had asserted and maintained American independence and the rights of American citizens; and the country at last began to look upon the navy as its best protection, and as the stanchest supporter of the national honour.

The frigate actions of 1812 had produced results almost as marked in England as in America. For twenty years English ships had been accustomed to victory over every enemy, even in the face of heavy odds. The nation looked upon them as invincible. About the Americans it knew so little and cared so little that it had hardly felt any general interest or concern in the war. The loss of the *Guerrière* came upon it like a clap of thunder in a clear sky. Of course some reason must be discovered for so extraordinary an event, and it was said that the frigate was old and rotten, and her powder, was bad. But as capture followed capture, as the *Frolic*, the *Macedonian*, and the *Java* were surrendered in quick succession, the first murmurs of discontent swelled to an angry outcry.

The naval administration was bitterly assailed, and called upon to take more energetic measures. It was necessary to devise something to serve as an excuse for defeat. Then arose that foolish clamour that the frigates of the Americans were not frigates at all, but ships-of-the-line in disguise, and that the naval authorities of Great Britain had been hoodwinked by a Yankee trick into sending frigates to fight them. As if they had not had scores of opportunities—in the Mediterranean, on the American coast, and even in their own ports of Southampton and Gibraltar—to find out what the *Constitution* and her sister ships were like; and as if anything but their own folly and arrogance had prevented them from seeing long before that our constructors had built for us superior frigates!

CHAPTER 12

Captain James Lawrence

The two earliest actions of importance in the year 1813, though nearly six months apart in time, belong together, for they form the two great events in the career of one of our bravest officers; and unless I am much mistaken, the second of these events, which ended so tragically in defeat and death, was in great measure a consequence and outcome of the first. All our captains who were actively engaged during the first months of the war had carried out their enterprises gallantly, but still with discretion and circumspection, as became them in fighting against the greatest naval power in the world; but Lawrence, borne beyond the bounds of prudence by one brilliant success, risked most where the danger was greatest, and so came to an untimely end.

We left the *Hornet* in December, 1812, blockading the *Bonne Citoyenne* at San Salvador, where Bainbridge and Lawrence had found her. As she was just equal to the *Hornet* in force,—what little difference there was being in favour of the Englishman,—Captain Lawrence, according to the gallant fashion of those days, sent a challenge to Captain Greene, who commanded the *Bonne Citoyenne*, proposing a fight between the two sloops. He gave his pledge, in which Commodore Bainbridge joined, that the *Constitution* should not interfere, in order that it might be an equal match, where skill and pluck alone should decide the battle. Such a thing is hardly likely to happen now, when war is carried on so much more with an eye to business; but at that time a battle between two well-matched ships was looked on as a sort of tournament,—a rough kind of play perhaps, but still little more than a game where men went in to win as much for the sake of the sport as for the real earnest. It had this of good about it, that it made men look upon their enemies in some sort as friendly rivals, and it took away part of the bitterness which war engenders.

JAMES LAWRENCE.

Of this generous and chivalric spirit no man had more than Lawrence, and it was a deep disappointment to him when Captain Greene refused to accept his challenge. Here is what the Englishman's letter said:—

I am convinced, sir, if such rencontre were to take place, the result could not be long dubious, and would terminate favourably to the ship which I have the honour to command; but I am equally convinced that Commodore Bainbridge could not swerve so much from the paramount duty he owes to his country, as to become an inactive spectator, and see a ship belonging to the very squadron under his orders fall into the hands of an enemy. This reason operates powerfully on my mind for not exposing the *Bonne Citoyenne* to a risk upon terms so manifestly disadvantageous as those proposed by Commodore Bainbridge. Indeed, nothing could give me greater pleasure than complying with the wishes of Captain Lawrence; and I earnestly hope that chance will afford him an opportunity of meeting the *Bonne Citoyenne* under different circumstances, to enable him to distinguish himself in the manner he is now so desirous of doing.

How little Captain Greene meant of these bold professions, and how small was the confidence he really had in his pretension that the result would be favourable to him, was shown soon after; for on the 6th of January the *Constitution* sailed for home, leaving the *Hornet* alone before the port. Here she remained until the 24th, nearly three weeks, waiting for the *Bonne Citoyenne* to redeem her captain's promise. At length the *Montague*, a seventy-four which had sailed from Rio on purpose to relieve the English sloop, hove in sight, and chased the *Hornet* into the harbour, where she was safe for the moment in neutral waters. But Lawrence placed no great reliance upon such protection, for he knew that naval officers under strong temptation did not always show a due respect for neutral territory; and in the night he wore ship and stood out to the southward, thus eluding the enemy. In this way the *Bonne Citoyenne* got safely off; but the *Hornet* got off too, although a seventy-four had come out for the purpose of capturing her.

After leaving San Salvador the *Hornet* cruised off Surinam and the neighbouring coasts. On the 24th of February, at the entrance of the Demerara River, she discovered an English brig-of-war, the *Espiègle*, at anchor outside the bar. Lawrence was forced to beat around Carobano Bank in order to get at her; and while thus manoeuvring, about the middle of the afternoon he discovered another brig edging down for him. Soon the stranger hoisted English colours, and Lawrence beat to quarters and cleared ship for action, keeping close by the wind in order to get the weather-gage. The new enemy was the brig *Peacock*, under Capt. William Peake. It was nearly half-past five when the two ships passed each other and exchanged broadsides at half-pistol shot.

As the *Peacock* was endeavouring to get about, Lawrence bore up, and running close up to her on the starboard quarter, began that furious and well-aimed cannonade which nothing in this war had thus far been able to withstand. In fifteen minutes the enemy's ship was riddled,—literally cut to pieces; her captain, Peake, was killed, and the lieutenant who took his place, seeing that he could hold out no longer, surrendered. Immediately after, the ensign was hoisted union down in the fore-rigging as a signal of distress, and presently the main-mast fell.

Lieutenant Shubrick was sent on board the prize, and reported that she had six feet of water already in her hold. No time was to be lost, for she was sinking fast. The two ships came to anchor, and boats were hurriedly lowered and sent to rescue the prisoners, and first of all the wounded. Some of the shot-holes were plugged, the guns were thrown overboard, and everything was done to lighten the ship, by pumping and bailing her out, so that she might float until the men could be taken off. But it was too late; the water was rising higher and higher, and in a few brief moments the brig went down, carrying with her several of the crew and three of the American blue-jackets who were trying to save them. The rest of the *Hornet's* people who were still on board only saved themselves by jumping to a boat that swung at the stern; and four of the enemy, who succeeded in climbing up to the foretop, clung there till they were taken off by the Americans.

The *Hornet* had but two of her crew killed, having lost more men in saving the enemy than in fighting the battle. Three others were wounded. The ship's rigging and sails were cut here and there, but her hull had not a single scar.

The *Peacock*, on the other hand, was a sinking wreck; her sides showed numerous shot-holes, and she had forty casualties among her crew. The English chroniclers in their descriptions of this as well as other naval actions lay much stress upon the fact that the *Hornet* was armed with heavier carronades, carrying thirty-two's where the *Peacock* had only twenty-four's; but as someone has well said, "the weight of shot that do not hit is of no great moment." It is clear that in this fight, as in the others, it was skilful gunnery and firing low that settled the result. The *Peacock* was a smart and well-kept ship, her decks well cleaned, her bright-work spotless; in fact, so well known was Captain Peake for his attention to these small details, that his ship was called the "yacht of the navy." But polished brass-work and well-scrubbed decks are not the things that win battles, as poor Captain Peake found in that bitter quarter of an hour when he met his death and his ship was riddled till she sank.

The *Hornet* was now crowded with prisoners, and she turned her head toward home, arriving at Holmes's Hole in Martha's Vineyard some four weeks after the fight. Lawrence, always generous and true-hearted, kept a watchful eye to the comfort of his prisoners, treating them not as enemies, but as unfortunates whom the chance of war had thrown into his hands. So strongly did they feel the captain's courtesy, that upon their coming to New York the officers of the captured ship wrote him a letter, in which were these words:

"So much was done to alleviate the distressing and uncomfortable situation in which we were placed when received on board the sloop you command, that we cannot better express our feelings than by saying we ceased to consider ourselves prisoners."

If all officers would follow the good example of Lawrence, how much might be done to lessen the sufferings of war and soften its ferocity and bitterness!

In the following spring Lawrence was given a larger ship as a recognition of his services and merits. This ship was the *Chesapeake*, which from her earliest history had been unlucky upon nearly every cruise. She was then refitting at Boston, and her former captain, Evans, having been sent on sick-leave, Lawrence was ordered to take his place, and arrived in Boston about the middle of May.

Not only was the ship an unlucky ship, which is always a bad thing among the simple-minded blue-jackets, but she was at this time in bad condition. The crew had come home from their last cruise dissatisfied; and having some dispute about their prize-money, many of them had left the ship. New hands were being shipped from day to day, but it was difficult to get good men, and several foreign sailors were taken,—some English and some Portuguese,—who showed a mutinous disposition. Some of the officers too had lately left the ship, and others less experienced had been ordered in their place. In time, no doubt, a captain like Lawrence would have made his ship's company as good as the *Hornet's* had been when she destroyed the *Peacock* so quickly and so easily; but he had orders to go to sea as soon as he could get the chance.

Outside the harbour lay one vessel of the enemy, the frigate *Shannon*, commanded by Capt. Philip Broke. She was of nearly the same force as the *Chesapeake*, though whatever difference there might be was in favour of the American. But discipline and training are of far greater moment than a slight difference in the number either of guns or men, as the sequel proved; and in these things Broke's ship was far superior. She had been long at sea, and most of her crew were veteran tars, whom Broke, one of the ablest of the English captains, had trained and drilled and practised until they worked like a machine.

Now it must be confessed that it was a little rash in Lawrence, who knew how far his crew was from being shipshape, and ready to meet an enemy, to go out thus hurriedly and give battle. But there were his orders, which he must obey. He did not like to say—who would have liked to say it in his place?—that his ship was not ready; for Captain Broke had sent away the other ships that had been with him so that he might give the *Chesapeake* just such a chance as Lawrence himself had given the English sloop at San Salvador, and by remaining there alone, Broke offered him a sort of challenge to come out. In fact Broke wrote a challenge, as fine and manly a letter as was ever written by a gallant officer, but it happened that Lawrence sailed before it was delivered. Besides all this, it was to be expected that Lawrence, after what he had seen of the *Peacock*, and after the victories of Hull and Decatur and Bainbridge, should somewhat underrate his foe; forgetting that this time his ship, besides being of lesser force than the other American frigates, was wanting in that very quality which had insured them their success,—the discipline and training of the crew.

On Tuesday morning, the 1st of June, while the *Chesapeake* was lying at anchor off Fort Independence, in Boston Harbor, the *Shannon* appeared outside, evidently waiting to join battle. As soon as the enemy was seen, Lawrence fired a gun and hoisted his flag; then, after making the last preparations, when everything was ready, the anchor was hove up, and with all her studding-sails set, and colours flying at each masthead, the *Chesapeake* left President's Roads and put out to sea. Along the shore, upon every hill-top and headland, people had gathered to see the battle; but both the frigates, their great clouds of canvas filled with the light southwesterly breeze, made off to the eastward and before long were lost to view.

About the middle of the afternoon the *Shannon* hove to, to await

"Along the Shore, Upon Every Hill-Top and Headland, People Had Gathered."

the coming of the *Chesapeake*. The latter, having already cleared for action, presently took in her top-gallant sails and royals, and hauled the courses up, and a little before six o'clock shot up alongside of the enemy. In an instant the battle has begun in all its fury. Lawrence if he desires can pass under the *Shannon's* stern and rake her, but he is confident of success, and scorns his advantage. So he turns, and pressing close along the enemy's side, receives the fire of each gun as it is brought to bear. Half the *Shannon's* cannon have been loaded with kegs of musket-balls, and at the short range these make terrible havoc, and as mischance will have it, above all among the officers. At the first fire White the sailing-master is killed, and Lawrence is wounded, but he does not leave the deck. The guns of the *Chesapeake* reply, but the raw crew are not equal to such work as is required of them in opposing Broke's well-trained gunners.

Presently the helmsman is shot down, and the ship, coming up in the wind, loses headway and falls off with her stern and quarter exposed to a raking fire. The enemy makes the most of this; broadside after broadside comes pouring in, smashing in the after-ports of the *Chesapeake*, and killing the men at the guns or driving them away. The slaughter among the officers goes on; the third lieutenant is killed, then the marine officer and the boatswain. A moment later and the ships are foul, the *Shannon's* anchor hooking in the quarter-port of her antagonist. The withering fire of the enemy continues,—the heavy round shot, followed, now that the ships have closed, by the rain of grape and musket-balls. Ludlow, the first lieutenant, the captain's main reliance, is twice wounded and falls; and last of all the gallant Lawrence himself, who until now has kept his post, though weak from loss of blood, receives his mortal wound and is carried below, exclaiming as he leaves the deck, "Don't give up the ship!"

It was of no use now,—this last injunction,—for there was none to heed it. The quarter-deck had been stripped of all its officers except the midshipmen, who after all were only boys, and three of whom have fallen. Lawrence, before he is carried off, orders the boarders to be summoned, but the frightened bugler cannot sound the call. The captain's aides were sent below to pass the word, but the gun's crews on the main-deck, in the confusion, fail to understand the order. On the upper deck the men, uncertain, without a leader, are flinching from their guns. Broke, from his forecastle, sees that the Americans are weakening, and calls away the men to board. His boatswain, a veteran of Rodney's fleet, lashes the ships together, and in an instant twenty of the crew, led by their captain, have leaped the rail and gained the *Chesapeake's* quarter-deck. The deck is piled with bodies, but there is no one here to make resistance. On the forecastle are gathered a fragment of the frightened crew, and against these the enemy now advances. They are in no condition to resist: a few struggle to reach the hatchway; others climb over the bow; the rest throw down their arms and call for quarter.

For a moment there is now a pause, but presently some of the men below make a rush for the deck, and the fight begins anew. It is a scene of wild confusion. The enemy is now crowding on board,— officers, marines, blue-jackets; there seems no end to their numbers. The *Chesapeake's* topmen, who as yet have taken no part in the struggle, now pick the boarders off with small arms, but they are soon driven from their stations. The two remaining lieutenants, Budd and Cox, who have meantime come up from the deck below, are both wounded. The gallant Ludlow, striving, mortally wounded as he is, to drag himself up the ladder, is cut down as he reaches the hatchway. The chaplain, Livermore, seizes a pistol and fires without effect at Broke, who in return makes one furious cut with his sword, nearly dividing his assailant's arm.

The *Shannon's* first lieutenant hauls down the flag and bends an English ensign; but in the hurry he hoists it with the old colours still above, and the guns' crews, whom he has left on board his ship, suppose from this that the boarders have been defeated. So they open again, and kill their own lieutenant and several of his men. Captain Broke, urging his boarders on, is half stunned by a blow from the musket of a marine, who clubs with his gun since he cannot fire; and a sailor, following the marine, cuts down the captain, only to be himself cut down by one of the enemy. A few minutes of desperate hand-to-hand conflict with pike and pistol and cutlass, and the Americans on deck are overpowered and yield. The crew below, not daring to come up, are still making a show of resistance; but a few shots fired down the hatchway put an end to the struggle, and the *Chesapeake* is in the hands of the enemy.

In this wonderful action, which from beginning to end lasted only fifteen minutes, the *Chesapeake*, out of twenty officers, lost seventeen in killed and wounded. Even had this worst of all disasters not befallen her, she might perhaps have still been captured, for as we know her crew were not prepared to fight, having had no training. But had not Lawrence and Ludlow both fallen at the critical moment when the two ships fouled, it is certain that one or the other of them would have prolonged the contest, and that the enemy's loss, large as it was, would have been larger yet. The two ships were carried into Halifax with their wounded captains still on board, but Lawrence died before he reached the shore. Captain Broke, whose wounds were not so serious, recovered, and was made a baronet for his victory, which, as neither friend nor enemy could deny, had been gallantly and bravely won. Of the officers engaged on one side or the other in that eventful battle, many were killed or died of their wounds, and nearly all who survived the fight have long since been gathered to their fathers; but it is a strange fact that the highest officer in Her Majesty's navy today, the senior admiral of the fleet, Sir Provo Wallis, was the lieutenant who took the *Shannon* into Halifax after her bloody victory three quarters of a century ago, (as at time of first publication).

CHAPTER 13

The Cruise of the "Essex"

Of the vessels in commission at the opening of the war, a fine frigate of the third class was the *Essex*, very fast, but poorly armed with carronades. She had been for some months under the command of Captain Porter, of whom we have heard in the war with France, and whose life had already been so full of active service, that though only two-and-thirty years of age, we think of him as a much older man.

The *Essex* had first got to sea for a war-cruise on the 3rd of August, and soon after, on a hazy night, she came up with a fleet of the enemy's transports sailing under the convoy of a frigate. Stealing up silently alongside the rearmost transport, Porter ordered her to draw out of the convoy on pain of being fired into. This order the transport hastened to obey; and the convoying ship, fearing that by delay she might lose all her convoy, went on her way without molesting the captor. The transport had one hundred and fifty troops on board; and Porter, putting all the prisoners on their parole, ransomed the prize and left her to make her own way into port.

A few days later the *Essex*, being then disguised as a merchantman, with her ports closed and her upper masts housed, made a strange sail, which proved to be the enemy's sloop-of-war *Alert*. The English sloop ran down for her, deceived by the disguise. The *Alert* was not a good ship for her size, and her size was only half that of her antagonist; but when she found out what the *Essex* was, she made no effort to escape. No doubt the English, who were accustomed, in fighting Frenchmen and Spaniards, to engage a ship of almost any force, thought that the Americans would be so frightened by an Englishman's attack that they would strike immediately; for this was before the *Guerrière* had surrendered to the *Constitution*. But they received a needed lesson from this engagement, for in ten minutes after the firing had begun they found their ship in a sinking condition, with seven feet of water in her hold; and after a resistance so feeble that the encounter could hardly be called a battle, they yielded her a prize. She was the first vessel of the enemy's navy that was captured in the war.

The *Essex* now ran in to the Delaware, where she remained some time, making preparations for a more extended cruise. This cruise was a cherished plan of the captain's own devising, and the scene of it was to be a hitherto untried field,—the Pacific Ocean. At that day the Pacific, with its vast stretches of sea-coast, and the innumerable islands studding its broad surface, was almost unknown, except to the English and American whalers. The United States had no settled territory bordering on the great ocean, and our ships-of-war had hardly been seen at all upon its waters. The *Essex*, on her first cruise in 1798, under Captain Preble, had gone as far as Batavia, by way of the Cape of Good Hope; and she was now to be the first vessel of the navy to go around Cape Horn.

What, then, was Captain Porter's object in sailing into this remote and almost unknown sea? It was this: he knew that the enemy would never expect to find our cruisers there, and therefore would have sent none of their own. If, then, he could evade the frigates that were patrolling up and down the Atlantic from Halifax to Bermuda, and from Bermuda to Jamaica, and all through the Windward Islands, and on the South American coast as far as Rio de Janeiro, and if he could once double the Cape and find his way into the Pacific, he would have before him a field of operations where he might be almost free from interruption. He would find there numbers of American whaling-ships, which generally went unarmed, and which he could protect and succour if they found themselves in any danger; and he would find also numbers of British whalers which were fitted out as privateers, carrying from five or six to twenty guns, to whom the Americans that they might meet would fall an easy prey.

To assist the first and to capture and destroy the second was now Porter's object. Sooner or later, he thought the enemy's government would no doubt hear of his depredations, and send out ships-of-war to capture him. But in those days of slow communication between distant places it would take a long time to accomplish this, and meanwhile the bold American would be able to carry everything before him; and even when the enemy arrived in force, he was prepared to take his chances either in flight or in battle as circumstances might require.

The original plan, as I have said already, was for the *Essex* to go to the Pacific with two other vessels,—the *Constitution* under Commodore Bainbridge, and the *Hornet* under Captain Lawrence. She was to start alone from the Delaware when the others sailed from Boston, and the three ships were to rendezvous near the coast of Brazil. The *Essex* went first to the Cape de Verde Islands. Proceeding thence to the westward on his way to the appointed place of meeting, Captain Porter fell in with an enemy's brig-of-war, the *Nocton*. The *Nocton* was a small ship for the *Essex* to fight, and Porter would not order the guns to be fired at her, supposing that she would surrender. But she began to manoeuvre to get into a raking position, thinking that perhaps she might fire one broadside and then escape in the confusion.

So Porter concluded to make short work of her, and coming close alongside he poured a volley of musketry upon her decks. This was enough, and the *Nocton* immediately struck. She was a stanch vessel, and therefore Porter sent her to the United States in charge of one of his lieutenants. It was a fortunate capture, for the brig had on board more than fifty thousand dollars in gold and silver; and as the *Essex* was to be gone on a long cruise, with no prospect of receiving money from the United States, the captain needed all that he could get.

The *Essex* now continued on her way to the island of Fernando Noronha, near the Brazilian coast, where Porter expected to meet Commodore Bainbridge, or at least to hear something of his movements. It had been arranged that both the ships should be disguised as Englishmen, in order that the enemy's squadron might not discover their presence in those seas. So when the *Essex* arrived off the island she lay to outside, and Lieutenant Downes went in a boat to the town and told the governor that she was the ship *Fanny* of London. Captain Johnson, bound for Rio. On his return Downes reported that the governor had told him that two British ships-of-war, the *Acasta* of forty-four guns, and the *Morgiana* of twenty, had departed from the island only the week before, and that Captain Kerr of the *Acasta* had left a letter for Capt. Sir James Yeo of the *Southampton*, which was to be sent to England by the first conveyance.

As soon as Captain Porter got this message, he knew that the pretended English ships were not the *Acasta* and *Morgiana* at all, but the *Constitution* and the *Hornet*, and that the letter from Captain Kerr to Sir James Yeo was really from Commodore Bainbridge to himself. He therefore sent word to the governor that the "captain of the *Fanny*" knew Sir James Yeo, and would willingly take him the letter if the

"When the 'Essex' Arrived off the Island She Lay to."

governor would send it to him; which the governor immediately proceeded to do. Here is the letter:—

My dear Mediterranean Friend,—Probably you may stop here. Don't attempt to water; it is attended with too many difficulties. I learned before I left *England* that you were bound to Brazil coast. If so, perhaps we shall meet at San Salvador or at Rio Janeiro. I should be happy to meet and converse on our old affairs of captivity. Recollect our secret in these times.

Your friend of H.M. Ship *Acasta*,

Kerr.

Sir James Yeo, of H.B.M. Ship *Southampton*.

This was apparently all the letter, and it would not have given Sir James much information about the Americans if he had received it, though its mysterious phrases would have puzzled him not a little. But on holding the letter before the fire these words could be read between the lines:—

I am bound off San Salvador, thence off Cape Frio, where I intend to cruise until the 1st of January. Go off Cape Frio, to the northward of Rio, and keep a lookout for me.

As soon as he read this, Captain Porter made sail at once for Cape Frio. He remained cruising about here for two or three weeks, waiting for the *Constitution*, and occasionally going in chase of a strange sail. Once he succeeded in making a capture of an English schooner, which he sent in as a prize in charge of one of his midshipmen. He could get no information that was to be relied on, but was all the while disturbed by vague rumours of something going on among the English and American ships in the neighbourhood. At last, upon putting in at St. Catherine's, he heard that an American sloop-of-war had been brought into Rio by the *Montagu* ship-of-the-line, and that an American frigate had sunk an English frigate. He concluded then that the captured sloop must be the *Hornet*, and the victorious frigate the *Constitution*, and that there was not much reason for his delaying longer in those parts.

As it turned out, the rumour about the frigate was true, for, as we have already seen, the *Constitution* had captured and sunk the *Java*; but the other story was false, for instead of being captured, the *Hornet* had gone off to the coast of Guiana, where she succeeded in sinking the *Peacock*, after which she had followed the *Constitution* home. "At any rate," thought Porter, "the cruise in the Pacific can be made just as well without the help of the other ships, and they do not seem to be anywhere hereabout, so I may as well go on without them."

This determined, the *Essex* laid in a stock of fresh provisions, and made her final preparations for the passage around the Cape. The captain expected to be gone for a long time, and in fact it was nearly two years before he finally returned. During the whole period, he was to be cruising in those distant seas, with no word of direction or encouragement from home, and with the whole care and responsibility of his ship's company resting upon him alone. But he was a man of such iron nerve and self-reliance and strength of purpose, that there was little danger that his spirits and his energy would ever flag. It was to him that all on board the ship were to look for support and guidance, and as they soon found out, they could have had no better man for their commander. For Captain Porter was a bold and hardy seaman, who knew his business well, and who feared neither the elements nor the enemy; and though he believed in strict obedience, and insisted upon having it, he believed too in lightening as far as in him lay the burdens of his men.

He despised the cat-o'-nine-tails, which in those rough times was always used to flog the sailors on board our ships-of-war, and never would inflict this punishment when he could bring about his object by other means. Two hours in every afternoon, from four o'clock till six, when there was no serious work on hand, he allowed the bluejackets to skylark as they liked, and at these times they could throw off the restraints of discipline and frolic to their hearts' content. The captain was always careful too about the men's health, and their sleeping-places, and all the little matters about their daily life which added to their comfort and their strength. So that the men in turn forgot their hardships, and were his devoted followers in storm and battle, only waiting for his word to do their duty in any way that it might please him to ask it of them.

After a stormy passage round Cape Horn the *Essex*, about the middle of March, 1813, appeared off the port of Valparaiso. At this time our relations with Spain were not over-friendly, and Captain Porter did not expect a very cordial reception. He learned, however, that Chili had shaken off the Spanish authority not long before, and being a young and small American republic, she was only too glad to welcome a ship from the oldest and most powerful of the free States of the Western Continent. Instead of indifferent or nearly hostile Spaniards, the *Essex* found in the Chilian inhabitants only devoted friends. The ship fired a salute in honour of the town, and the captain visited the Chilian governor, and received his visit in return. All was hospitality and cordial good-feeling, and stores and provisions were supplied in abundance.

The Government of Chili could thus be relied on as at least a neutral in the war. It was far otherwise with Peru, which was still a Spanish province. On the day before Captain Porter left Valparaiso, an American whaler had come in with the report that several English whaling privateers were off the Peruvian coast, and that the news of the declaration of war had just reached them. The *Essex*, though she had only been in port a week, lost no time in putting out to sea, to reach the enemy's cruising-ground. Soon Porter fell in with another American, the *Charles*, whose captain told him that the Englishmen were not the only enemies to be found there, for a Spanish privateer out of Callao, the principal port of Peru, had recently chased the *Charles* and had captured two of her companions, the *Walker* and the *Barclay*. Here was a fine state of affairs! It was well that the *Essex* was on the spot, and she had arrived only just in time, for it was evident that between open enemies and piratical neutrals the unarmed Americans would have little hope of safety.

The *Essex*, keeping the *Charles* in company,—for the whaler was only too glad to stay under the wing of her new and powerful protector,—now crowded all sail for the Peruvian coast. After a few hours she sighted a vessel in the distance which had the appearance of a ship-of-war disguised as a whaler, and which hoisted the Spanish flag. The American frigate, as a ruse, showed English colours, and fired a gun to leeward, which is the signal all the world over that a ship comes on a peaceful errand. At the same time the *Charles* sent up a union-Jack over her American flag, which meant that she was an American whom the pretended Englishman had made a prize.

The stratagems were successful, and the stranger, which was a Peruvian privateer, the *Nereyda*, was completely deceived, thinking that the *Essex* was one of the English whalers, and she fired a shot across the latter's bow. This was an insult; but Captain Porter wisely thought he could put up with it, as it was an insult to the English colours. In a short time a boat came from the *Nereyda* bringing her lieutenant, who, little thinking to whom he was talking, told the captain that he was cruising after American vessels, and had captured the *Walker* and *Barclay*, whose crews were then prisoners on board the *Nereyda*; but that the *Nimrod*, an English privateer, had taken possession of the ships.

"You know," he added, "that the Spaniards are faithful allies of the British, and that we always respect your flag; and we are now endeavouring to clear the seas of these Americans."

When the lieutenant had finished his communication, and told Captain Porter all there was to tell, great was his surprise at seeing the British ensign lowered, and the stars and stripes going up to the peak of the *Essex*. He was still more astonished when she fired two shots point blank at the *Nereyda*, and the latter immediately hauled down her flag. He realized, too late, that he had been entrapped, and that he had revealed his perfidious acts to the very man from whom he most desired to conceal them.

As there was no war with Spain, the *Nereyda* could not well be made a prize, for the captain knew that two wrongs do not make a right, and that, treacherous as had been her conduct, he could not stoop to retaliate. He released the twenty-three Americans that were confined in her hold, threw overboard her guns and light sails, and sent her back to the Viceroy of Peru, with a letter that was courteous and dignified, but whose language could not be misunderstood. His spirited action had the desired effect, and taught the Spaniards such a good lesson that the American whalers were never afterward molested by Peruvian *corsairs*.

The *Charles* now sailed to Coquimbo, and soon after the *Barclay* was recaptured. The *Walker*, however, and her captor the *Nimrod*, which Porter most desired to find, had by this time disappeared. Taking the *Barclay* along, the *Essex* made for the Galapagos,—a group of uninhabited islands much used by the whaling-ships as a refuge and rendezvous. Good anchorage was to be found here, and whales abounded in the neighbourhood; but the principal product of the islands was the land-turtle. There were great numbers of these of large size, some of them as much as five feet across, and they would live for months in the ship's hold without food or water. They made delicious food, and the sailors found them an agreeable change from salt pork and hard-tack; so that every ship calling at the islands took great quantities of them on board.

Some years before, an Irishman named Patrick Watkins had deserted from a whale-ship, and had settled on one of the islands at a place which came to be known as Pat's Landing. Here he had built himself a little cabin and planted a potato-patch, and he would sell potatoes and pumpkins to the whaling-crews for rum, to the use of

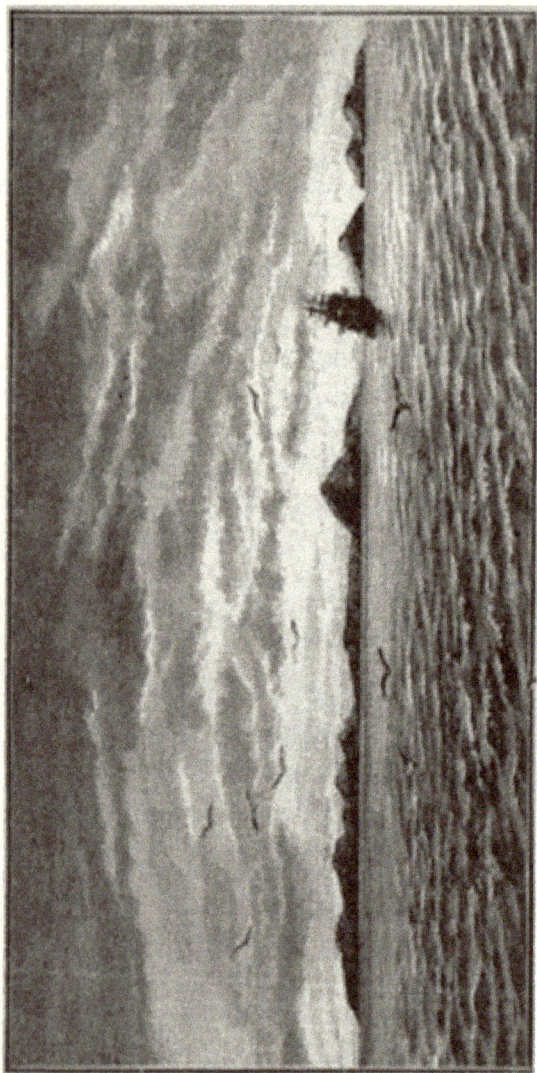

APPROACHING THE GALAPAGOS ISLANDS.

which he was much addicted. He led a wretched life, becoming like a savage in appearance, his hair and beard matted, and his clothes in rags. He spent his time in wandering about the island, doing enough work to keep his garden-patch in order, but as soon as he had laid in a supply of liquor, keeping himself drunk until it was exhausted. He was a half-crazy creature, and once he frightened a negro boat-keeper into leaving the boat and going off with him as his slave. For this he was severely punished by the captain to whom the boat belonged, and ever after he sought to wreak vengeance upon the whalers. At last by some means or other he got a boat and sailed away to the mainland, where he was locked up by the authorities.

All this happened shortly before the arrival of the *Essex*, so that the islands were now deserted. But on one of them was found a rough sort of post-office, made of a box nailed to a tree, in which the whalers touching at the island left letters containing news of their movements. From these it was learned that six whalers had put in here some time before with two thousand and five hundred barrels of oil. One of the letters was from the master of the American ship *Sukey*, and read as follows:—

Ship *Sukey*. John Macy. 7½ months out, 150 barrels, 75 days from Lima. No oil since leaving that port. Spaniards very savage lost on the Braziel Bank John Sealin apprentice to Capt. Benjamin Worth fell from the fore topsaill yard in a gale of wind left Diana Capt. paddock 14 day since, 250 barrels I leave this port this day with 250 turpen 8 boat load wood yesterday went up to Patts Landing east side to the starboard hand of the landing 1½ miles Saw 100 turpen 20 rods a part road very bad.

Yours Forever

John Macy.

This was a fair sample of the letters left at the Galapagos post-office. Captain Porter remained a fortnight among the islands, searching every hole and corner to find the whalers, and in the intervals exploring the land, and making sailing directions of the coast, while the men spent the time when they were not busy with their duties, in catching turtles and in killing iguanas,—the big lizards that swarmed on the islands, which though not very pleasant to look at, were excellent to eat. Jack always likes a frolic on shore when he is not too much hampered by the restraints of civilization; and the sailors of the *Essex* took great pleasure in their sports, although the heavy turtles had to be dragged over the rocky slopes a long distance to bring them to the ship. There was plenty of fishing, too, for those that stayed on board the ship, and flocks of penguins and pelicans and other strange birds lined the shore. Altogether it was a pleasant break, this stay at the Galapagos, and the ship revisited the spot several times, making it a sort of headquarters for the next six months.

But all this was not war, and the men began to remember that it was not prize-money; so when, after a fortnight of it, on the morning of the 29th of April, the cry of "Sail ho!" was heard, everyone was glad, and all the crew rushed eagerly on deck. A large sail was seen to the westward, and the *Essex* started in pursuit. Soon two more sail were discovered farther off. They were evidently whalers. If they should only prove to be enemies! The crew went to work with willing hands, and bearing down under British colours, by nine o'clock the *Essex* had overtaken the nearest of the strange ships, the British whaler *Montezuma*. The master came on board and was shown into the cabin, where he spent an hour in giving his supposed countryman such information as would help him to capture the Americans. While this interview was going on, his people were taken on board the frigate as prisoners, and a prize crew was thrown into the whaler; and when the master came on deck he was overcome with surprise at finding himself in the hands of an enemy.

The *Essex* lost no time here, but moved on to reach the other vessels. Soon the wind fell, and it became a dead calm, while they were still eight miles away. The boats were then got out, and the men pulled away for the whalers, under the command of Lieutenant Downes, the first lieutenant of the *Essex*. After a hard row for nearly two hours they approached the largest of the strangers, which flew the English flag, and which opened fire upon them. Nothing daunted, Lieutenant Downes kept steadily on and prepared to board. As he ran up alongside he hailed the ship and demanded a surrender. "We surrender," was the reply, and down came the flag.

No sooner had Downes taken possession than the second ship hauled down her colours without waiting for an attack. The prisoners were quickly secured, crews were placed on board the whalers, and soon after the frigate was rejoined by her men, bringing with them the new prizes,—the *Georgiana* and the *Policy*. It was a good day's work, for the three ships, together with their cargoes of oil, were valued at half a million. The *Georgiana*, a fast, fine vessel, was made a tender, and the command of her was given to Lieutenant Downes, the

"We Surrender," and Down Came the Flag.

other ships being placed in the charge of the older midshipmen.

The *Essex* now returned to the Galapagos. Here it was found that vessels had visited the island during her absence, and the *Georgiana* was sent out under Lieutenant Downes to look for them. The other prizes were refitted, and after a stay of several days the commodore, as we may call him now that he had a squadron to command, got under way again with all his consorts, leaving instructions for Lieutenant Downes in a bottle, which according to a previous agreement was buried at the foot of the tree that marked the post-office. After a week's cruising, in which all the vessels were spread out so as to cover as much ground as possible, one of them sighted a strange sail, and the *Essex* started in chase.

In a short time it fell calm, and the boats were got out, with the intention of coming near enough to the stranger to keep her in sight all night, but not to attack her unless it could be done by surprise. Soon after the boats got away, however, a breeze sprang up and the *Essex* again took up the pursuit. The enemy, who carried the British flag, waited for her to come up, supposing that she was British too; and he was not undeceived until Porter had got alongside and made him a prize. The new capture was the whaler *Atlantic*, carrying six 18-pounders, and like the others engaged both in privateering and in whaling. She was very fast, and with her little battery of heavy guns made a valuable addition to the squadron.

No sooner was the capture of the *Atlantic* completed, than another whaler was reported in sight, and she too was quickly overhauled and taken. She was called the *Greenwich*, and like the *Atlantic* was a good sailer. On board the two ships were great quantities of supplies of all kinds, including water and provisions and naval stores, of which the *Essex* stood much in need; especially of water, which is so scarce in the Galapagos that it is sometimes taken from the stomachs of the turtles,—the only sure place to find it.

The captain now proceeded with his prizes toward the coast of South America, stopping on the way at the island of La Plata, where he left instructions for the *Georgiana* in case she should visit it. The letter was put in a bottle which was hung upon a tree, and the letters "S.X." were painted on a rock to attract attention. Lieutenant Downes would know that this meant *Essex*, but no one else would suspect it. Soon afterward a Spanish brig from Panama was spoken, whose captain took the squadron for an English convoy and gave a full account of the affair with the *Nereyda*; only he said that the *Nereyda* had attacked the American frigate and shot away her mainmast, but having suffered much in the action she thought it best to make her escape by running away, which she accomplished by throwing overboard her guns,—all which, as we know, was very different from what had actually happened.

On the 19th the squadron arrived at Tumbez, on the South American coast, where it remained several days. The Governor of Tumbez, a ragged old gentleman, who would be of assistance—so Commodore Porter thought—in selling the prizes, came to the *Essex* by invitation, and was received with full military honours.

After staying a week at Tumbez the commodore began to be anxious about the fate of the *Georgiana*, which had parted from him at the Galapagos four weeks before, and of which nothing had since been heard. At last, on the morning of the 24th of June three vessels were seen coming into the harbour, one of which was the missing tender. The others were English whalers—the *Hector* of eleven, and the *Catherine* of eight guns—which the *Georgiana* had captured. A third prize, the *Rose* of eight guns, had also been seized by the tender, but she was a dull sailer, and rather than be impeded by her slow movements Lieutenant Downes had sent her to England with all the paroled prisoners, after throwing overboard her guns and cargo.

Commodore Porter now had with him a fleet of nine excellent vessels, several of which were well armed, and all of which had been supplied by the enemy. The best of the prizes in every way was the *Atlantic*, and she was fitted out as a new tender in place of the *Georgiana*, mounted with twenty guns, and christened the *Essex Junior*. Lieutenant Downes was transferred to her, and the chaplain was placed in command of the *Georgiana*, which would seem to be a very strange arrangement; but the chaplains in those days were employed to teach navigation to the younger officers as well as to administer spiritual advice, so that there was much that they would know about the management of a ship. Besides, the supply of regular officers was now almost at an end, even the youngest midshipmen being placed in charge of prizes.

A plan of action for the remainder of the cruise was now drawn up by the commodore. The *Essex Junior* was to go to Valparaiso with the *Montezuma. Policy, Hector*, and *Catherine*, which were to be laid up or sold or sent to the United States; though there was small chance that any of them would reach port in safety, while British cruisers swarmed in the Atlantic Ocean. The *Barclay*, the recaptured American whaler, was to accompany the others to Valparaiso, there to remain and await further developments. The *Greenwich* was converted into a store-ship, and all the spare supplies and provisions were put on board of her. She now carried twenty guns, and with her and the *Georgiana* as tenders to the *Essex*, Commodore Porter proposed to continue his cruise against the whalers that were still at large in the neighbourhood of the Galapagos Islands. Here the *Essex Junior* was to rejoin him.

This plan was exactly carried out. Early in July the two squadrons parted company, Lieutenant Downes proceeding to Valparaiso, and the commodore making his way once more to the Galapagos. The sailors were rejoiced to return to their rambles on shore and their dinners of turtle; but they were still more pleased with the prospect of making new prizes in the neighbourhood where they had already been so fortunate. They did not have long to wait. Hardly had they dropped anchor in the familiar roadstead, when three sail were reported in sight, and all were soon under way in pursuit. The *Essex* headed for the ship that seemed midway between the others, which last made off in opposite directions.

The centre vessel ran off before the wind, and for a while the *Essex* had a hot chase; but in the end she came up with the stranger, the English whaler *Charlton*, of ten guns. The *Greenwich* made for the second vessel, which opened fire, but after receiving one or two well-directed broadsides she hauled down her flag. She was called the *Seringapatam*, and was the finest ship of the Pacific whaling-fleet, having been built for a ship-of-war. She carried fourteen guns, and did not trouble herself much about catching whales when it was so much more profitable to catch the American whalers, one of which she had already made a prize. The last of the three strangers, the *New Zealander* of eight guns, was soon after overtaken and captured by the *Essex*.

The *Charlton* was now sent to Rio with the prisoners, and the *Georgiana* was despatched with orders to proceed to the United States; but she was captured by the enemy on the way home. If the United States had at this time had a port on the Pacific, all the prizes might have been easily disposed of. As it was, they were compelled to run the gantlet of British squadrons in the Atlantic, where they were almost sure to be retaken.

For two months the *Essex*, now accompanied by the *Greenwich*, the *Seringapatam*, and the *New Zealander*, cruised about among the islands. There was now only one British whaler left to capture,—the *Sir Andrew Hammond*, commanded by another Captain Porter. At last, one morning toward the latter part of July she was discovered some distance off; but the *Essex*, unfortunately getting into a dangerous situation among the rocks and currents, was delayed in following her, and soon she was lost to view. The next day she was seen again and pursued, but when the frigate had come within four miles of her it fell calm. The boats of the *Hammond* were hoisted out, to tow her out of reach.

The *Essex* then called away her boats,—not to tow, but to pull for the whaler and board her. The commodore was sure that if they could only reach the enemy they would succeed in taking her. But this time his hopes were vain. The boats had covered more than half the distance, and were nearing their object, when suddenly a breeze sprang up, filling the *Hammond's* sails, and she lost no time in making off. The *Essex* lay immovable, for she was still becalmed and did not get a breeze until after sunset. So the Englishman was again lost in the darkness, and next day no sign of him was to be seen.

Six weeks were now spent at the Islands, during which the *Essex* was repainted, and her whole appearance so completely changed that her own officers could hardly recognize her. At the end of this time she started off alone, hoping to fall in with the *Hammond*, which was almost sure to be somewhere in the neighbourhood. The commodore's search was soon rewarded, for he had been out but a few days, when one morning at daylight he discovered her some distance to windward, to all appearance lying to, but really fastened to a whale, which she was in the act of taking. The disguise of the *Essex* now served her in good stead, for if she frightened away the enemy there would be little chance of making a capture.

The commodore had learned from the *New Zealander* that a private signal had been agreed upon between her and the *Hammond*; and he now came up in a lazy and careless fashion, under British colours, and showing the private signal. He proceeded on in this way for some hours, and had got within three or four miles, when suddenly the *Hammond*, suspecting a stratagem, took alarm, and casting off the whale, made sail to escape. But she had waited too long. In a few minutes the *Essex* was within gunshot, and after firing half a dozen rounds the Englishman struck his colours.

The last of the British whalers in the Pacific had now been captured, and Commodore Porter could feel that his year's work had accomplished substantial results. The Americans were safe from attack, for there were none of the enemy left to attack them. The commodore could now carry out his plan of retiring for a while with his fleet to some obscure harbour in the South Seas, where he could refit at leisure, and where his men could rest from the fatigues of their long voyage. Soon after the *Essex Junior* came in, with the news that she had taken the prizes safely to Valparaiso and laid them up, and that the cruise of the *Essex* had caused so great a commotion in England that three ships-of-war had been sent out specially to seize her. These had already arrived at Rio, and before many weeks would make their appearance in the Pacific.

But the Pacific Ocean is broad, and the Southern Seas are dotted with innumerable islands, unfrequented at that time by civilized man, with deep and safe anchorages in their land-locked bays, where ships might remain for years lost to the world outside. Among all the South Sea Islands none seemed to offer the needed advantages more than the beautiful Marquesas, a group inhabited only by native tribes who lived in primitive simplicity, uncorrupted by the influences of European civilization. Thither the commodore now shaped his course in the frigate, taking with him his tenders, the *Essex Junior* and the *Greenwich*, as well as his four latest prizes.

It was about the middle of October when the squadron came to anchor off the island of Nookaheevah, in the Marquesas group, and here it remained for two months, during which the *Essex* was thoroughly repaired. The natives of this part of the island became very friendly, as soon as they had recovered from their first suspicions. They were like children, and showed great delight at receiving the simple presents that were given them,—knives, or fish-hooks, or even pieces of iron hoops or glass bottles; while a whale's tooth, which the islanders valued above all other possessions, would purchase, almost anything they had. The king of the tribe, Gattanewa, an old man of seventy, tattooed from head to foot, came on board the *Essex* and vowed eternal friendship with the Americans, ratifying the bond by exchanging names with the commodore,— "Tavee" or "Opotee," as he was called, which was the nearest approach that the Nookaheevans could make to David Porter.

The island of Nookaheevah was eighteen miles long and crossed by ranges of mountains between which lay beautiful and fertile valleys filled with streams and waterfalls, and little villages, and forests of sandal-wood, and groves of cocoanut-palm and bread-fruit and banana. In that tropical climate,—for the place lies near the equator,— where Nature gives with a liberal hand all that man can ask for, amid

162

the luxuriance of forest growth, of tree and fruit and grass and flower, with its simple-minded and childlike people, the sailors of the *Essex* were now to pass two months of rest and refreshment. It was like the fabled land of the Lotus-eaters,—a land

> *In which it seemèd always afternoon.*
> *All round the coast the languid air did swoon,*
> *Breathing like one that hath a weary dream.*
> *Full-faced above the valley stood the moon;*
> *And like a downward smoke, the slender stream*
> *Along the cliff to fall and pause and fall did seem.*
> ★★★★★★
> *The charmèd sunset lingered low adown*
> *In the red west: through mountain clefts the dale*
> *Was seen far inland, and the yellow down*
> *Bordered with palm, and many a winding vale*
> *And meadow.*

No sooner had the captain established friendly relations with the natives, than he saw how great the danger was that his men, intoxicated by the delights of this enchanted land, would forget their duties, and like Sir Amyas Leigh's companions sink into the captivating indolence of the life around them. He wished that they should have relaxation, but he was not a man who would suffer discipline to grow slack. It was therefore not without satisfaction that he learned that his sailors might have some hard work; for the Happahs—the native tribe dwelling in the next valley—were at war with his friends, and unless he took part in the conflict he would soon lose their respect and with it their friendship. So he joined forces with them and landed his men, and after mounting a six-pounder, which his allies transported for him, on the intervening range of hills, he drove the Happahs from their fort and compelled them to ask for peace.

In the valley beyond the Happahs dwelt the Typees, a warlike tribe whom all the other natives of the island held in great awe because of their martial prowess. Hearing of "Opotee's" arrival, and of the subjugation of their neighbours the Happahs, the Typees now declared war against him, sending him defiant messages and declaring that he dared not fight them. This challenge the commodore suffered to pass unnoticed, as he did not wish to run any serious risks where no great object was to be gained. But he soon discovered that his inaction was having a bad effect upon the others, who began to think the Americans as much afraid of the Typees as they were themselves. So he resolved to attack the warlike tribe.

After his experience with the Happahs the commodore somewhat underrated his new enemies, and on his expedition against the Typees he took with him only Lieutenant Downes and about thirty men. The native allies appeared in great force, but they were not overzealous when it came to fighting, their purpose being to witness the combat and take sides with the party that might win. The attacking force proceeded in boats and canoes to the landing at the end of the Typee valley. After he had disembarked and made a reconnoissance, Porter found that he would have to march with his handful of men to the enemy's stronghold through an almost impenetrable jungle, which was filled with hundreds of hostile savages, armed with clubs and slings which they used with no little skill. But it was impossible to go back now; and the Americans, advancing with great difficulty, fought their way slowly through the forest.

Early in the day Lieutenant Downes was wounded, having his leg broken by a stone. Sometime after this mishap the Americans reached a river which they forded, the enemy retreating as the sailors charged gallantly up the opposite bank. Here their progress was checked by a strong fort, and they could not storm it, for the ammunition was nearly exhausted. The situation was very serious, or would have been so had the Typees shown more boldness. But they were afraid of the "*bouhis*," as the muskets were called, and did not venture to attack; so that the Americans were able by great care and coolness to extricate themselves from their dangerous position and retreat through the woods to the beach.

It was now evident that the Typees must be subdued at any cost. A few days later Porter, taking with him two hundred men, marched over the mountains and attacked the natives in their forts. These were captured one by one, and the men then proceeded up the valley, burning the native villages. It seemed a pity to do this, but it was the only way in which the savages could be really reduced; and from that time forward the Typees and the Americans were fast friends.

At length the time came for the *Essex* to depart from the island. The sailors were not happy at the prospect of leaving so pleasant a refuge, and there was some disposition to murmur, as might have been expected. But the captain sternly checked all insubordination, and on the 9th of December the *Essex* and the *Essex Junior*, repaired, and well supplied with provisions and stores, sailed away for Valparaiso.

The *New Zealander* sailed soon after on her way to the United States, and the *Greenwich*, with the *Hammond* and *Seringapatam*, was left in the harbour in charge of Lieutenant Gamble of the marines, who was ordered to start for home in five months unless the *Essex* returned before that time.

The *Essex* did not return, however, and Lieutenant Gamble found his position full of difficulty. The few men who were left behind became demoralized, and in May a party of the sailors, among them several who had deserted from the prizes, mutinied, and seizing the *Seringapatam*, made their escape from the island. The natives now became hostile, and Gamble, after losing some more men through treachery, set fire to the *Greenwich* and left the Marquesas in the *Hammond*. He took with him all that remained of the force,—a midshipman, three marines, and three seamen. On her way to the Sandwich Islands the *Hammond* was captured by the enemy's sloop *Cherub*; and Gamble and his midshipman, with their feeble crew of half a dozen men, were made prisoners.

Meanwhile the *Essex*, with her consort the *Essex Junior*, made her way safely to Valparaiso, arriving there early in February. Four days later the English frigate *Phœbe* appeared off the harbour accompanied by the sloop-of-war *Cherub*, which had been sent out to capture the *Essex*. The two ships were much more than a match for Commodore Porter's force, for the *Essex Junior* carried such light guns that she was of no use at all, and the *Phœbe* alone was about as large as the American frigate. Besides, the *Phœbe* was armed with long guns, while the *Essex* had mostly carronades; so that if Captain Hillyar, the English commander, could choose his distance, he would have the *Essex* at his mercy; for, as we must remember, the long guns carried much farther than the carronades, and if the ships were far apart would hit their mark at every shot, while all the projectiles from the small guns would fall short.

The English ships lay in or about the harbour for several weeks, and during this time Commodore Porter made repeated efforts to draw the *Phœbe* into action alone. The sailors in the *Essex*, when the enemy was near them in the harbour, would amuse themselves by singing songs about the victories over the English frigates, which were set to the tune of Yankee Doodle; and the English crews retaliated in like manner by songs whose object was to banter the Americans. Commodore Porter and Captain Hillyar were old acquaintances, having been together in the Mediterranean, and they often met on shore and con-

versed about their situation as amicably as if they were great friends instead of being mortal enemies. On one occasion Porter, speaking of his prizes which were laid up in the port, said,—

"They are in my way, captain, and I mean to take them outside and burn them at the first opportunity."

"I dare you to do it," rejoined Captain Hillyar, "while I am in sight."

"We shall see," said Porter.

So choosing a day when the *Phœbe* and *Cherub* were at some distance outside the harbour, the *Essex* towed the *Hector* out and set fire to her. The English ships tried their best to head the *Essex* off from the harbour, but without success, and by evening she was lying safe and sound at her old anchorage.

Commodore Porter now decided on a judicious plan of action. He had found by trial that the *Essex* outsailed the *Phœbe*, and he proposed to put to sea with both his ships, the two taking different directions; by which means either the enemy's ships would be separated, or if they both followed the *Essex*, the *Essex Junior* would escape. Besides, as the *Cherub* was a dull sailer, the *Phœbe* in attempting to overtake the *Essex* would be drawn away from her consort, and so might be engaged alone. At any rate, it was necessary to seize the first opportunity to escape, for other frigates of the enemy were shortly expected on the coast.

An accident, and a most unlucky one for the *Essex*, finally brought about the battle. On the 28th of March the wind was blowing fresh, and the *Essex* parted her cable, and dragging the other anchor drifted out. Sail was made, but at the moment when she was rounding the point a squall struck her and carried away her main-topmast. The *Phœbe* and *Cherub* were close upon her, and finding that she could not regain the harbour, she ran over to a bay on the western side, where she anchored half a mile from the shore. This was in neutral waters, just as much so as in the harbour, and as Captain Hillyar had given assurances that he would respect the Chilian neutrality, the American commander felt that he could repair his injuries in security.

It is much to the discredit of Captain Hillyar that he did not keep his word. When he found the *Essex* thus placed at a disadvantage, he took a position under her stern, where no guns could be brought to bear on him, and opened an attack. The *Cherub* joined him, and the two ships together raked the *Essex* almost unopposed, inflicting heavy losses, until Porter managed to get three long guns out of his

"A SQUALL STRUCK HER AND CARRIED AWAY HER MAIN-TOPMAST."

stern-ports. These he worked as well as he could for half an hour, after which the enemy's vessels hauled off to make repairs, although their damages were in no degree serious.

The *Essex* was now in a very bad way. Many of her men had been killed or wounded, and her rigging was so much cut that she could carry hardly any of her sails. The enemy had suffered no loss worth speaking of. Commodore Porter nevertheless determined to take the offensive. It was a desperate measure, but the only one that seemed to promise any hope. Setting his flying-jib—the only sail he could use—and cutting his cable, he stood down for the enemy. He could not manoeuvre much, but for a little while he was near enough to use his broadside of carronades with some effect. But it was only for a little while. The English were fighting a safe battle, and meant to use the safest tactics, which of course it was perfectly right that they should do; and in a little while both ships had withdrawn out of range of the carronades, and the *Phœbe's* long 18-pounders were once more covering the decks of the "Essex" with the bodies of her unlucky men.

Still the *Essex* would not give up. She had been on fire in several places, but the flames were extinguished. Her carronades were many of them disabled,—as always happened with carronades,—and as the guns' crews fell, others took the places of the killed. The cockpit was filled with wounded, so that there was no room for more. The slaughter on board was fearful, for in the smooth water every shot from the enemy told with deadly effect; and at length the captain resolved to run the ship ashore, as the wind was blowing that way, and land the remainder of his men and then destroy the frigate. So he made for the land. But just as he had nearly reached the point where he must touch, the wind shifted and drove him out again.

At this juncture the *Phœbe*, being somewhat injured aloft, began to drift to leeward, and Porter, in the hope that she might drift out of range, bent a hawser to the sheet-anchor to hold on where he was. This would have enabled him to gain a little time; but the hawser parted, and with it went the last chance for the *Essex*. The boats had been destroyed, but Porter told the men that such as wished might swim for the shore. Most of the crew preferred to remain by the ship, although they knew her hours were numbered. The flames were now coming up from all the hatchways, the hull was riddled, the enemy was still keeping up a raking fire, and the men were falling at every shot. At last, finding all the chances against him, the commodore yielded to fate and gave the order to haul down the flag. Never had the honour

169

of that flag been more gallantly sustained.

Out of two hundred and twenty-five men on board the *Essex*, one hundred and fifty-five were killed, wounded, or missing. Captain Hillyar, upon receiving Porter's surrender, entered into an agreement by which the *Essex Junior* was to be converted into a cartel-ship, and so be exempt from capture. In her the captain and the remnant of his crew took passage for the United States, where they at length arrived after nearly two years of absence. Thus ended the eventful cruise of the *Essex*.

CHAPTER 14

Perry and Lake Erie

Returning now, we take up the story of a young officer who, although he had passed fifteen years in the service, had never been so fortunate as to take part in any of its more striking operations, but who was now to leap at one bound to a height of glory and renown unsurpassed by any of his comrades in the navy. This was Oliver Hazard Perry. He had entered the service in 1798, during the hostilities with France, when he joined his father's ship as a midshipman at the age of thirteen. He had served in the Tripolitan war in the squadron of Commodore Morris, and later with Commodore Rodgers; but during Preble's command, when all the great achievements of the war had been performed, it was his ill luck to be at home, and he was thus almost the only one of the victorious commanders of the war of 1812 that had not received his training in the squadron of the great commodore.

Perry was now twenty-seven years old, and a master-commandant,—that is, he was higher than a lieutenant, but lower than a captain. When the war was expected, he went to Washington and begged that he might be ordered into active service against the enemy and given a post suitable to his rank. His request could not at once be granted, and meantime he was placed in command of a gunboat flotilla at Newport. For nine months he carried on his duties here with energy and zeal, but all the time chafing and fretting that he should be concerned with such trivialities while others were winning distinction in great enterprises and fighting battles with the enemy's ships-of-war.

During this year the northern lakes, and especially Erie and Ontario, were the scene of great preparations for combat, as might be expected upon waters which washed the frontier of two hostile countries. Upon their shores on either side were opposing armies, and the

OLIVER HAZARD PERRY

movements of the troops depended upon which side gained control upon the lakes. During the winter of 1812-13 the work of building and equipping ships was going briskly forward on Lake Ontario, where Commodore Isaac Chauncey was in command. But little had as yet been done upon Lake Erie, where the enemy had a considerable force of vessels, which gave him almost undisputed mastery on the water.

At this stage of affairs it occurred to Perry to write to Commodore Chauncey and offer him his services, at the same time renewing his entreaties to the department by letters and through friends. The commodore was just now looking for an officer who could take charge of matters on the western lake, of which he still desired to retain command, and knowing Perry well, and knowing too his worth, he gladly consented to his coming for this service. Accordingly on the 18th of February, 1813, Perry received his orders to proceed to Sackett's Harbor with the best men of his flotilla. So eager was he to be off, and so quick to carry out the order, that on that very day, before nightfall, he had started his first detachment of fifty seamen under one of his lieutenants. Five days later one hundred more had been despatched, and Perry had set out for his new command.

It was a severe journey at that inclement season, bitterly cold, and the way from Albany over the frozen roads led through a thinly settled country still covered by its virgin forests. Perry had with him his little brother Alexander,—a boy twelve years old, whom he was taking to be a midshipman on board his ship. After eleven days of travelling the two brothers reached their destination, and reported on board the flagship *Madison*, which was lying at Sackett's Harbor. Here they were delayed a week; but at last they set out for Lake Erie, where they arrived about the middle of March.

For the next six months Perry was busily occupied in preparing his squadron,—indeed, one might say in building it, for the principal vessels were only just begun. These were two good-sized brigs, each designed to carry twenty guns, but at this time their keels only had been laid. The station of the proposed squadron was at the town of Erie, where there were also building three schooners, now about half finished. So far the work had gone on but slowly; but the young commander by his zeal infused new zeal into those around him, and by his energy and wisdom overcame all obstacles and difficulties.

It was a strange and difficult position in which Perry now found himself. The enemy with his squadron of five vessels controlled the lake. The building-yard at Erie was without protection. There were no guns, not even muskets or cartridges, and if there had been, there were no men to use them. Of the ship-carpenters who were sent on with their tools from Philadelphia only a few had come. All the supplies,— guns, sail-cloth, cordage, ammunition,—everything, in short, but timber, was to be brought a distance of five hundred miles over bad roads, through a country that was almost a wilderness. Finally, the little brig *Caledonia* and the four gunboats which together made up the whole of the squadron afloat were at Black Rock in the Niagara River, and were unable to make their way past the enemy's river batteries into the lake.

Perry began his work at once. He sent to Buffalo for seamen, and at his request some companies of militia were posted at Erie. He went himself to Pittsburg, where he procured small cannon and muskets to assist in the defence. Iron was bought at Buffalo, and when this supply was exhausted, every scrap that could be got in the neighbourhood was worked up for use in the construction of the fleet. Blacksmiths were found among the militia. To obtain the timber for the vessels, trees were felled and sawn up, and all was so quickly done that it often happened that wood which at daybreak had been growing in the forest was before nightfall nailed in place upon the ship. With such extraordinary despatch did the young commodore push forward his work, that by the third week in May all the vessels had been launched from the ways and were afloat in the harbour of Erie.

About this time Perry learned that Commodore Chauncey was preparing to attack Fort George, and he resolved to join him, for he knew that his services would be needed. The message was brought to him one day at sunset, and though the night was stormy, in an hour he had started in his four-oared boat for the Niagara River. It took him twenty-four hours to reach Buffalo, where he rested; then starting again he entered the river, and landing just before he reached the rapids, he resumed his journey alone and on foot, the rain pouring in torrents, directing his course to the camp at the mouth of the river, off which the squadron lay. Here he found the officers assembled, and as he walked into the cabin of the flagship, wet, bedraggled, and spattered from head to foot with mud, the commodore grasped him by the hand and told him that "no person on earth could be more welcome."

And it was fortunate that he came, for the fleet was sadly in want of just such a man as he; and the attack on the next day, in which he served in some sort as the commodore's chief of staff, was successful largely through his coolness and skill, his ready and unerring eye, and his untiring energy. For on this day he was everywhere,—pulling in his boat under a shower of musketry from one vessel to another, encouraging the men here, re-forming the line and altering a boat's position there, sometimes even going on board and pointing the guns himself so that their fire might tell with more effect, and finally landing to join in the assault on shore, which ended in the capture of the fort.

After the fall of Fort George, the English abandoned the whole Niagara frontier, and there was therefore at last some slight chance that the vessels at Black Rock might be enabled to make their way into Lake Erie. Leaving the Ontario fleet, Perry repaired to Black Rock, and with the help of oxen and two hundred soldiers the five boats were tracked up against the rapid current of the Niagara. A fortnight was consumed before they reached the head of the river, after laborious exertions, and "a fatigue," said Perry, "almost incredible." At last they were out upon Lake Erie, but before them there was still the difficult task of eluding the British squadron, whose flagship, the *Queen Charlotte*, was alone a match for all of them, and which had besides four smaller vessels. The enemy was in the neighbourhood, and the winds were contrary; but Perry with great skill managed to pass them unopposed, and at last brought his vessels into the harbour of Erie, thus joining in one squadron all his forces.

It was now the end of June, and for a month Perry was engaged in fitting out the vessels that had been launched in May, and in preparing their crews. One of the brigs was named the *Lawrence*, in honour of the captain of the *Chesapeake*, who had just before died of his wounds in the action with the *Shannon*; the other was called the *Niagara*. The seamen, who were mostly drawn from the Lake Ontario squadron, came in slowly. As soon as one detachment arrived, the men were placed on board and stationed, and every day when it was possible to do it they were exercised at the guns. But the hardest task was yet to come.

Upon the bar at the mouth of the harbour the water was only six feet deep, and outside lay the British squadron on the watch. To get the two brigs over the bar under the enemy's fire seemed hopeless, and Commodore Barclay, the British commander, well knew his advantage. But one day early in August, either because he thought the ships were not ready, or because he fancied that he could overcome the Americans in any case, he left his post of observation and took his squadron over to the Canadian shore.

The American commodore, as he was now called, saw his opportunity and made the most of it. Five of the small vessels were sent across the bar, where they were cleared for action. The *Niagara*, anchoring close inside, pointed her guns down the channel; and the *Lawrence* was towed down to be taken across. Every means was used to lighten her; her guns were hoisted out, and when all was ready, two great scows were fitted alongside, and filled with water so that they sunk to the edge. Huge cross-timbers were then run through the ports of the brig, their ends resting upon blocks of wood placed in the sunken scows. The scows were now pumped out, and as they came up they lifted the brig with them. It was anxious work, for the enemy might return at any moment, and finding the *Lawrence* defenceless and immovable, might riddle her until she could not float. The first trial failed, for there was little water on the bar and the brig could not be lifted high enough to get her over. But the men worked with might and main, the militia helping the blue-jackets; and the scows were readjusted, so that at last the ship had forced her way over the sands and passed into the deep water beyond. Here she was joined by the *Niagara*.

The fleet of Commodore Barclay now came in sight, and although it was a little late, a smart attack might yet have saved it the supremacy which it had held thus far. The guns were still to be put on board the *Lawrence*; and to gain time Perry ordered two schooners, the *Ariel* and *Scorpion*, to stand out toward Barclay's vessels and annoy them with their guns. The schooners advanced so boldly that the enemy were fully occupied. In a short time the *Lawrence* had received her battery and placed it in position, and she was ready for action. The enemy's opportunity was lost, and Barclay sailed away to the northern shore. From this moment Perry had the advantage on Lake Erie.

The American fleet was now only waiting to complete its crews before seeking its adversary. Soon a final detachment of one hundred men came from Lake Ontario, brought by Lieutenant Elliott, who was placed in command of the *Niagara*. The *Lawrence* was selected by Commodore Perry as his flagship. He had now through his energetic efforts a force superior to the enemy both in guns and men, and the next few days were spent in training the mixed crews, and in reconnoitring and manoeuvring on the lake.

At sunrise on the morning of the 10th of September, as the American ships were lying at anchor at Put-in Bay, the British squadron was sighted from the mast-head of the *Lawrence*, standing in for the bay. Lieutenant Forrest, the officer of the deck, reported the news to Commodore Perry, and immediately the signal was hoisted on the flagship. "Under way to get!" For a few moments all was hurry and bustle, and in a little while the American squadron was under sail, beating out of the harbour.

The breeze was light, and as the enemy had the weather-gage, several hours were now passed in manoevering. But in the course of the forenoon the wind shifted, bringing the English fleet to leeward, upon which Perry determined to advance without further preliminaries. The enemy were now in line of battle, hove to, the schooner *Chippeway* leading. Next came the *Detroit*, Commodore Barclay's flagship, with the brig *Hunter* astern. Next to the *Hunter* lay the *Queen Charlotte*, the second of the enemy's large ships; and the schooners *Lady Prevost* and *Little Belt* brought up the rear.

The American squadron was so arranged as to bring its largest vessels opposite to the largest of the enemy. The commodore led in his flagship the *Lawrence*, supported by the *Ariel* and *Scorpion* upon his weather-bow. He chose Barclay's flagship as his own antagonist. Following him was the brig *Caledonia*, which was to engage the *Hunter*. Next came the *Niagara*, Elliott's vessel, to oppose the *Queen Charlotte*; and the line was completed by the schooners *Somers*, *Porcupine*, and *Tigress*, and the sloop *Trippe*, which would take care of the enemy's rear.

The English lay in compact order, broadside on, their red ensigns opening to the light breeze. No picture could be drawn more peaceful or more beautiful than that upon which the sun shone on this September morning as it lit up with sparkling brilliancy the rippling waters of the lake. The long column of the Americans came slowly down with all sails set, led by the *Lawrence*, at whose mast-head was unfolded the lettered flag bearing the words, "Don't give up the ship,"—the last order of the ill-fated commander of the *Chesapeake*. It was Perry's battle-flag; and as it was displayed and the words were read by the different crews, cheer upon cheer rang out, caught up from ship to ship down the long line of the advancing column. The last preparations had now been made; the shot were in the racks, the pistols and cutlasses arranged at hand, and the decks sanded to give a foothold, when in a few moments they would become slippery with blood. All was in readiness, and the men only waited to join battle.

For more than an hour the squadron advanced slowly and in silence under the light wind. At length the notes of a bugle sounding

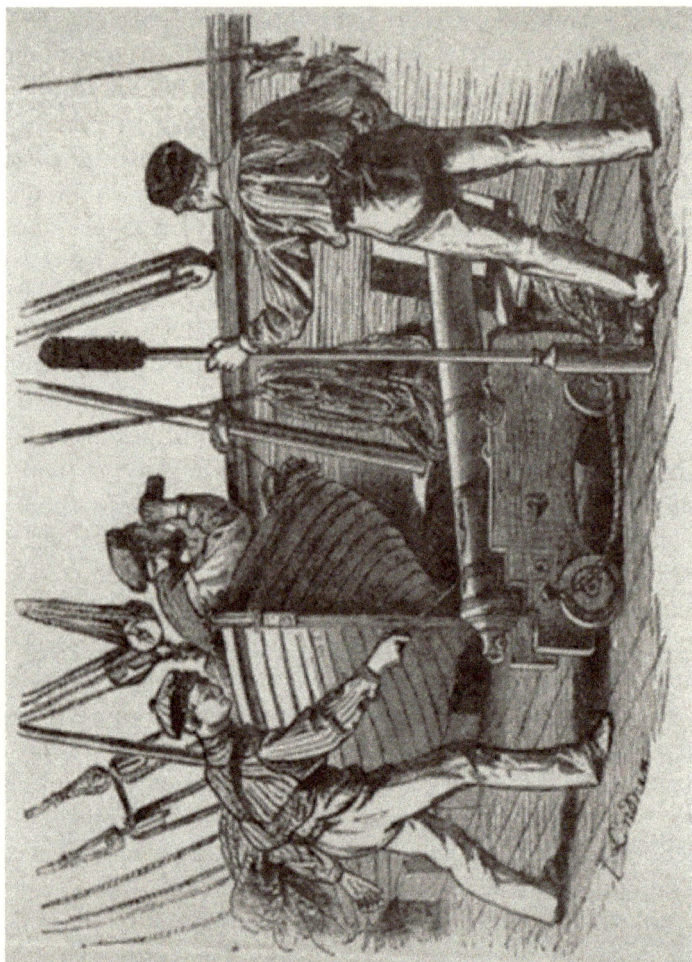

"A Single Gun Boomed from Barclay's Ship."

on the *Detroit* broke the still air, followed by cheers from the enemy's ships, and soon a single gun boomed from Barclay's ship as the signal for opening battle. His second shot passed through both bulwarks of the *Lawrence*, and Perry made reply. But his battery of carronades was useless at this distance, and for fifteen minutes more he continued to advance, receiving a terrific fire without being able to answer it. At length, arriving within three hundred and fifty yards, he hauled up and began the action.

The other American vessels, delayed by the lightness of the wind, had been slow in getting into position for battle. The *Ariel* and *Scorpion* supported the *Lawrence* efficiently. The *Caledonia* too, the next astern, closed with the *Hunter*. But the *Niagara*, upon which Perry mainly relied as one of his largest vessels, engaging only at long range, failed to close, and finally, moving ahead, passed to windward of the *Caledonia* and *Lawrence*, thus placing them between herself and the enemy and throwing herself out of the battle. It was represented afterward that this was due to the lightness of the wind; but however this may be,— and there is no event in naval history which has been the subject of more wrangling and disputation,—certain it is that never was a ship made to do so little to help her consorts as the *Niagara* during the time when Elliott was directing her movements. The *Queen Charlotte*, finding that her opponent had thus placed himself out of harm's way, filled her main-topsail and passed ahead of the *Hunter*, thereby doubling the odds against the already injured *Lawrence*.

For two long hours the *Lawrence* now sustains an unequal contest, receiving the concentrated fire of nearly the whole of the enemy's squadron. The rigging is cut, the sails are torn to shreds, one by one the spars are shattered or fall upon the deck. Gun after gun is dismounted, and fearful is the slaughter of officers and men. The wounded are taken below so fast that the surgeon can barely serve them, hurriedly amputating a leg or an arm, one after another, and binding up as best he may the bleeding wounds. Cannon-shot enter the quarters for the wounded, striking men whose limbs have just been taken off by the surgeon's knife.

The first lieutenant, Yarnall, wounded in the forehead and the neck, his face streaming with blood, continues to fight his guns until his men are killed, and sending to the commodore for more, is answered that there are no more to give him. The second lieutenant, Dulany Forrest, standing beside Perry, receives a spent grape-shot in the breast which throws him to the deck. A gun captain whom Perry has addressed to give a word of caution is just about to fire, when a cannon-ball passes through his body and he falls without a groan at the commodore's feet. Brooks the marine officer, a dashing young lieutenant, is making a smiling response to Perry's cheerful words, when a heavy shot crushes his thigh and throws him across the deck. In an agony of pain he implores the commodore to shoot him dead and put him out of misery.

All the guns but one are now dismounted, but this one still keeps up its fire; for the commodore, with the brave purser Hambleton, and Chaplain Breese, aided by two or three men, are working it themselves. At last the purser falls, his shoulder shattered by a grape-shot. Presently this gun, too,—the last one,—is disabled, and the *Lawrence* cannot fire a shot. There are less than a score of sound men left on board.

At this terrible moment, when, though untouched himself, nearly all his companions had fallen, when his ship was beaten, and himself exhausted with the stress of two hours of battle, there came to Perry one of those resolutions which can only be called inspiration. He saw that if the flagship surrendered, the whole fleet would follow. He saw that the two leading ships of the enemy had suffered much in his attack, though their force was not so nearly spent as his own. He saw too that the *Niagara* and the schooners in the rear were almost fresh, if they could only be brought into action. Upon this he formed his resolution. Calling away his boat, and taking with him his little brother, who like himself had passed through the fearful ordeal unscathed, except for the bullets in his cap, he rowed under the enemy's fire to the *Niagara*. It was a daring act, for the enemy's shot broke the oars, and the spray was dashed in the faces of the rowers. But it was more wonderful in the coolness and bravery which enabled the young commander at such a time and after such a trial to carry out with promptness and judgment the only plan to retrieve disaster.

Arriving on board the *Niagara* Perry at once assumed command, hoisting his flag, and a moment later he sent Lieutenant Elliott, who volunteered for the duty, to bring up the tardy schooners. Then, setting the signal for close action, he formed his ships in line abreast and dashed at the enemy. The *Lawrence* had now struck, but the enemy had no chance to take possession. The onset of the fresh fleet was irresistible. The *Detroit* and the *Queen Charlotte*, seeing the blow coming, attempted to wear, so that fresh broadsides might be brought to bear. In doing this they fell foul, and as they lay entangled, the breeze freshening, the *Niagara* plunged through their line, firing both broadsides

"Calling Away His Boat, He Rowed Under the Enemy's Fire."

as she passed through the narrow gap.

At the same moment the *Caledonia* with the *Scorpion* and *Trippe* broke through the line at other points, and turning with the *Niagara* brought the enemy between two deadly fires. The shrieks of the wounded mingled with the roar of the American cannon; the British commodore could not resist this new attack, and in seven minutes from the *Niagara's* passage of the line, four of the enemy had surrendered in their places in the column. The two remaining vessels sought to escape under cover of the smoke, but they were pursued and brought back by the *Trippe* and *Scorpion*.

As soon as the prisoners had been secured, the prizes manned, and orders given for the necessary repairs, Perry sat down in his cabin and wrote to General Harrison, commanding the Army of the West, who had been waiting anxiously for the issue of the battle. Here is his letter:—

Dear General,—We have met the enemy and they are ours,— two ships, two brigs, one schooner, and one sloop.
Yours with very great respect and esteem,
O.H. Perry.

Well might the general be elated when he got the news. The victory had saved the whole Northwest, which until then had been desolated by the most savage and barbarous of enemies. No time was lost in following it up, and in carrying the war into the enemy's country. The army was quickly embarked on board the ships and landed in Canada.

After marching inland it attacked the enemy, and in the great victory of Moravian Town the English troops were annihilated, and Tecumseh, the relentless enemy of the United States, was killed. From that time forth until the close of the war the British were compelled to abandon all operations on Lake Erie.

CHAPTER 15

The Sloop Actions

So far most of the engagements which had taken place on the ocean were fought by frigates. Only two of them,—the first between the *Wasp* and *Frolic*, and the second between the *Hornet* and *Peacock*— were sloop actions. But the sloops formed at this time a very important part of our navy, and no less than six sloop actions were fought later in the war, all but one of them resulting in victory for the Americans. The sloops-of-war of this period were generally small three-masted vessels, though in the brig-sloops, like the *Argus* and *Pelican*, there were but two masts. They were armed with carronades, of which the American sloops carried either eighteen or twenty, and the British sixteen; and each of them carried also two long guns. The batteries varied slightly in the different vessels; but whatever the variations, it seemed that we had always a little the advantage in armament.

Two of the sloop actions took place in the summer of 1813,—the same summer which opened so badly with the loss of the *Chesapeake*. The first was that of the *Argus* and the *Pelican*, and like the frigate action it proved a disastrous battle for the Americans. The *Argus* had sailed from New York in May, having on board as passenger Crawford, the Minister to France, who was on his way to his new post. She was under the command of Lieut. William Henry Allen. This was the same Lieutenant Allen who, it will be remembered, fired the gun with a live coal in his fingers on board the *Chesapeake* when she was assailed by the *Leopard* in 1807. He was the same, too, who had been for five years Decatur's first lieutenant in the United States, ending his cruise with the capture of the *Macedonian*.

After landing his passenger at Lorient, Captain Allen was ordered to make a cruise in English waters. It was almost impossible for him to send to America any prizes he might make, even if he could weaken his ship to man them; and his instructions, therefore, were to sink, burn, and destroy all he captured. It was a daring enterprise, like the cruises of Paul Jones and Wickes and Conyngham in the older war, though with the increased numbers of the enemy's navy it was presumably attended with greater danger. But strangely enough, with the lesson of the earlier war before them, so little had the British provided for the defence of their own seas against commerce-destroyers, that the *Argus* was able to cruise for two months, often within four leagues of their coast, without being disturbed in her operations.

During this time she captured twenty-three prizes, most of which were burned. The value of the ships and cargoes destroyed amounted to near two millions of dollars; and as happened in the Revolution, the rate of marine insurance in England was raised far in advance of its usual figure. The naval administration, which at this period of defeat was roundly abused by English writers, must have been more than usually sluggish, to have allowed a 20-gun brig to continue for two months such depredations.

At length the British sloop *Pelican*, which had just come in from the West Indies, was sent out from Cork expressly to fight the *Argus*. She was a little superior in force, but the difference, as in most of these actions, was not great enough to be of any consequence. The *Argus* was now destroying prizes right and left, and the *Pelican* was guided to her by the smoke of the burning merchantmen. When the English sloop first sighted her in the evening, she was busy with a prize; and though the *Pelican* lost her in the night, another fire disclosed her position in the morning.

As the *Pelican* bore down to engage, Captain Allen shortened sail to give the enemy a chance to close. At six o'clock in the morning the *Pelican* had come within grape-shot distance, and Allen fired his first broadside. It was his last too, poor fellow! for the enemy returning the fire with spirit, a round shot carried off his leg; and though he would not leave the deck, he was soon unconscious from loss of blood, and his career was ended. The rigging of the *Argus* was at the same time badly cut; but when the enemy tried to get under her stern and rake her, Lieutenant Watson, who was now in command, cleverly threw all aback and thwarted the attempt.

But alas! the gun's-crews on this day were not up to their work; for whether, as some have said, the hard work of the night before had worn them out, or whether they had got hold of the spirit-cask in their last prize, certain it is that their firing was weak and wild, and far

184

"THE 'PELICAN' WAS GUIDED TO HER BY THE SMOKE OF THE
BURNING MERCHANTMAN."

below the example which had been set by American blue-jackets in other battles. The enemy remained almost unhurt, and by no means got as good as they sent. Lieutenant Watson was disabled by a grape-shot in the head; two round shot passed through the warrant-officers' cabins; the running rigging and wheel-ropes were shot away, so that the brig became unmanageable; and finally, three quarters of an hour after the action had begun, as the enemy was about to board, the *Argus* struck her colours.

★★★★★★

The next engagement was happily more creditable to the Americans. Early in September the *Enterprise*, commanded by Lieut. William Burrows, a brave and skilful officer who was much respected and be-loved in the service, put out from Portland, and the day after, being the 5th of the month, fell in with the enemy's brig *Boxer*, Captain Blyth. The two ships were about a match in guns, but the American, as usual, had a larger crew. As Burrows approached he manoeuvred to try his powers of sailing; and finding that his ship had greater speed, he bore up for close action, setting three ensigns and firing a gun of defiance.

Blyth had nailed his flag to the mast, telling his men that it should never be struck while he had life in his body. And he kept his word. As the *Enterprise* ranged up, her crew gave three cheers, and opened on the enemy at half-pistol shot. At the first fire a round shot passed through the body of the gallant English captain. The *Boxer* returned the fire. A moment later Captain Burrows, encouraging his men, seized a tackle to help the crew in running out their carronade; and as his leg was raised to brace it against the bulwark, a canister-shot struck it, and glancing upwards to his body, gave him a frightful wound. In an agony of pain he lay on the deck, crying out that the colours must never be struck, and refusing to be taken below.

The two ships were now fought by their lieutenants. McCall, the lieutenant of the *Enterprise*, finding that he ranged ahead, sheered across the *Boxer's* bow, pouring in a raking broadside. Presently the *Boxer* lost her main-topmast, and McCall, hanging on her bow, kept up his raking fire. There could now be but one result, and soon the *Boxer* hailed to say that she had surrendered. The flag which had been nailed to the mast was now lowered, but Blyth had already breathed his last. Burrows kept his place on the deck until he had received the sword of his adversary. Then he exclaimed, "I am satisfied; I die contented," and with that word breathed his last.

★★★★★★

The next of the sloop actions was in the spring of the following year. The *Peacock*, one of the new sloops, named after the British vessel which the *Hornet* had sunk in the Demerara River, was cruising in April under the command of Capt. Lewis Warrington, when she met the enemy's brig-sloop *Epervier* off the coast of Florida. Though the *Peacock* had the larger crew, the ships were not far from a match in guns. But the *Epervier's* battery was not in fighting condition, and she had practised so little with her carronades that her officers did not know of their defects; or if they did, they had not done anything to remedy the difficulty. Indeed, the whole service of the *Epervier*, both at the guns and in other ways, was most slovenly, and far behind what one would expect in a British sloop-of-war. The vessels as they neared opened on each other, but at the first broadsides the *Epervier's* carronades were dismounted, the bolts giving way. For three quarters of an hour the fight continued, the guns of the brig getting worse and worse, until she could hardly fire a shot. At length the English captain gave the order to board, but his men showed no zeal or courage, and even refused to follow him; so he gave up and struck his colours.

There was hardly any other action in the war in which the enemy did so poorly as in this. The *Epervier* had twenty-two men killed or wounded in the battle; the *Peacock* had none killed and only two wounded. The enemy was almost a wreck. Her hull was riddled, her main-topmast and boom were shot away, her foremast was nearly cut in two, her sails tattered, her bowsprit badly wounded, her battery disabled, and there were four feet of water in her hold; while the *Peacock*, except for the loss of the foreyard, was as fresh as ever, and not a shot had struck her hull. It was a profitable hour's work for her crew; for a large amount of specie was found on board the enemy, and the government bought the captured sloop for more than fifty thousand dollars. The two vessels made for Savannah, where, though several times chased by the enemy, they arrived safely a few days after the battle.

★★★★★★

On the day that the *Epervier* entered the Savannah River, the new sloop-of-war *Wasp*—named for that other *Wasp* which had captured the *Frolic*—sailed from Portsmouth on a cruise. She was commanded by Capt. Johnston Blakely, a most resolute officer, and had as fine a crew of stanch New Englanders as ever trod the deck of a Salem clipper. Running the blockade off the coast, the *Wasp* stood over toward the English channel, and soon she was burning and sinking merchantmen as actively as the *Argus* had done before her. But when it came

Captain Lewis Warrington.

her turn to meet the enemy in battle, her crew showed themselves to be made of different stuff from the sailors of that unlucky brig.

The *Wasp* had been nearly two months out, when she fell in with one of the enemy's sloops. This was the *Reindeer*, commanded by Capt. William Manners, a young officer whose gallantry was unsurpassed by that of any of his comrades in the English service. His ship was less in force than the *Wasp*, for she carried twenty-four-pound carronades instead of thirty-twos; but nevertheless he no sooner sighted the American than he made sail to attack her. Blakely too was ready for the combat, and shaped his course to meet the enemy.

So the vessels approached under a light breeze during the whole forenoon, and it was not till after one o'clock that they beat to quarters and cleared ship for action. For two hours both were now manoeuvring for an advantage as deftly as two skilful fencers, but the two captains were equally good at this, and neither could score a point against his adversary. At length, soon after three o'clock, the *Reindeer*, being then at a distance of sixty yards on the *Wasp's* weather-quarter, opened on her with careful aim from the shifting carronade on her top-gallant forecastle, to which the *Wasp* could not reply. Five times this was repeated, at intervals sometimes of two, sometimes of three minutes, the fire of round and grape shot making destructive work on board the unresisting American.

The *Wasp's* crew were well trained, and nothing showed it more than the quiet steadiness and nerve with which they bore this trial. But Captain Blakely, finding that the enemy did not advance beyond his quarter, luffed, and so brought his broadside to bear. Then began a furious and deadly conflict, for the ships were close abreast, and in the smooth water there was no motion to disturb the pointing of the guns. But it was on board the *Reindeer* that the carnage was most dreadful. In fifteen minutes her upper works became a wreck, and more than half her crew were killed or wounded. The topmen of the *Wasp* picked them off with their muskets one by one.

The gallant Manners was badly wounded early in the action, but remained on deck. A grape-shot passed through both his thighs. He fell, but raised himself; and staggering to his feet, the blood streaming from his wounds, he fought on, encouraging his men. At last the two ships fouled, and Manners, true hero that he was, climbed up by the rigging, calling out, "Follow me, my boys, we must board!" But at that instant two bullets pierced his head, and he fell lifeless to the deck. A moment later the crew of the *Wasp* had rushed on board his ship, and she surrendered.

After this battle, so glorious for both sides, Blakely put into Lorient. His prize was so disabled that he burned her the day after the fight, and the wounded prisoners were sent to England in a Portuguese brig. Refitting at the French port, Blakely set sail again toward the end of August. On the 1st of September he was on the edge of the Bay of Biscay. He had already made two prizes since leaving port, and on this day he was hanging about a fleet of English merchantmen bound for Gibraltar, under convoy of the line-of-battle ship *Armada*. The clumsy seventy-four twice tried to catch him, but the sloop was too nimble for her, and ended by cutting out one of the convoy under her very eyes.

Blakely was now on the spot most frequented by British cruisers; for all that went to and fro between England and the Mediterranean must pass that way, and it behooved him to be upon his guard. At dusk that same evening he discovered four sail whose character he could not make out. But he stood boldly down for one of them, and after a two hours' pursuit, in which the chase had made repeated night-signals that he could not answer, he discovered that she was a large man-of-war brig. An hour later, and the ships were near enough to hail.

"What ship is that?" asked the stranger through the darkness.

"What brig is that?" asked Blakely in return.

"What ship is that?"

"Heave to, and I'll let you know what ship it is."

But the stranger did not heave to, and presently the *Wasp* opened on her.

Soon she got alongside, and both ships began to fire in dead earnest. Dark as it was, the *Wasp* made splendid practice with her guns, yet was herself but little hurt. The enemy's gaff and rigging were cut and broken, the round shot penetrated her hull, and, half an hour after the first gun, her mainmast went by the board. Captain Blakely now hailed to know if she would yield, for her fire had ceased. Soon it began again, and to Blakely's second demand the answer came that the brig surrendered.

A boat was now lowered, but at the same moment a second brig appeared, just visible a short distance off in the darkness. The boat was hoisted in, the men were called again to quarters, and as Blakely made off before the wind to reeve new braces, the new-comer followed him, firing, but without effect. Two more sail were now discovered, and it seemed that the American might have hard work to escape.

Meantime guns of distress were firing from the *Avon*, Blakely's first opponent, and the second brig hauled off hastily to go to her assistance. But she was none too soon, for the *Avon* sank before all her people could get on board the rescuer. The two other ships—one of which, the *Castilian*, had joined in the battle, and the other, the *Tartarus*, had only just come upon the scene—did not attempt pursuit, while Blakely, seeing that it was idle to remain in a neighbourhood surrounded thus by enemies, quickly made sail to leave it, and proceeded on his cruise.

Three weeks later the *Wasp* captured the merchant brig *Atalanta*, and by her sent home despatches. This was the last that was ever seen or heard of the gallant sloop. Whether she foundered in a gale, or caught fire, or ran upon a rock, no one can say; and to this time the fate of her brave Yankee crew is one of the buried secrets of the deep.

★★★★★★

The last of the sloop actions of the war was between the *Hornet* and the *Penguin*. The *Hornet*, the same vessel which Lawrence had commanded two years before, left New York near the end of January, 1815, and proceeded to the remote island of Tristan d'Acunha, where she had a rendezvous with the *Peacock*. She was commanded by Lieutenant James Biddle. The voyage out lasted two months. On the day that she reached the island, the 23rd of March, she met the *Penguin*, a British sloop of force almost exactly equal. The *Penguin* was to windward and bore down upon her, while Biddle hove his ship to and awaited her coming. As she came up alongside, the fight began broadside to broadside. It did not take long to show which was the better crew. The *Hornet's* fire was steady and precise, the *Penguin's* wild and ineffective.

At the end of fifteen minutes the English sloop had lost her captain and many of her men in killed or wounded, and her sides had been battered by the American fire. One round shot entered her aftermost port, and in its passage killed the powder-boy, took off six legs of seamen at the gun, dismounted a carronade, and fell into the water beyond. Just before the captain had received his mortal wound he had put his helm over to throw the ships afoul, so that his men might board the *Hornet*. But when the first lieutenant would have led them over, they fell back. The American crew were eager to board the other ship, but Biddle wisely restrained them; for he knew that the loss of life might be great, and that the victory was his without it.

A moment later the enemy cried out that they surrendered,—or

191

at least so Biddle understood, and leaping on the taffrail, he gave the order to cease firing. But it seems that there was some mistake, for an English marine now took aim at him and shot him in the neck, fortunately wounding him but slightly. The crew were indignant at what seemed like treachery; but the captain checked their ardour, and wearing so that he might bring a fresh broadside to bear, he again called upon the enemy to surrender. Her foremast and bowsprit had now gone, and her mainmast was ready to go, so the colours were hauled down, just twenty-two minutes after the action had begun. The *Penguin's* loss in killed and wounded was forty-two, and she was such a wreck that Biddle had to destroy her, while the *Hornet's* loss was only eleven, and she was ready for action again a few minutes after the fight was over.

"One Round Shot Entered Her Aftermost Port."

CHAPTER 16

Macdonough and Lake Champlain

Once more our story goes back to the northern waters, this time to Lake Champlain. Little had been done here by either side during the first two years of the war. There was hardly a naval force on the lake worthy of being mentioned, and the only operations that took place were mere raids or forays. In June, 1813, Lieutenant Smith had been despatched with the two sloops *Growler* and *Eagle*, which were the only vessels then possessed by the Americans, to annoy the British gunboats at the northern end of the lake; and rashly pursuing them into the Sorel River, from which he was unable to make his way out, he had been attacked by the boats, and by the troops that lined the banks, and his whole force had been captured.

This gave the enemy control of the lake, and they were not slow to use their advantage. Four weeks later a body of troops were sent up from the Canadian territory to Plattsburg, along with the captured sloops, which had now been named the *Chubb* and the *Finch*; and the troops, landing, wrought great havoc at the post by destroying the buildings, and the supplies which had been stored there.

The American commander at this time on Lake Champlain was Capt. Thomas Macdonough, of whom it may be truly said that no one in the old navy has left behind him a more spotless reputation, either as an officer or as a man. Brave and energetic, but prudent beyond his age,—for at this time he was but twenty-eight years old,—he was also earnest and sincere, grave but gentle, full of ardour, but of an even and kindly temper. He had been one of Preble's gallant band of officers, and he had sailed with Decatur in the *Intrepid* when the *Philadelphia* was burned; and again he was at his brave leader's side when with nine men they boarded and carried the Tripolitan gunboat in the first battle before Tripoli. Formed in that school of chivalrous devotion, his own lofty spirit had gathered in these later years added strength and judgment; and as events were now to show, no better man could have been chosen to defend the frontier at this its most vulnerable point.

During the second year of the war, Macdonough was engaged, as Perry had been on Lake Erie, in building the vessels that were to form his fleet, but under difficulties even greater, in the want of workmen and materials. The British, too, were busily employed, and by the midsummer of 1814 the work of building was so far advanced that they began to think of taking the offensive, and to make the needful preparations for a great combined movement by land and water. An army of invasion numbering ten thousand men, many of them veterans, and commanded by Sir George Prevost, was massed at Montreal to march up the shores of the lake as soon as the fleet should be ready to support them in their advance. Their commander, fortunately for us, was a most unfit officer, else he would have made short work of the handful of troops under General Macomb at Plattsburg, which was the only army to oppose him.

The naval force, under Com. George Downie, as yet consisted only of the brig *Linnet* and the two captured sloops; but there was also on the stocks, and nearly finished, the fine frigate *Confiance*, which carried thirty long 24-pounders,—a very heavy battery for this lake warfare. To oppose this force Macdonough had one ship, the *Saratoga*, mounting eight long 24's, and eighteen carronades of heavy calibre; but being carronades they were by no means equal to long guns, and the *Saratoga* was therefore far from a match for the *Confiance*. He had also the schooner *Ticonderoga* and the sloop *Preble*; and the *Eagle*, a brig of fair size and metal, was still under construction. In the latter part of August both the "*Confiance*" and the *Eagle* were launched, so that by September both sides had made up their complete numbers. The two fleets had in addition a little flotilla of gunboats, numbering ten or perhaps more upon each side.

The opposing squadrons, in the number of men and in the weight of broadside, were as nearly matched as two naval squadrons well could be, and what difference there was between them was in favour of the enemy. But it amounted to so little that it is hardly worthwhile to consider it at all. In all kinds of naval equipment the ships were poorly fitted and supplied, but both sides shared equally in these deficiencies.

Macdonough had been informed of the enemy's intentions, and made his plan to await their attack at Plattsburg, where the fleet and

"On the stocks, and nearly finished,
the fine frigate 'Confiance.'"

the army might stand or fall together. The formation of the bay at Plattsburg gave him a strong position. It lies on the western side of Lake Champlain, and is enclosed in part by a long neck of land which juts out into the lake, and curving like a hook or a bent finger, makes some distance to the southward. The enemy in advancing up the lake from the northern end must pass along this promontory on the outside, and then double its extreme point in order to enter the bay, passing to the northward again along its inner side. If they came up the lake with a leading wind, as they would doubtless do, they must beat up against the wind after they doubled the point; and thus during their slow advance, while manoeuvring in a confined space, they would be exposed to the broadsides of the ships that lay at anchor within.

With this in view Macdonough decided on his order of battle. His line was formed heading directly north and well inside the bay, the leading vessel, the brig *Eagle*, being so near the inner curve of the bight that the enemy would not be able to turn the line by passing between her and the shore. Next came the flagship *Saratoga*, and astern of her the schooner *Ticonderoga*. The sloop *Preble* brought up the rear. In the intervals of the line the gunboats had their stations; and these were to check any attempt of the enemy to turn the rear by passing through the narrow opening between the *Preble* and Crab Island shoal, which closed the bay on the southern side. A small battery on Crab Island aided still more in giving this protection.

In these arrangements Commodore Macdonough showed great foresight and judgment; but he was not satisfied with this, and it was by the additional precautions that he took, which few commanders would have thought of, that he evinced his greatest skill, and indeed in the end saved the battle. Knowing that with his battery of carronades his engaged broadside would in time become disabled, he made the most careful preparations to wind his ship,—that is, to turn her round,—so that she might bring a fresh broadside to bear. This would be no easy matter for a ship at anchor in a narrow space in a crowded bay, and under the enemy's fire; but he resolved that it should be done. So besides the usual anchors, he planted kedges broad off on his ship's bows, with hawsers hanging in bights under the water, and leading to her quarters. The stream anchor was suspended astern. We shall see presently how important these precautions became.

★★★★★★

Soon after daybreak, on the 11th of September, 1814, just a year and a day after the battle of Lake Erie, the picket boat of the American squadron, lying outside the bay, descried the advancing enemy, and falling back, announced to Commodore Macdonough their approach. The ships were at once cleared for action. At eight o'clock the masts of the enemy's vessels could be seen across the neck of Cumberland Head, and soon they had rounded the point and were standing in, formed in line ahead, the *Chubb* leading, toward the van of the American squadron. The *Chubb* and *Linnet* were to engage the *Eagle*. Next came the *Confiance*, with her powerful battery, marked out to engage the *Saratoga*, and the *Finch*, with the greater part of the gunboats, to attack the rear, and endeavour to turn the line.

The water in the bay was smooth, and the English squadron filled, and came down on the starboard tack, without a sound to break the stillness. On board the American ships the men awaited in silence and expectation the order to fire. The *Eagle* was the first to open, discharging in succession her 18-pounders, but the shot fell short. On board the *Saratoga* a rooster which had been set free in clearing away the hen-coops, startled by the report of the guns, flew upon a gun-slide, and flapping his wings, crowed cheerily. This little incident relieved the strain of waiting, and the blue-jackets, taking it as a good omen, broke out in cheers and laughter. Commodore Macdonough stood on his quarter-deck unmoved, watching the play of the *Eagle's* shot.

As soon as he saw them reach the mark, he walked to one of the 24-pounders, and pointing it carefully himself at the bow of the *Confiance*, touched the match and fired. The shot entered near the hawse-hole of the enemy's ship and passed the whole length of the deck, killing and wounding several men in its passage, and ended its course by carrying away the wheel. All the long guns of the *Saratoga* now began to play upon the enemy's frigate, every shot telling with deadly effect. Still the *Confiance* continued to advance without replying, with a stubborn bravery that moved to admiration all who witnessed it. At last she swung into position and came to anchor, not so near as Captain Downie could have wished, but as near as he could venture under the galling fire. The *Chubb* and *Linnet* took their places ahead of him, engaging the *Eagle*; but not a gun was fired from the frigate until the anchoring was complete and everything had been secured in true seamanlike manner.

Suddenly a sheet of flame seemed to burst from the side of the *Confiance*, as her whole broadside was fired. The guns, double-shotted and aimed at point-blank range, in smooth water, sent flying their volley of huge 24-pound shot; and under the shock the *Saratoga* shivered as though a ram had struck her. Half the crew were thrown down to the deck, and forty were killed or wounded by the cannon-balls or flying splinters. The first lieutenant, Gamble, struck in the breast by a split quoin or gun-wedge, fell dead without so much as a break in the skin. For an instant the *Saratoga* ceased her fire, but the next moment it was resumed with redoubled energy. Macdonough, pointing one of the guns himself, was knocked senseless by a blow from a shattered spar, but regaining consciousness he sprang to his feet and went back to his work at the gun. A moment later a shot struck the gun-captain, taking his head clean off, and the head struck Macdonough with such force that it threw him across the deck into the scuppers.

On board the other ship, Downie, standing in the rear of the gun at a moment when a shot from the *Saratoga* struck its muzzle, received a blow in the groin as the gun was driven from its carriage, and fell to the deck; he never spoke again.[1] After this the broadsides from both ships gradually became less and less deadly. The British sailors, inexperienced in handling the guns, loaded hurriedly, sometimes putting in the ball or wad before the cartridge, and as the quoins were loosened, the breech of the gun fell lower and lower, raising the muzzle, until the shot passed harmlessly through the air. The *Saratoga's* carronades, too, were overloaded, and what with that and with the enemy's fire, those on the engaged or starboard side were disabled one by one, until at last only a single carronade remained; and as the crew were taking a final shot with this, the recoil broke the weakened bolt, and the gun jumped down the hatchway.

Ahead of the two flagships the battle had all this time been raging, but with no more certain result. The little *Chubb*, it is true, manoeuvring at the head of the line, lost her bowsprit and main boom under the *Eagle's* fire; and drifting down on the American line, a shot from the *Saratoga* made her a prize, and a midshipman in the *Saratoga's* boat towed her in shore. The fight at this end was now between the *Eagle* and the *Linnet*, and the enemy was getting the best of it. Indeed, the *Eagle*, having lost her springs, could not return the *Linnet's* fire with advantage, so sheeting home her topsails, she cut her cable and ran down the line, taking a new berth astern of the *Saratoga*, and bringing a fresh broadside to bear.

Meantime a separate battle was going on at the rear of the line. Here the British had their strongest gunboats, and the Americans their weakest. It was upon the *Preble* that the attack was first directed, and

1. This gun with its cracked muzzle is still (1887) preserved at the Naval Academy.

after a time the gunboats succeeded in making her berth too warm, and cutting her cable she drifted in to leeward. After this repulse she was not again engaged. In a short time the *Finch*, attempting to carry the *Ticonderoga*, was disabled by two well-aimed broadsides, and she also drifted out of the fight, at last going ashore on Crab Island, where she struck to the neighbouring battery. The *Ticonderoga* was now pressed hard by the English gunboats, which attacked her with great dash and energy; but Lieutenant Cassin, who commanded her, defended her valiantly, standing on the taffrail amid a shower of grape and canister, and beating back the assailants as they crowded around his little sloop. It was thus due to Cassin's vigorous efforts that the rear was held so firmly on that trying day.

The fight had now been going on for an hour or more, and the critical point in the battle had been reached, when the forces of both sides were nearly exhausted, and the next move meant victory or defeat. The *Ticonderoga* might still hold the rear, and the *Eagle* could make some reply to the *Confiance*; but the *Saratoga* had not a gun left on her starboard side, which was toward the enemy, and the *Linnet*, unopposed, had stationed herself off the American flagship's bow, and was raking her without resistance. To remain where she was meant destruction to the *Saratoga*. Now, then, was the time to use the appliances which MacDonough's careful forethought had provided. He resolved to wind the ship, so that his port broadside could be brought to bear. It was a difficult and dangerous process in the face of the enemy's fire, for if once his men should be thrown into confusion all would be lost.

But with the captain standing on the quarter-deck, calm and collected, there was no danger that anyone would lose his head. The stream anchor was let go astern, and the hawser, bent to the kedge on the starboard bow, which had been carried to the starboard quarter, was hauled in until the ship was half-way round. Then the men clapped on a line bent to the stream anchor, and pulled and tugged, but with all their efforts they could only swing her far enough to make one gun bear on the *Confiance*. Instantly this was manned and opened fire. But this was not enough. The ship now hung with her stern exposed to the raking fire of the *Linnet*. Something must be done, and quickly. What should it be? There still remained the other kedge, planted broad off the port bow. That alone could accomplish the result. Its hawser, leading to the port quarter, was carried forward, passed under the bow and then aft on the other side, where the crew roused on it with a will. It seemed not much, but it was enough, and in a few minutes more the *Saratoga* was heading south, and firing at the *Confiance* from a clean, fresh, broadside battery.

This ended the battle. The *Confiance* herself, attempting to wind, was caught when half-way round, and after enduring a few moments of the *Saratoga's* fresh fire, struck her colours and surrendered. The *Linnet* held out a little longer, but it was a useless struggle, and she too hauled down her flag.

It was a complete victory. The enemy were more than defeated,— they were annihilated, their squadron wiped out of existence. Lake Champlain, which till this point in the war had been almost a British lake, was now delivered up without a possibility of recovery. Sir George Prevost, seeing the issue of the battle in the bay, made only a feeble demonstration against Plattsburg, and soon he was in full retreat to Canada, and New York was saved from the threatened invasion.

CHAPTER 17

Stewart and "Old Ironsides"

During the latter part of the war, as might have been foreseen, there was little opportunity for American frigates to show that they could keep up the fame they had so gloriously won. The British were determined that none of them that ventured out to sea should escape; and by stationing a squadron, which their great resources enabled them to do, before each port where a frigate lay, they succeeded in keeping it cooped up and inactive. No longer were offers made by British captains, like that of the chivalrous Broke before Boston, to send away part of their vessels, leaving one to fight a duel with the frigate that was in the harbour. A steady watch was kept up before each port by the whole blockading squadron. The *Constellation*, which had won such high renown under Truxtun in the French war, sailed from Washington down the Chesapeake Bay; but falling in with the heavy squadron of the enemy near Hampton Roads, composed of ships-of-the-line and frigates, she took refuge at Norfolk, and here or in the river below she remained blockaded till the end of the war.

The *President* was lying at New York, and off the port were the *Majestic* (*razee*) and three frigates,—the *Endymion*, *Pomone*, and *Tenedos*. The *United States* and *Macedonian*, after getting out from New York though Hell Gate, encountered the British squadron of a line-of-battle ship and two frigates at the eastern entrance of the Sound, and put in to New London, where they lay in the mud for eighteen months unable to get out. The *Constitution*, under Captain Stewart at Boston, found herself checked in the same way by a squadron of heavy frigates.

The *Adams*, which had been a 28-gun frigate, but which was now a corvette, managed to slip out from Washington in January, 1814, under the command of Charles Morris, who had been promoted to a captain for his service in the battle with the *Guerrière* seventeen months before. Six months were passed in cruising, part of the time off the Irish coast, but with no great success; for Morris was not fortunate in meeting prizes of any value, and once or twice he narrowly escaped the enemy's larger frigates. At length the scurvy showed itself among the crew, and the ship was turned toward home. But it was almost as difficult for American ships to get in as to get out. About the middle of August Morris arrived off the coast of Maine, where unluckily for him he sighted the English sloop *Rifleman*, which he chased, but which escaped in the fog. Soon after the *Adams* went ashore at the mouth of the Penobscot River, and when she got off, Morris found her so much injured that he resolved to go several miles up the river to Hampden, where he could refit, as there were ship-yards all along the bank.

A short time before Morris's arrival a large force made up of seventy-fours and frigates had left Halifax to make a descent on the Maine coast, and near Castine it received news from the *Rifleman* of the presence of the *Adams*. This was exactly what the enemy wanted. Some light vessels and boats, with about six hundred troops, were at once detached and sent up the river to capture her. Morris had dismantled the ship and landed her guns and stores preparatory to making the needed repairs. By dint of hard work nine of the guns were mounted in battery on a neighbouring hill-top, but without protection, and the remainder were placed in position on the wharf where the ship was lying. Farther up the river was a creek crossed by a bridge; but the bridge was not strong enough to allow the guns to be carried over, and the Americans were thus prevented from taking up their position in rear of the creek. There was a sufficient force of men to defend the position, supposing that it had been well taken, with proper preparations, and that the men were good men. But more than half of them were militia, whose officers knew nothing of war, and whose men had no steadiness under fire.

The enemy landed at sunset on the 2nd of September, and early the next morning made a sharp attack. The day was chill and rainy, and a heavy fog hid the hill, which the militia were to defend, from the view of Morris and his command on the wharf. Soon the enemy's bugles were heard on the road below the hill-battery, followed by three discharges from one of the guns. A few moments later word was passed by the marines, who had been posted at intervals between the hill-battery and the wharf, that the militia had broken and were flee-

CAPTAIN CHARLES STEWART.

ing in disorder. There was no time to be lost; for if the enemy should gain the bridge in the rear, the retreat of the sailors would be cut off. The ship was set on fire, the guns were spiked, and Morris and his men retired to the creek. Here they found the panic-stricken militia crowding over the bridge, and the seamen, being without firearms, could make no real resistance. So they forded the creek, and being now safe from pursuit, they marched through the woods to the Kennebec. Here they separated into detachments, taking different routes, as in this way it was easier to obtain provision on the journey, and finally all arrived safely at Portsmouth.

★★★★★★

At this time the *Constitution* was, as I have said, lying at Boston, watched by a squadron of the enemy. She had proved a lucky ship, just as the *Chesapeake* and *Adams* had proved unlucky; and her present captain, Charles Stewart, who had been one of Preble's lieutenants at Tripoli, was certainly a man well fitted to make the most of any chance he had. The frigate had been in port since April, at first repairing, and later unable to get out owing to the presence of the enemy's squadron. In December, 1814, this squadron was composed of the *Newcastle* of fifty guns, under Lord George Stuart, and the *Acasta* of forty guns, under Captain Kerr. About the 12th of the month the *Newcastle*, for some unexplained reason, ran down into Cape Cod Bay, where she grounded for a short time on a shoal. Here she was joined by the *Acasta*. Captain Stewart was on the watch, and when he found out the situation, he did not wait long.

All was quickly in readiness, and having quietly weighed her anchor, the *Constitution*, setting all her sail with a fair wind, was soon dashing at full speed down the harbour and out to sea; and before the enemy could learn of her flight, she was ploughing the waves of the broad Atlantic. With what delight her officers and men, after their long confinement and inaction in port, felt once more the salt breezes speeding the good ship on her course, the spray dashing from her bow as it cut the surging billows! Now at last there was a hope that with such a ship and such a captain they might win for the navy new victories, and add to the laurels which their companions had already gathered.

The *Constitution* stood across the Atlantic to the coast of Spain and Portugal, and thence stretched over to the Azores and down to Madeira. On the 20th of February, being then about sixty leagues distant from Madeira, at one o'clock in the afternoon she sighted two vessels sailing apparently in company, but at the moment some ten miles apart. These were discovered after a time to be two British ships-of-war,—the corvette *Cyane* of twenty-two guns, Captain Falcon, and the sloop *Levant* of twenty guns, Captain Douglas. The *Constitution* made all sail in chase, hoping to be able to engage the vessels separately. The *Levant* was the nearer of the two, and soon she was seen straining every nerve to join her consort, and making signals that the stranger was an enemy. Captain Stewart had crowded on everything the ship would carry, even to topmast, top-gallant, and royal studding-sails; indeed it was a little more than she could carry, as the main royal mast presently snapped off, and another had to be prepared.

The enemy's ships were thus enabled to effect a junction, and after manoeuvring to delay the action until dark, which they thought would give them an advantage, they hauled by the wind on the starboard tack, and formed in column, the *Levant* leading. Their united force was not so strong as that of the *Constitution*, but as there were two of them, the American frigate was required above all things to be alert in her movements, so that she might not be taken at a disadvantage. For this special purpose she could have no better commander than Stewart, who excelled in skilful seamanship. Soon after six she ranged up on the starboard or weather quarter of the *Cyane*, the rearmost ship, and fired her broadside at a distance of two hundred yards. The *Cyane* replied with spirit; and as the *Constitution* forged ahead, the *Levant* in turn opened on her, receiving her fire at the same time. The ships were now in a triangular fight, but as the *Constitution* moved on, she became engaged with the *Levant* alone.

Presently the smoke lifted, and Stewart saw the *Cyane* luffing up for his port quarter. Without an instant's hesitation, without stopping to wear or tack, which would have exposed his bow or stern to a raking fire, he simply braced aback his topsails, at the same time giving the *Levant* a parting broadside, and backed astern till he had the *Cyane* abeam, so that she was compelled to bear up again to avoid a rake. A furious cannonade now silenced her, and the *Levant* wore, to come to her assistance. But Stewart was on the alert again, and seeing this manoeuvre he filled and shot ahead, and catching the sloop in the midst of the operation he gave her two terrific stern-rakes. Then, wearing himself in the smoke, his movements as quick and as nimble as those of a trained gymnast, he bore down again on the *Cyane*, who, thinking him gone, was herself beginning to wear, and arriving in the nick of time, he raked her stern as he had just raked her consort's. Ranging up immediately after on her quarter, Stewart had the satisfaction of receiving her surrender.

Lieutenant Hoffman and a few men were now thrown hastily on board the prize, and the *Constitution* went in search of the *Levant*, which had made sail after her last encounter. But she had only hauled off to repair damages, and coming back she passed the *Constitution* on the opposite tack, the two ships exchanging broadsides. This last was enough, and the sloop now sought to escape in good earnest. But it was of no avail; the frigate was on her heels, and after receiving a few shot from the bow guns of the *Constitution*, the *Levant* struck her colours.

Captain Stewart had now completed a good day's work, and putting Lieutenant Ballard on board the *Levant*, he proceeded to Port Praya, in the Cape de Verde Islands, where he came to anchor. Here we must leave him for a moment, to return to the blockading squadron which he had left before Boston. The *Newcastle* and *Acasta* returned to their station, and discovered to their dismay that the *Constitution* had given them the slip, and had got off in their absence. This was a serious mishap. Of all the American ships, the *Constitution*—*Old Ironsides*, as she was called—was the worst offender. She had captured two frigates, the *Guerrière* and the *Java*, and there was no telling what mischief she might be up to now. At this juncture the squadron was reinforced by another 50-gun ship, the *Leander*, under Sir George Collier, K.C.B.; and Sir George, being the senior officer, decided that there was but one thing to be done, and that was to go in pursuit.

It seemed like a wild-goose chase, to search for a ship that might be anywhere on the Atlantic Ocean. But fortune favoured the pursuers in a most wonderful manner; for it so happened that on one foggy morning at Port Praya, as the *Constitution* was lying snugly at anchor, with a large part of her crew at work on board the prizes, Lieutenant Shubrick, the officer of the deck, as he was looking idly seaward, gazing at vacancy, was startled at catching sight, through a rift in the fog, of the sails of a great ship-of-war looming up distinctly, though her hull was hidden from view. He rubbed his eyes, thinking that some illusion must have deceived him; but there was the great spread of white canvas, and the ship that bore it was making for the anchorage. He rushed below to tell the captain.

"Well," said Stewart, calmly, as he repaired to the deck, "she is either an English frigate or an Indiaman. Call all hands at once, and get the ship ready to go out and attack her."

But when they came on deck it was a different story, for the fog had lifted a little, and two more sail were seen following the first. Sure enough; these were Stewart's old friends, the blockaders,—the *Newcastle* and *Acasta*,—and with them was another and equally formidable ship, the *Leander*. They had started from the American coast a week behind the *Constitution*, and after cruising about vainly in search of her for over two months, they had chanced upon the very spot which she had chosen as the best place in which to refit.

Port Praya was in neutral territory, and by the established laws of war the *Constitution* and her prizes, as long as they lay there, should have been safe from molestation. But so little respect had been paid by the British to these rules, that Captain Stewart decided in an instant that he would place no reliance upon neutral protection. That settled, there was not a moment to be lost, for the enemy would soon be at the entrance of the harbour. Loosing his topsails, the captain signalled to the prizes to follow him, and cutting his cable, in seven minutes from the time when the first frigate was sighted the three ships were standing out of the harbour. That was rare discipline and organization, for not one crew in twenty could have accomplished the task.

It was blowing fresh as the *Constitution*, followed by the prizes, passed close under the point of land at the entrance, within gunshot of the enemy's squadron, and being to windward of them, she crossed her top-gallant yards, and set the foresail, mainsail, spanker, flying-jib, and top-gallant sails. The enemy immediately tacked, and made sail in chase. The six ships were now all upon the port tack, the *Constitution* racing along at the head of the line. Next came the prizes. Of the enemy, the *Newcastle* was leading, the *Leander* two miles astern of her, and the *Acasta* on her weather quarter. At half-past twelve the *Constitution* cut adrift the boats that she had been towing astern. Half an hour later Captain Stewart perceived that the *Acasta* was luffing up, and thereby gaining his wake.

At the same time the *Cyane*, the rearmost of the prizes, was dropping astern and to leeward. "If she keeps on in this way," he reasoned, "it will be impossible to save her without bringing the *Constitution* into action, which will certainly result in her capture. If the *Cyane* tacks, the *Acasta* may go off in pursuit, but the prize will gain the anchorage at Port Praya before the enemy can catch her; that is probably her only chance. On the other hand, if the enemy fail to pursue her, she can escape." The signal was therefore made to the *Cyane* to tack, which she accordingly did, and finding that the English squadron took no notice of her, she went off in good style, and laying her course for the United States, she arrived there safely just a month later.

At three o'clock the *Levant* found herself losing ground, exactly as the *Cyane* had been doing two hours before. She also was therefore signalled to tack, which was immediately done. Now came the singular part of this day's proceedings. Seeing the *Levant* making off, Sir George Collier, instead of keeping on and attempting to come up with the *Constitution*, which, if he could have overtaken her, would surely have become his prize, abandoned the pursuit, and tacking with all his vessels, went off after the *Levant*. The latter immediately made for the harbour; but Stewart's surmises about British respect for the neutrality of the port turned out to be correct. The prize anchored close under the batteries of the port, and the *Leander* and *Acasta* immediately opened fire with a broadside, most of which, however, passed above her, and did more damage in the town than on board the vessel. After this illegal attack the squadron completed its work by an inglorious capture.

The British officers who were prisoners on board the *Constitution* had all the while been eagerly watching the manoeuvres of the squadron, which they expected presently to set them free. Great was their chagrin and disappointment when they saw this overwhelming force diverting its course in pursuit of the little prize sloop whose capture was of no earthly moment to the British Navy, and leaving *Old Ironsides*, the frigate which more than any other under the American flag that navy longed to take, to go on her way rejoicing. Yet so it happened; and the *Constitution*, now freed from all anxiety, shaped her course comfortably for home, where she arrived in May without any further mischances.

The only other frigate that left port in the last year of the war was less fortunate than the *Constitution*. This was the *President*, now under Commodore Decatur. She was at New York, and for some time had lain at anchor off Staten Island watching for an opportunity to pass the blockading squadron. On the 13th of January, 1815, a heavy snowstorm drove the enemy off the coast; and next day, as the wind was favourable, Decatur determined to make the attempt in the night. Unfortunately the *President* in going out grounded on the bar, and by this accident lost an hour or two of darkness. Unfortunately also the shrewdness of the British commander, Captain Hayes, had led him to stand away to the northward and eastward, in what would probably be the course of an American ship if any such came out, in preference to closing the land to the southward.

Hence at daybreak, being then about fifty miles from Sandy Hook, and steering southeast, the *President* found herself close upon the very ships she was trying to avoid, and within two miles of the largest of them, the *Majestic*, a *razee* of sixty guns. The others were the frigate *Endymion* of fifty guns, and the *Pomone* and the *Tenedos*, of forty-four each. Seeing such an overwhelming force directly in his path, Decatur changed his course to the northeast, and crowded sail to pass the enemy. The whole squadron immediately gave chase, and when the pursuit was fairly begun, the *Majestic* was some five miles astern, the *Endymion* following, and the *Pomone* a little farther off on the *President's* port quarter.

For six hours the chase continued, with no change in the position of the ships. The *President*, laden with all the stores for her cruise, was deep and sluggish in the water, and it was only by vigorous efforts that she kept her distance from her pursuers. At length, about noon, the wind became light and baffling. The *Majestic* was now falling astern, but the *Endymion* began to gain rapidly. All hands on board the *President* were busy lightening the ship, starting the water, cutting away the anchors, and throwing overboard provisions, cables, spare spars, boats,—everything, in short, that could be got at,—while the sails were kept wet from the royals down. The uncertain wind now blew only for the enemy; the *Endymion* had a good breeze, while it fell light upon the sails of the *President*. At five o'clock the English frigate got a good position on the *President's* quarter, where none of Decatur's guns could be brought to bear on her. Still she did not close, preferring to yaw from time to time so that her broadside would bear, and then resume the chase, rather than risk anything by a close action.

The pursuit had lasted all through the short winter's day, and it was now dusk. Seeing that the *Endymion's* tactics must end in his being crippled, Decatur suddenly altered his course to the southward, which compelled the enemy to do the same, and so brought her abeam, and a battle began between the two ships, broadside to broadside, Decatur encouraging and cheering his men, and fighting as steadily as if there were no other enemies in sight. His guns were aimed rather at the *Endymion's* spars than at her hull, seeing that his object was to destroy her power of sailing, and thus his loss in men was far greater than that of the enemy. Nevertheless, after two hours of a running fight the *Endymion* drew out of the battle, and dropped astern to repair her injuries.

Decatur now continued on his course, hoping against hope that in the darkness of the night he might yet escape. But his pursuers were close at his heels and never lost sight of him for a moment. So well did he hold his own, that for more than two hours after the fight with the *Endymion* the enemy only gained on him inch by inch. At last, at eleven o'clock, the *Pomone* ranged up alongside, and planting herself within musket-shot on his port bow, she opened fire. At the same moment the *Tenedos* had taken a raking position on his quarter. If this had been the beginning of the action, it would have been right for the commodore to resist the attack, even though his resistance had lasted but a few moments and had accomplished no result. But in his two hours' action with the *Endymion* he had upheld with gallantry the honour of the flag, and with sixty men already killed or wounded it was probable that an attempt to fight the new assailants would only cause a useless slaughter. So he surrendered, and the *President* became from that day forth what she still remains,—a British frigate. It was a defeat indeed, but one which left the vanquished as much credit as the victors.

★★★★★★

The actions of the *President* with the British squadron, and of the *Constitution* with the *Cyane* and the *Levant*, were the last frigate engagements of the war. Indeed, the treaty of peace had already been signed, and it only awaited ratification. What had been the results of the naval war? The British Navy, numbering more than forty times our own, had met in the battles on the ocean with more defeats than victories, and on the lakes its squadrons had been twice annihilated. Its naval prowess, of which the wars with Dutch and Danes and French and Spaniards gave it so much cause to boast, was now matched by the naval prowess of a new rival in the Western Continent. The people who for twenty years had submitted to aggression, learned that those to whom their defence upon the ocean was intrusted were worthy of the trust, and would prove brave and efficient champions against a foreign foe, however great his power or prestige; and from that time forward no political party in the United States dared to rely for popular support upon a platform of tame submission to foreign encroachment.

CHAPTER 18

The War With Algiers

When the war with Great Britain broke out in 1812, it was no longer possible to keep ships cruising in the Mediterranean to over-awe the States of Barbary. It was true that the severe lesson which Tripoli had received from Commodore Preble in 1804 was well remembered, and the Pasha had no desire to have it repeated. But Algiers, the most powerful State upon the northern coast of Africa, had always cherished a contemptuous feeling for the United States, which was still weakly paying tribute; and no sooner did the *dey* learn that England, the mistress of the seas, was at war with the American Government, than he resolved to take advantage of the stress thus put upon the American Navy to break his treaty obligations. In order that he might have some pretext, he made complaint that the naval stores sent to him were not so good as the treaty called for, and after extorting by savage threats a heavy payment from the Consul of the United States, he finally expelled him, with all the other Americans, from his dominions. He even went beyond this, and took up again his old trade of pirate, capturing the brig *Edwin*, of Salem, and imprisoning her officers and crew, whom he refused to release even on payment of the heaviest ransom.

So matters continued during the war, it being impossible, as we have seen, to send out ships-of-war to the Mediterranean. But the moment that peace was declared, all this was changed. The navy, which had for nearly three years successfully defied the power of Great Britain on the sea, was not likely to shrink from an encounter with the corsairs of Algiers; and the American people, who had learned their strength, were no longer willing to submit to the encroachments of a petty barbarian prince. Besides, the navy, so far from having been destroyed in the war, was stronger than at the beginning. Of the larger frigates there still remained the *Constitution*, the *United States*, the *Constellation*, and the *Congress*; and during the last year of the war others had been built, too late, indeed, to be of service against Great Britain, but ready now for conquests over a new enemy. There was the *Independence*, the first American line-of-battle ship, of seventy-four guns, and there were the splendid frigates *Guerrière* and *Java*, named after the prizes of 1812.

It was with joyful prospects that the new squadron, composed of eleven sail, under the command of Commodore Decatur, who hoisted his broad pennant in the flagship *Guerrière*, set out from New York on the 20th of May, 1815, bound for the Mediterranean. The squadron stood directly across the Atlantic, making a quick passage, and heading cautiously for the Strait of Gibraltar, arrived before any news of its departure had reached that quarter of the globe. It was Decatur's hope to take the Algerines by surprise while they were cruising, and his precautions were rewarded by success.

Touching at Tangier for information, and learning that the Algerine vessels had been heard from but a short time before, the commodore proceeded up the Mediterranean, and off Cape de Gatt he fell in with the enemy's flagship, the *Mezourah*, commanded by the Rais Hammida, the bravest and most skilful officer in the Algerine Navy. The *Mezourah* was a beautiful frigate, originally a Portuguese, and sailed uncommonly fast. Hammida at first supposed that the ships were English, as no one could dream that an American squadron of such force was in that neighbourhood; but one of the vessels having hoisted American colours by mistake, he was undeceived, and speedily took to his heels.

The *Constellation*, being nearest to him, opened fire; but Decatur could not resist the temptation, and signalling to her to sheer off, he dashed up in the *Guerrière* until he was alongside the enemy. Then he gave her one of those thundering broadsides which had so many times carried dismay and destruction to English frigates. The *rais* was killed, his body cut in two by a shot; his ship was shattered, and his people fell on all sides about the decks. The survivors were demoralized, and hardly returned the fire. A second broadside was discharged, and the *Mezourah* turned to flee; but the little *Epervier*, herself a trophy of the last war, was in her path, and the Algerine surrendered.

Two days later the squadron fell in with another of the enemy's ships, the brig *Estedio*. She took to flight, and being near the Spanish coast, ran into shallow water, where the large ships could not follow her. The brigs and schooners were sent in after her, and attacking her hotly, she was run ashore, and presently surrendered. She was floated off without much delay, and was sent with the other prize to Carthagena.

Further concealment was useless; and the commodore, having now nearly five hundred Algerine prisoners, decided to proceed to Algiers, and on the 28th of June he entered the bay. The *dey* was amazed at the sight of the squadron, and, fearful for the safety of his cruisers, all of which were now out, he sent the captain of the port with the Swedish consul-general to ascertain the purposes of the American commodore. Decatur received them with due ceremony, dressed in his full uniform and surrounded by his officers. After exchanging courtesies, he asked the captain of the port what had become of the Algerine squadron.

"By this time," answered the wily Turk, "it is safe in some neutral port."

"Not the whole of it," rejoined the commodore; and then he told the story of Hammida's death, and the capture of the *Mezourah* and the *Estedio*.

This did not satisfy the official, who shook his head and smiled, as much as to say, "That is all very well, but you don't expect *me* to believe your story."

"Wait a moment," said Decatur; and he sent for the *Mezourah's* lieutenant, who, coming on deck enfeebled by his wounds, briefly recited the circumstances of the two captures.

The captain of the port was no longer incredulous, but began to realize the seriousness of the situation. Alarmed and anxious, he asked the commodore what terms he offered. Decatur's reply was brief: "No tribute; no ransom; liberation of all American captives; immunity of all American ships and crews in future."

Hearing this answer, the captain of the port hesitated and proposed a truce, during which the commissioners should negotiate on shore. But the commodore declared that all the discussion should be on board his flagship, and that he would not cease from hostilities a moment until the treaty had been signed. With this answer the captain of the port returned to his master.

The *dey's* wrath was great when he learned the news, but his alarm was even greater. On the next day the captain of the port returned, and the commodore gave him a copy of the proposed treaty. Still he demurred, seeking to gain time. He asked again for a truce, and again it was refused. He begged for three hours to consider the terms, but

"Accompanied by Abdallah the Dragoman, I Left the Canal."

the commodore answered, "Not a minute;" and he added to the messenger, "If your squadron or one of your ships appears in sight off the port before the treaty is signed, I will capture it." All that he would promise was that if the boat, returning with the treaty signed, should hoist a white flag, hostilities should then cease. The captain of the port then took the treaty and pulled for the landing five miles away.

Not long after his departure an Algerine *corvette* hove in sight at the entrance of the bay. The flagship made signal for a general chase, and Decatur himself bore down upon her in the *Guerrière*. All this the *dey* saw from his palace, and bitterly as he felt the humiliation, he did not long hesitate in affixing his signature and sending the treaty back. Soon the returning boat made its appearance, with the white flag hoisted which had been agreed upon as the signal that the treaty had been signed; and the commodore, who had prepared to board the Algerine and have a battle like the old contests before Tripoli, hauled off shore and returned to his moorings.

The boat approached rapidly, her progress quickened by the anxiety with which the captain of the port had watched the squadron's movements.

"Is the treaty signed?" asked the commodore in his peremptory way when the Swedish consul came on deck.

"It is here," replied the consul, as he delivered the document.

"And the prisoners?" continued Decatur.

"They are in the boat."

As they were speaking, the Americans, who after three years of confinement and suffering were now to be set free, reached the quarter-deck, where they were warmly greeted by their deliverer.

This prompt action of Decatur at Algiers, and the treaty which resulted from it, put an end forever to the piratical depredations of the Barbary States upon American commerce, and the example set by the United States was soon after followed by England, so that Mediterranean piracy in a short time thereafter ceased to exist. On the 8th of July the squadron weighed anchor and proceeded to Tunis. During the late war the neutrality of this port as well as that of Tripoli had been violated by British cruisers, which had seized within the two harbours the prizes of an American privateer, without opposition from the authorities. Commodore Decatur now proposed to obtain satisfaction for the outrage.

The consul of the United States at Tunis, Major Noah, was waiting for Decatur's arrival. He says:—

On the 30th of July, about noon, we observed signals for a fleet from the tower at Cape Carthage, and shortly after the American squadron, under full sail, came into the bay and anchored. Nothing can be more welcome to a consul in Barbary than the sight of a fleet bearing the flag of his nation; he feels that, surrounded by assassins and mercenaries, he is still safe and protected, and an involuntary tribute of admiration is paid by the Mussulmen to that nation which has the power and the disposition to command respect. The flags of all the consulates were hoisted, and I lost no time in riding to Goletta, for the purpose of communicating with the squadron.

On my way, a Mameluke on horseback presented me a letter from Commodore Decatur, announcing peace with Algiers, and desiring to know the nature of our differences with Tunis. I had already prepared the documents and arranged the plan of procedure which I intended to suggest to the commodore. On my arrival at Goletta the Minister of Marine ordered the *dey's* barge of twelve oars to be prepared for me, and arranged the silk cushions in the stern, and, accompanied by Abdallah the dragoman, I left the canal.

The squadron lay off Cape Carthage, arranged in handsome order; the *Guerrière*, bearing the broad pennant of the commodore, was in the centre, and the whole presented a very agreeable and commanding sight. In less than an hour I was alongside the flagship, and ascended on the quarter-deck. The marines were under arms, and the Consul of the United States was received with the usual honours. Commodore Decatur and Captain Downes, both in uniform, were at the gangway, and most of the officers and crew pressed forward to view their fellow-citizen.

After an interview with the consul, Commodore Decatur wrote a letter to the *dey* demanding an indemnity for the captured prizes. This was duly delivered, and the consul, going ashore, had several interviews with the Tunisian minister. Next day Captain Gordon and Captain Elliott were presented to the *Bey*, who consented, much against his will, to pay the money.

Three days later the squadron sailed for Tripoli, where a similar demand was made. The *pasha* hesitated; but on learning what had happened at Tunis and Algiers, and remembering what this same Captain

Decatur had done ten years before in his own harbour, he concluded that it would be wiser for him to yield. So he paid the money, and in addition released ten Neapolitan captives, whom Decatur desired to restore to their native country, as a return for the favours which the King of the Two Sicilies had shown the squadron in the earlier war.

Thus was accomplished the whole object of Decatur's mission in fifty days after his arrival in the Mediterranean. Since that day there has been no trouble with the States of Barbary. The effect of Decatur's acts was rendered tenfold greater by the appearance of another squadron a month later, under Commodore Bainbridge, with his broad pennant on the new line-of-battle ship *Independence*, and having with him besides the frigate *Congress* and three other vessels. The three ports of Barbary were visited in succession; and great was the astonishment of the Turks at this second display of naval strength. "You told us," said the Algerine Prime Minister to the British Consul, "that the Americans would be swept from the seas in six months by your navy; and now they make war upon us with some of your own vessels!"

Late in September the frigate *United States* with four sloops in company arrived at Gibraltar, and here all the squadrons assembled in one great fleet under Commodore Bainbridge,—the grandest fleet which had ever been gathered under the flag of the United States. There was the great seventy-four the *Independence*; five frigates,—the captured *Macedonian*, the *United States* which had captured her, the new *Guerrière*, the *Congress*, and the *Constellation*; the sloops "*Erie*" and "*Ontario*;" the brigs "*Firefly*," "*Flambeau*," "*Saranac*," "*Boxer*," *Enterprise*, *Spark*, and *Chippewa*; and the schooners *Torch*, *Lynx*, and *Spitfire*,—in all eighteen sail. And it was no slight satisfaction to the officers of the American squadron, when in this British port, that its two commodores were Bainbridge and Decatur, each of whom had taken a British frigate, and that the *Macedonian* and the *Boxer* were in the squadron, and flying the stars and stripes of the country that had captured them.[1]

---

1. It is an interesting fact, and one which, as far as I know, has never before been published, that when the practice squadron under Captain (now Rear-Admiral) Luce, sailed in 1865 to Europe, having on board the midshipmen from the Naval Academy, a singular rencontre took place in the English Channel. Meeting an English frigate, Captain Luce hailed from the quarter-deck,—"Ship ahoy! What ship is that?" —"Her Majesty's ship *President*," came the answer. "What ship is that?"— "The United States ship *Macedonian*," replied Captain Luce; for, strangely enough, the two vessels which half a century before had changed sides as prizes in the War of 1812 were now exchanging peaceful greetings under the flags of their respective conquerors.

CHAPTER 19

The War With Mexico

We now come to a long break of thirty years, during which the United States were at peace with all the nations of the earth. But in this period the navy was by no means idle. There was first a long and arduous campaign against the pirates of the West Indies, which ended at last in sweeping from the seas the gangs of cut-throats that had so long infested the Spanish Main. When this important work had been successfully accomplished, the navy was actively occupied in putting down the slave trade on the coast of Africa, and in protecting American commerce from the depredations of savage tribes in distant countries, above all on the coasts and islands of the Pacific and the Indian Oceans.

The navy too was busy with its peaceful occupations; for as the coadjutor of the nation's commerce it is a part of its duty to survey and explore the waters upon coasts hitherto unknown, to map out the channels, and to warn against the rocks and shoals and other dangers to the ships that will someday have to navigate these remote seas. It was in this period that the great exploring expedition was sent out to the Pacific under Lieutenant Wilkes, whose researches gave us our first accurate knowledge of the waters of this region, and form a lasting monument to the memory of the commander, and to the zeal and energy and skill of the navy which planned and carried out the enterprise.

But the long period of peace was now to be rudely interrupted, and the complications that followed the annexation of Texas at last brought on hostilities with Mexico. The possibility of this war had been long foreseen by the government, and the navy was found prepared for it. For several years a squadron had been maintained on the western coast of America, from Valparaiso to the Columbia River; and at the declaration of war, May 12, 1846, a considerable force was assembled in the northern cruising-ground. A still stronger force, composing the Home Squadron, was concentrated in the Gulf. The two coasts continued during the war to be two distinct bases of operation; but as the Mexicans had no naval force, the operations consisted mainly in blockade, and in attacks upon the cities along the coast.

Of the officers who held successively the chief command on the western coast, Commodore Stockton had the largest share of the work. Commodore Sloat, who was in command of the station when the war broke out, was there only long enough to make a beginning. This he did promptly and well. He had with him the frigate *Savannah* as flagship; the sloops *Portsmouth*, *Warren*, *Levant*, and *Cyane*; the schooner *Shark*; and the storeship *Erie*. These were all sailing-ships. At this time the coast south of the forty-second parallel of latitude, including the whole of California, belonged to Mexico, that parallel having been the boundary of the United States as fixed by the treaty of cession of Louisiana in 1803.

North of this point was the unsettled and hardly-organized territory of Oregon. The squadron was therefore without a base of supplies in the Pacific, and as it took months to communicate with Washington, its commander was obliged to act largely on his own responsibility. The enemy's coast, including the peninsula of lower California, extended over four thousand miles. To cover such a range of coast even with steamers would require uncommon activity; and with a force of half a dozen sailing-vessels the task was much more difficult.

Commodore Sloat's instructions of the 24th of June, 1845, which were written a year before the war broke out, contained these words:—

It is the earnest desire of the President to pursue the policy of peace; and he is anxious that you and every part of your squadron should be assiduously careful to avoid any act of aggression. Should Mexico, however, be resolutely bent on hostilities, you will be mindful to protect the persons and interests of citizens of the United States near your station; and should you ascertain beyond a doubt that the Mexican Government has declared war against us, you will at once employ the forces under your command to the best advantage.

On the 7th of June, 1846, while at Mazatlan, Commodore Sloat received satisfactory information that the Mexican troops had crossed the Rio Grande and had attacked the army of General Taylor in Texas. At the same time he learned that our squadron in the Gulf had put some of the Mexican ports under blockade. Of course he had not yet heard of the declaration of war passed on the 12th of May; but he knew that according to the policy of the administration this meant war, and that under his instructions he was to begin offensive operations. Leaving the *Warren* at Mazatlan, he sailed at once in the *Savannah* for Monterey.

The commodore showed great foresight in striking his first blow in California. The country was mostly unexplored, and only sparsely inhabited, many of the settlers having come from the United States. Its resources were not fully known, but they were supposed to be considerable, though nothing was looked for like the Eldorado that was afterward discovered. It embraced an immense territory, comprising, besides the State of California as its boundaries are fixed today, (1887), Nevada, Utah, New Mexico, Arizona, and part of Colorado. Its position pointed it out as the part of Mexico which could most advantageously be transferred in case of an annexation of territory at the end of the war. Annexation would be made much easier by an early conquest, and indeed a conquest was in some degree necessary to make the ground of cession. It was a vulnerable point, because it was garrisoned only by a small force of Mexican troops, and it lay too far from the scene of active hostilities to be recovered from the Americans if they once got full possession.

The *Savannah* arrived at Monterey on the 2nd of July, and found there the *Cyane* and the *Levant*. Commodore Sloat hastened to demand a surrender from the Mexicans, and upon their refusal, two hundred and fifty seamen and marines were landed, who took possession of the town without resistance. Soon after a proclamation was published declaring that California had become a part of the United States. A company of volunteer dragoons was organized among the Americans on shore, and preparations were made to seize the neighbouring towns.

While this was going on at Monterey, Commander Montgomery in the *Portsmouth*, which was at Yerba Buena, or San Francisco, as it is now called, having received an order from the commodore, took like measures to assert the authority of the United States. He also organized his military companies, and assumed control of all the posts in the neighbourhood,—Sonoma, Sutter's Fort, and the Presidio. Not far off, in the interior, Frémont, a young captain of topographical engineers, who was at work upon his duties of surveying, had raised the American flag, and at various points he too had taken a nominal possession. On the 19th of July he joined Commodore Sloat at Monterey.

With these vigorous preliminary measures the commodore's command came to an end. He had been for some time past in bad health, and when, late in July, the *Congress* arrived, under Commodore Stockton, a younger man and a most brilliant officer, Commodore Sloat turned over the command to him. The campaign had been opened, and it remained for the new commander-in-chief to follow up the blows that had been struck.

At this time the Californian Legislature was in session at Los Angeles, the capital of the province, which was defended by a body of Mexican troops under General Castro. Commodore Stockton at once determined to strike a decisive blow at the city. As Los Angeles was not on the sea-coast, and as it was defended by a trained army, it required an extraordinary degree of boldness and enterprise on the part of the naval commander to resolve to attack it without the aid of regular soldiers. But the result only shows how much may be done in case of necessity by blue-jackets on shore under a capable commander. The commodore organized the volunteer dragoons as a battalion of mounted riflemen, and appointed Captain Frémont major and Lieutenant Gillespie captain.

On the day after he took command the battalion embarked on board the *Cyane*, and next day it sailed for San Diego, from which place it was to march toward the capital. A few days later Commodore Stockton sailed in the *Congress* to San Pedro, a point some distance to the northward of San Diego, and only thirty miles from Los Angeles. On his way down he landed a garrison at Santa Barbara, an intermediate port. Arriving at San Pedro he organized a little army—a naval brigade, as we should call it now—of three hundred and fifty seamen and marines, drilling them daily on shore by a rough manual which he devised hastily for the purpose. For artillery he had some 6-pounders and a 32-pounder carronade.

After a few days' delay, to exercise his men and to give Major Frémont time to begin his advance, the commodore set out for Los Angeles. His force was only one third of that of the enemy, who were strongly intrenched in a fortified camp in the valley of the River Mesa. The road from San Pedro contained many narrow defiles, which the Mexicans might easily have defended; but, strange to say, they neglected this advantage. On his way Stockton was twice called upon to surrender by envoys from General Castro; but he talked to them so boldly that he succeeded in deceiving them about the actual size of his force. Soon they became alarmed at the invasion, and when the Americans arrived at Castro's camp, it was found that the general had fled, and that his followers were scattered in all directions. On the 13th of August the commodore entered Los Angeles and took possession of the capital of California.

Commodore Stockton now set about to organize his conquest, and first of all he issued a proclamation declaring California a territory of the United States. A tariff of duties was established and collectors were appointed to receive them at the different seaports. A constitution was drawn up and put in operation, in which the powers and duties of the various branches of the government were laid down. Major Frémont was appointed governor of the territory, and directions were given for elections to be held for civil magistrates, the conquered country meanwhile remaining under martial law.

It had been the commodore's purpose to enlist a force of volunteers, and taking them to Mexico, to land at Acapulco or some other convenient point, and create a diversion of the Mexican army by an invasion from the west coast, and for this reason he had installed Frémont as governor; but circumstances soon after compelled him to change his plan, which after all was perhaps somewhat visionary. In the month of September, while he was busily occupied in northern California, a rising took place at Los Angeles, under General Flores, and Pico the governor, whom the Americans had released on their parole at the capture of the city. The garrison left by the commodore was driven out and took refuge in San Pedro.

Thither Captain Mervine was ordered at once in the *Savannah*, and thither the *Congress* shortly followed him. Arriving at San Pedro late in October, the commodore found that Captain Mervine had just been defeated by the enemy, who were then besieging the little town. The naval brigade was again landed, and presently the besieging forces were driven off. From this time till the 1st of January the fleet was occupied with preparations for a second and more serious attack upon Los Angeles. The great advantage of the enemy was in his cavalry. Every Californian was an expert horseman, and the Mexican ponies are trained to the severest work.

On the other hand the naval brigade, as might be expected, was badly off in this essential arm of service. Commodore Stockton was a man of bold and original mind, but even his mind did not go to the length of forming a corps of marine cavalry; and besides, there were no horses, for the Mexicans had taken care to strip the country of ponies in the neighbourhood of the southern ports. Parties were sent out in all directions to obtain them, but with no success. Finally Major Frémont was conveyed to Monterey with his battalion, with the understanding that he should march south by land as soon as he had completed his preparations; but as he was delayed from one cause or another, and as Monterey was three hundred miles north of Los Angeles, he did not arrive in time to take a part in the attack.

Early in December the force at San Diego was joined by Gen. S. W. Kearney, of the army, a brave and devoted officer, who, after having seized several points in New Mexico, had crossed the mountains from the eastward with a few squadrons of dragoons. The Californians met him at San Pasqual, not far from San Diego, where they gave him battle and nearly cut to pieces his command. The remnant of the force, after their gallant struggle, was only saved by the arrival of reinforcements from Commodore Stockton, which escorted the general into San Diego. The commodore now generously offered to give up the command to General Kearney and to act as his *aide*.

Kearney with equal magnanimity declined the offer, and he was placed in charge of the land troops for the proposed expedition, the commodore retaining the chief command. Preparations were completed on the 29th of December, and the little army set out. It was indeed a mongrel force, but it was none the less a good army for the work in hand. It consisted of sixty dismounted dragoons who had come with General Kearney; sixty mounted riflemen of the California battalion; five hundred seamen and marines from the "Congress," *Savannah, Portsmouth,* and *Cyane*; and six pieces of artillery. The force was poorly armed, many of the sailors having only boarding-pikes and pistols, and the cavalry were badly mounted.

After a march of one hundred and forty miles, lasting ten days, the Americans, on the 8th of January, came upon the enemy strongly posted on the heights of San Gabriel, with six hundred mounted men and four pieces of artillery, commanding the ford of the river. In a position where an officer with a soldier's training would perhaps have hesitated, Commodore Stockton's confidence and resolution influenced him to advance. He forded the river under the enemy's guns without firing a shot, dragged his guns through the water, and formed his men in squares on the opposite bank. Here he repelled an attack of the enemy, and after a stubborn conflict carried the heights by a charge.

Next day, on the march across the plains of the Mesa, the Mexicans made another desperate effort to save the capital. They had a strong position, being concealed with their artillery in a ravine till the commodore came within gunshot; then they opened a brisk fire on his flank, at the same time charging him both in front and rear. The squares of blue-jackets coolly and steadily withstood the cavalry charge, and the enemy, after being twice repulsed, were finally driven off the field and dispersed. Immediately after the battle Commodore Stockton entered the city of Los Angeles, and for the second and last time California was conquered.

The object of the government was now accomplished. When the time came to settle the conditions of peace, the territory of the United States was increased by this immense district, comprising over 650,000 square miles, and by far the largest part of the work had been done by Stockton and his naval brigade.

Soon after these events Commodore Shubrick came out in the *Independence* to take command of the station. He was followed by the *Lexington* with a detachment of troops belonging to the regular artillery. These were landed at the important points in California and left to garrison them, and the fleet could now turn its attention to the coast of Mexico, where vigorous demonstrations were soon after made. Mazatlan, the principal seaport of Mexico in the Pacific, was captured by a landing force of six hundred men from the fleet. Its garrison retreated, and the victorious Americans held the town until the end of the war, collecting duties at the custom-house, which went far to defray the cost of maintaining the squadron.

Other towns were taken, some of them several times over. At Guaymas and Mulejè attacks were made by the *Dale*, under Commander Selfridge. After defeating the Mexican chief Pineda, whose band of guerilla infested the country about Mulejè, Captain Selfridge obtained a schooner, and stationed her there under Lieutenant Craven to blockade the port. At Guaymas a force was landed, and a severe fight took place with the Mexicans, in which Selfridge was wounded. Though the force of the *Dale* was too small to leave a garrison on shore, she remained off the town and made it untenable for the enemy.

At San José, at the extremity of Lower California, a post was established on shore in an old mission-house, which was garrisoned by fifty-seven men,—seamen, marines, and volunteers,—under Lieutenant Heywood. It was attacked in November, 1847, but the Mexicans failed in their attempt to carry the place by assault. The town had been deserted, and fifty or more women and children had taken refuge in the mission-house. In February the attack was renewed by a large force of Mexicans. Not wishing to risk an assault, they occupied the houses about the mission and laid siege to the post. Twice Lieutenant Heywood made a sortie with his gallant little force and drove them from their position; but they recovered their ground as soon as he returned.

The situation was now becoming critical, for the supplies of the garrison began to fall short, and the fugitives under their protection shared their rations. At last they could not even get water; for with the close watch maintained by the enemy, any man who ventured out was shot down. The siege had lasted ten days, and the garrison would presently have been starved into surrender, when by a fortunate chance the *Cyane* came into the harbour. Commander Dupont, who was in command, immediately landed a force from his ship and raised the siege, bringing off the heroic garrison in safety. This was the last affair of importance on the west coast.

★★★★★★

In the Gulf the outbreak of the war had found a large squadron already assembled. There were three fifty-gun frigates and half a dozen sloops and brigs. There were also two steamers, the first that the United States had used in war,—the large paddle-wheel vessel *Mississippi*, and the *Princeton*, which had gained a melancholy notoriety from the bursting of one of her guns while on an experimental trip in the Potomac, by which the Secretary of State, the Secretary of the Navy, and other high officers of the government had lost their lives. The vessels, however, were all too large for the service. The Mexican coast is a long stretch of sand exposed to the sudden and tempestuous "northers," as they are called,—furious northerly gales which blow frequently in the Gulf.

The important sea-coast towns lie mostly in deep bights or recesses at the mouths of rivers, sometimes two or three miles up, with a bar having but ten feet of water, and currents that render difficult the pilotage of sailing-vessels. Vera Cruz, a large town with strong fortifications, was an exception, for its harbour was deep and accessible. The other points of importance—Tuspan, Tampico, Alvarado, and Tabasco, the last of which lay some distance up the Tabasco River—were partially protected by earthworks, but their principal safeguard lay in the

226

difficulties of a shallow and frequently shifting entrance.

The headquarters of the squadron were fixed at Anton Lizardo, a harbour formed by a group of small barren islands a few miles south of Vera Cruz. A blockade was declared and maintained by vessels stationed off the ports or cruising up and down the coast. In the course of the first summer the squadron was reinforced by four sloops and brigs; and, what was of much more importance, by two steam gunboats, the *Vixen* and *Spitfire*, each of which carried an 8-inch gun and two lighter guns. These were the ideal vessels for service on the Mexican coast, with their heavy gun and their light draught,—only seven feet; and it is a curious fact that one of them, the *Vixen*, was actually designed and under construction for the Mexican Government in New York when she was purchased by our own.

Other steamers were added later, one of them a revenue cutter: and a number of gunboat schooners were also sent down to the station. The peculiar dangers and difficulties of the coast were seen in two catastrophes that befell the squadron during the summer. The brig *Truxtun*, attempting to move against Tuspan, grounded on the bar in the river, where it was necessary to abandon her, and where the Mexicans left her after carrying off her guns; while another brig, the *Somers*, was sunk with half her crew in a "norther" which came down on her without warning. Among the saved was her captain, Raphael Semmes, the future commander of the *Alabama*.

The first eight months of the war on the east coast, while the squadron was under the command of Commodore Conner, were not marked by any great success. In August an attempt was made to capture Alvarado, thirty miles southeast of Vera Cruz. The large ships anchored off the bar, with the gunboats close in, engaging the batteries during the afternoon and evening, and a boat expedition was organized to attack in the morning; but when the morning came, the fleet was called off on account of threatening weather. In October the attempt was renewed, but with no better success. This time the gunboats were arranged in two divisions, each in tow of a steamer. After the first division had worked safely in, the towing steamer of the second grounded on the bar, and the schooners in tow got foul, and the van was left unsupported. This check was enough to decide the commodore against prosecuting the attack; the van was recalled, the grounded steamer got afloat, and the squadron sailed away a second time from Alvarado.

In November the fleet made an important capture,—the seaport of Tampico. Great preparations were made for the expedition, the force despatched consisting of the two principal frigates,—the steamers *Mississippi* and *Princeton*,—the sloop *St. Mary's*, and a large fleet of gunboats. The gunboats, with the boats from the large ships, were safely towed over the bar and appeared before the city. The authorities thereupon surrendered without any resistance. The city was occupied, and a military government was established, which continued to the end of the war.

Meanwhile another commodore had joined the squadron,—Matthew Calbraith Perry, an officer whose reputation was second to that of no one of his time in the service. At first Commodore Perry was chiefly employed in detached enterprises. His first important success was an expedition in October against Tabasco, a town lying seventy miles up the Tabasco River. Leaving the *Mississippi* outside, he entered the river in the *Vixen*, and after having seized the shipping at Frontera, near the mouth of the river, the expedition proceeded up to Tabasco. At its approach the enemy abandoned the fort, but the Mexican commander, occupying the town with his troops, refused to surrender. Fire was opened on the town, but the commodore presently desisted from his bombardment, at the entreaties of the foreign merchants who owned most of the property. Nothing could be gained by laying the town in ruins; and after a scattering fight on shore the troops were re-embarked, and the flotilla returned, leaving two vessels at the entrance to continue the blockade. The expedition had taken nine prizes and destroyed four more, and had broken up the contraband trade in the river.

In December Commodore Perry commanded an expedition against Laguna, in Yucatan. Yucatan was an uncertain friend, with a disposition to become an annoying enemy by supplying the Mexicans with arms and munitions of war from British Honduras and other points. Perry therefore occupied Laguna, and installed Commander Sands in charge of the post as a temporary governor.

The government had now decided that it would be wise to change the plan of campaign which had so far been followed in the war. General Taylor's army, which had invaded Mexico from the Rio Grande, though it was victorious at Monterey, and later at Buena Vista, could hardly hope to penetrate into the heart of the country without great loss of time, troops, and money. It was resolved to take a shorter route to the interior and so decide the war. General Scott was to command the army of invasion, and Vera Cruz was the point selected for the beginning of its march.

By the middle of February the transports containing General Scott's army began to rendezvous at the island of Lobos, and store-ships to arrive at Anton Lizardo with materials for the expedition, including sixty-seven surf-boats in which the troops were to be landed. The preparation for the landing was made by the squadron, still under Commodore Conner's command, with such despatch and thoroughness that though General Scott and his staff only arrived on the 6th of March, on the 9th the army was disembarked. Early on the morning of this day the men-of-war, with the troops on board, sailed from their anchorage to Sacrificios, an island just south of Vera Cruz, and by ten o'clock that night the whole body of twelve thousand men had been landed without mishap or loss.

No opposition was made to the landing, though the position offered great advantages for defence. A line of investment five miles in length was drawn about the city, and the erection of batteries was begun at once, the naval forces being still employed in landing munitions of war. By the 22nd some of the batteries were ready, and the city having refused to surrender, General Scott opened the bombardment.

On the day before the attack began, Commodore Conner, who had long been in bad health, and who would have done more wisely to give up the command before, was relieved by Commodore Perry. As the heavy guns provided by the army for the siege—the battering train—had not arrived, the army had only its mortars and a few light guns. These had no effect upon the walls and bastions of the city, and General Scott suggested to Commodore Perry that he should land some of the heavy cannon from the ships.

Perry answered that he would land the guns, and moreover that he would fight them. Six heavy guns, each weighing three tons, were landed, and, drawn by two hundred seamen and volunteers, they were moved during the night of the 23rd three miles from the landing-place to their position in battery, seven hundred yards from the city wall. On the morning of the 24th they opened, and immediately drawing upon themselves the concentrated fire of the fortifications, they did more real execution than all the batteries which had been hitherto engaged.

The Mosquito fleet, as it was called, seconded the shore batteries in the bombardment. This was a detachment of vessels composed of the steamers *Spitfire* and *Vixen*, and the five sailing gunboats, and commanded by Commodore Tattnall, a very gallant officer, in the *Spitfire*. On the first day the flotilla lay off Point Hornos, and at three in the afternoon, when the bombardment began, it opened upon the city, continuing the fire till night. The next day, leaving one of his schooners at the anchorage as a blind, Commander Tattnall took out the six other vessels, the steamers having the gunboats in tow, as if to rejoin the squadron. As soon as he had cleared the point he turned and steamed up to within eight hundred yards of Fort San Juan d'Ulloa, and directly between it and Fort St. Jago. From this position Tattnall discharged a heavy fire into the city.

As soon as the forts recovered from their surprise they opened a concentrated fire upon the audacious flotilla, which nevertheless kept at its post until Perry, fearing that all the vessels would be lost, recalled them by signal. It was a splendid sight to see Tattnall with his little vessels, without protection,—for there were no ironclads in those days,— holding his perilous position under the fire of the great forts, with his crews loading and firing as coolly as if their work were but pastime. As the surgeon stood for a moment on the deck of the *Spitfire*, Tattnall paused in his work to say, "Ah, doctor, this may not make life longer, but it makes it a great deal broader!"

The bombardment by the batteries on shore lasted four days, during which the unprotected inhabitants of the city were the chief sufferers; for the strong castle of San Juan d'Ulloa, in its secure position on a reef to the northward, was hardly injured at all. But perhaps there is no more effective method of reducing a town than by the sufferings of its inhabitants, cruel as the method is; and on the 26th of March negotiations were opened by the besieged, which were concluded the next day by the signing of a capitulation including both the town and the castle.

On the day after the surrender of Vera Cruz an expedition was planned for the third time against Alvarado. Extensive preparations had been made, and a brigade from the army under General Quitman was detailed to co-operate by land. The enterprise had a truly singular ending. Commodore Perry had sent the sloop-of-war *Albany* and the small steamer *Scourge* as an advance force to lie off the bar of the river and reconnoitre. The *Scourge*, commanded by Lieutenant Hunter, arriving before the *Albany*, stood close in to the land, abreast of the outer fort, and seeing indications of flinching, fired a few shot into it. The fort, having no intention of resistance after the fall of Vera Cruz, and understanding the fire as a summons to yield, sent a boat to the *Scourge* with an officer, who tendered a surrender.

Upon this, Lieutenant Hunter threw a midshipman and five men into the fort, and pushing on to the town took possession of it, as well as of another town nearby, and after capturing all the shipping, held his course up the river. When Commodore Perry arrived with his fleet and General Quitman with his brigade, they found the capture, for which they had made such large preparations, already effected, and the place was turned over to them by the midshipman in charge. Lieutenant Hunter was still up the river, where he could be heard firing this way and that in his career of conquest. It was stated that one of the secondary objects of the expedition, the capture of supplies, was partly defeated by this premature action. The commander-in-chief commented with extreme severity upon Lieutenant Hunter in his report, and caused him to be court-martialled, which seemed rather hard, as he had only erred through excess of zeal.

Commodore Perry next resolved to attack Tuspan, a town about one hundred miles northwest of Vera Cruz. It was the only point of importance on the coast remaining in the enemy's hands. The squadron, which was now well equipped for service, rendezvoused at Lobos, off the mouth of the Tuspan River. Two days were spent here in organizing landing-parties and practising field exercises with a battery of light artillery which the commodore had organized. With the thoroughness that marked all his preparations, Perry spent another day in sounding on the bar and buoying the channel. At length all was ready, and on the 18th of April the attack was made. The flotilla was in three lines, each in tow of a steamer, the commodore leading in the *Spitfire*. Besides the gunboats and steamers there were thirty barges, each containing a detachment from the ships.

The river, about three hundred yards wide, was defended by three forts, enfilading the reaches of the stream and mounting seven guns, most of which had been taken from the *Truxtun* when she was lost on the bar of Tuspan the year before. The enemy were stationed as sharpshooters in the thick chaparral on the banks. As soon as the boats came within range, a hot fire of grape was opened on them from the forts. The detachment from the "Germantown," under Commander Buchanan,—an officer of whom we shall hear more in the later war,—was first in the advance, and was ordered to storm the nearest fort. This was gallantly done, and the enemy were driven out. The second and third forts were carried in the same way by storming-parties, the river-banks were cleared of their concealed sharpshooters, and before evening the town was in possession of the Americans.

In June a similar expedition was sent against Tabasco, which Commodore Perry had attacked successfully the year before, but which was again a centre of detached operations by Mexican guerillas. As at Tuspan, the details of the enterprise were prepared beforehand with the utmost care and skill; every contingency was provided for, and the machinery ran as smoothly as clock-work. The enemy were driven off, their forts destroyed, their stores removed, and to provide against a recurrence of operations, a force was left to occupy the place.

This was the last enterprise of importance in the naval war. The army was now fighting its way to the city of Mexico, but the coast was entirely reduced. At all the important ports the blockade had been converted into an occupation, and a military government under officers of the squadron had been established. The custom-houses were placed in charge of naval officers, a tariff was laid, and duties were collected in the name of the government. So matters remained until the end of the war.

LEONAUR

ALSO FROM LEONAUR

AVAILABLE IN SOFTCOVER OR HARDCOVER WITH DUST JACKET

THE RELUCTANT REBEL *by William G. Stevenson*—A young Kentuckian's experiences in the Confederate Infantry & Cavalry during the American Civil War..

BOOTS AND SADDLES *by Elizabeth B. Custer*—The experiences of General Custer's Wife on the Western Plains.

FANNIE BEERS' CIVIL WAR *by Fannie A. Beers*—A Confederate Lady's Experiences of Nursing During the Campaigns & Battles of the American Civil War.

LADY SALE'S AFGHANISTAN *by Florentia Sale*—An Indomitable Victorian Lady's Account of the Retreat from Kabul During the First Afghan War.

THE TWO WARS OF MRS DUBERLY *by Frances Isabella Duberly*—An Intrepid Victorian Lady's Experience of the Crimea and Indian Mutiny.

THE REBELLIOUS DUCHESS *by Paul F. S. Dermoncourt*—The Adventures of the Duchess of Berri and Her Attempt to Overthrow French Monarchy.

LADIES OF WATERLOO *by Charlotte A. Eaton, Magdalene de Lancey & Juana Smith*—The Experiences of Three Women During the Campaign of 1815: Waterloo Days by Charlotte A. Eaton, A Week at Waterloo by Magdalene de Lancey & Juana's Story by Juana Smith.

TWO YEARS BEFORE THE MAST *by Richard Henry Dana. Jr.*—The account of one young man's experiences serving on board a sailing brig—the Penelope—bound for California, between the years 1834-36.

A SAILOR OF KING GEORGE *by Frederick Hoffman*—From Midshipman to Captain—Recollections of War at Sea in the Napoleonic Age 1793-1815.

LORDS OF THE SEA *by A. T. Mahan*—Great Captains of the Royal Navy During the Age of Sail.

COGGESHALL'S VOYAGES: VOLUME 1 *by George Coggeshall*—The Recollections of an American Schooner Captain.

COGGESHALL'S VOYAGES: VOLUME 2 *by George Coggeshall*—The Recollections of an American Schooner Captain.

TWILIGHT OF EMPIRE *by Sir Thomas Ussher & Sir George Cockburn*—Two accounts of Napoleon's Journeys in Exile to Elba and St. Helena: Narrative of Events by Sir Thomas Ussher & Napoleon's Last Voyage: Extract of a diary by Sir George Cockburn.